ADVANCE PRAISE FOR *MY DEAREST LILLA*

"Jacob D. Cox's Civil War letters to his beloved wife 'Lilla' capture how the war transformed the civilian Cox to corps commander as he withstood significant combat in both the Eastern and Western Theaters and maintained a strong relationship with Lilla whom he considered both a confidant and an intellectual equal. Cox's letters provide a significant window into the intellectual, emotional, political, and military dynamics of the Civil War era."

—**ANGELA ZOMBEK**, associate professor of history at University of North Carolina Wilmington, author of *Penitentiaries, Punishment, and Military Prisons: Familiar Responses to an Extraordinary Crisis during the American Civil War*

"Cox's wartime letters to his wife effectively package his first-hand personal observations on a variety of themes—military, socio-cultural, even a sort of travelogue—which form a basis for Cox's historical work."

—**BENJAMIN FRANKLIN COOLING**, author of *To the Battles of Franklin and Nashville and Beyond: Stabilization and Reconstruction in Tennessee and Kentucky, 1864–1866*

"Dr. Gene Schmiel has done a great service to Civil War scholars here. Jacob Cox's letters home provide insights into his thinking about the conduct of war, his own experiences in battle, and the nation's postwar future. Anyone interested in nearly any aspect of the Civil War will find this book invaluable."

—**BENJAMIN T. ARRINGTON**, historian and author of *The Last Lincoln Republican: The Presidential Election of 1880*

My Dearest Lilla

Jacob and Helen Cox, circa 1862.

My Dearest Lilla

LETTERS HOME
FROM CIVIL WAR GENERAL
JACOB D. COX

Edited by Gene Schmiel

Voices of the Civil War
Michael P. Gray, Series Editor

The University of Tennessee Press / Knoxville

The Voices of the Civil War series makes available a variety of primary source materials that illuminate issues on the battlefield, the home front, and the western front, as well as other aspects of this historic era. The series contextualizes the personal accounts within the framework of the latest scholarship and expands established knowledge by offering new perspectives, new materials, and new voices.

Copyright © 2023 by The University of Tennessee Press / Knoxville.
All Rights Reserved. Manufactured in the United States of America.
First Edition.

Library of Congress Cataloging-in-Publication Data

Names: Cox, Jacob D. (Jacob Dolson), 1828–1900. | Schmiel, Gene, 1944- editor.
Title: My dearest Lilla : letters home from Civil War General Jacob D. Cox / edited by Gene Schmiel.
Description: First edition. | Knoxville : The University of Tennessee Press, 2023. | Series: Voices of the Civil War | Includes bibliographical references and index. | Summary: "The letters in this collection were written by General Cox to his beloved wife, Helen. The volume's editor, Gene Schmiel, wrote a well-regarded biography of Cox in 2014. In 2012, Schmiel was made aware that Oberlin College had a cache of letters that had been transcribed by Cox's great granddaughter, and the cache yielded 213 letters written by the general to his wife during the Civil War. Well-known for his incredibly detailed postwar writing about campaigns, Cox reveals himself in these letters an ambitious, warmhearted, and concerned observer of the progress of the war. The letters reflect his service in the Maryland, Atlanta, and Franklin-Nashville Campaigns"—Provided by publisher.
Identifiers: LCCN 2023018045 (print) | LCCN 2023018046 (ebook) | ISBN 9781621907978 (paperback) | ISBN 9781621907985 (kindle edition) | ISBN 9781621907992 (pdf)
Subjects: LCSH: Cox, Jacob D. (Jacob Dolson), 1828–1900—Correspondence. | United States—History—Civil War, 1861–1865—Personal narratives. | Ohio—History—Civil War, 1861–1865—Personal narratives. | United States—History—Civil War, 1861–1865—Campaigns. | Generals—Ohio—Biography. | Cox, Helen, 1828–1911—Correspondence.
Classification: LCC E467.1.C83 A4 2023 (print) | LCC E467.1.C83 (ebook) | DDC 973.7/81—dc23/eng/20230502
LC record available at https://lccn.loc.gov/2023018045
LC ebook record available at https://lccn.loc.gov/2023018046

Contents

Foreword	ix
Michael P. Gray	
Preface	xv
Introduction	xix
1. The Making of a Soldier, 1861	1
2. Baptism of Fire: The Hills of (West) Virginia	13
3. On the National Stage: The Antietam Campaign	75
4. Paper General	95
5. East Tennessee and the Struggle for Position	125
6. The Atlanta Campaign	153
7. The Taking of Atlanta	189
8. Final Campaigns: Victory in the West and in North Carolina	197
Afterword	227
Notes	233
Selected Bibliography	247
Index	253

Illustrations

Figures

Jacob Cox's Portable Field Desk	83
Jacob Cox at the Battle of Franklin, Kurz and Allison	203
Jacob Cox's Official Portrait as Governor of Ohio, 1866	228
The Cox Family, circa 1889	229
The Coxes' Gravesite Obelisk	230

Maps

1. The West Virginia Campaigns, 1861–1862	11
2. Battle of South Mountain, September 14, 1862	84
3. Battle of Antietam, September 17, 1862	88
4. The Taking of Atlanta, August 31–September 1, 1864	192
5. Battle of Franklin, November 30, 1864	201
6. The North Carolina Campaign, 1865	213

Foreword

As the United States stood at the brink of civil war, Jacob Dolson Cox consulted with his close friend, fellow Ohioan, and political ally James A. Garfield over their futures. Both in their early thirties, Cox and Garfield were trained lawyers rather than soldiers. Their lack of formal military training forced them to acquaint themselves quickly on the art of war, so they voraciously read up on military history and preparation. One might imagine, in the back of their minds, was that the country's nineteenth-century "great divide" could serve as a platform in propelling their careers, whether in the military or in civilian arenas. It might be hard to imagine, at least in the twenty-first century, that about such a life-altering decision, Jacob Cox never consulted his wife on the matter. Helen, whom he affectionately called "Lilla," was tasked with taking care of the children and the household, so the pressure of an absent husband might conceivably add strain on a marriage that was already impacted by her overbearing, famous father. Fortunately for posterity (and the marriage) Jacob's momentary lack of communication with his wife manifested into a slew of correspondence he wrote to her during the conflict. His letters to Lilla became a seemingly therapeutic exercise that he devoutly attended to, and Helen was updated on his latest movements while he was on duty.

The Voices of the Civil War series has brought forth a wide range of publications through letters, diaries, and memoirs, so our readers might gain deeper understanding of the participants and the cultures in which they lived. The publications feature a wide cast of characters who committed thoughts to paper during the conflict: civilians on the home front, battle-hardened soldiers, the latter ranging from enlisted men to officers. Other volumes capture voices of military engineers, surgeons, signalmen, editors, ministers, diplomats, and politicians. Still others feature youthful boyhood commentary, and many voices of women from all classes of society. The series strives to be holistic, while providing fine-grained contributions to current trends in the secondary scholarship and improving the overall historiography of the Civil War.

Recently, scholars have taken a deep look into the relationship of spouses during the Civil War. Carol Berkin's 2010 *Civil War Wives: The Lives and Times of Angelina Grimke Weld, Varina Howell Davis and Julia Dent Grant* probes into how women had avenues of influence, but also yielded power to their husbands by assuming traditional spheres of domesticity. The 2016 *Lincoln's Generals' Wives: Four Women Who Influenced the Civil War—for Better and for Worse*, by Candice Shy Hooper, finds personalities did in fact sway interactions and, in turn, decisions. Education, religion, politics, world views, and individual beliefs all played out in different ways in different families. Moreover, the familial dynamics and interpersonal relationships of spouses, affected by children, the loss of children, parents, in-laws, or other immediate family, found ways to trickle down to decision making on both sides. At the very least, women played a crucial role in being confidants.

The reader will find that our latest volume, *My Dearest Lilla: Letters Home from Civil War General Jacob D. Cox*, is more than the exploits of the citizen soldier, whom his wife lovingly referred to by his middle name, Dolson. Helen wrote, "My ambition has always, from childhood, been for fame, and although my own life has been in the quiet domestic lines, the fame of my father, my husband, my son has been dearer than life to me." Helen also wrote to future first lady Lucretia Garfield on matters, as our expert guide in the story, editor Gene Schmiel, weaves into the narrative other personalities: "the firm bonds between them [Helen and Jacob] were also exhibited in their correspondence to others." Helen wrote to Lucretia Garfield about the "complete happiness" after visiting Jacob, or if there was any hesitation in thinking she was not missed by him, she was "assured of my husband's loving appreciation of my work and self-denial, I should faint by the way." Women sought guidance, affirmation, and consolation from one another, as well as from their spouses. Indeed, these connections would be much needed on a variety of levels, especially after Helen and Jacob suffered the loss of a child during the first year of the war.

Another important objective of the Voices of the Civil War series is to recruit experts in the field who have already written extensively on their subject. Furthermore, newly discovered documents help add insight and fresh findings to a story that may have been missed. Both these circumstances meet at a confluence in this volume. A keen editing eye in piecing the story together, coupled with an extraordinary trove of newly found letters, has brought to our readership more than an excellent narrative. *My Dearest Lilla: Letters Home from Civil War General Jacob D. Cox* also combines family intrigues by prominent members, and insight into high-profile generals and politicians during Cox's military service in both the Eastern and Western Theaters.

Like his subject, Schmiel has had a fascinating career in the public sector. He earned his doctorate at the Ohio State University, wrote his dissertation, "The Career of Jacob Dolson Cox, 1828–1900: Soldier, Scholar, Statesman," then took an assistant professorship in history. Schmiel then moved on to a long career as a diplomat, becoming a foreign service officer in the State Department. Eventually, a revised version of the dissertation was published in 2014 under the title *Citizen-General: Jacob Dolson Cox and the Civil War Era* and won high accolades. It was also during that research that Schmiel discovered the newly accessioned writings to Helen, some 213 letters added to the Oberlin College Archives. Schmiel writes he was "astounded" and that the letters afforded "a treasure-trove of information, insights, and analysis. Within, the stoic, introverted Jacob Cox revealed—as he did to no one else—his inner thoughts and concerns to his beloved partner, providing her with in-depth discussions and analyses of the war, his changing life, his ambitions, and other related topics." Furthermore, "Cox's wartime letters were a key foundation of his Civil War writings, serving in effect as his first draft." And finally, "The letters he wrote to Helen are the most incisive and revealing of all. These in-depth missives are among the most useful collections of Civil War letters written by a self-made and not formally trained military man."

Helen and Jacob met at Oberlin College while he was attending to his studies. Helen was well educated and well traveled already, touring with her father at religious revivals; he was the famous revivalist and leader of the second Great Awakening, Charles Grandison Finney. As she matured, she ultimately found the household authoritarian and escaped by attempting to make her own family and married early. After the death of her first husband, Helen met Jacob while he was studying to be a minister or theology professor, and they married while he was enrolled at Oberlin. When a classroom debate between Cox and Finney, who was a professor and president of the college, became acrimonious, it led to a showdown between the two. Cox thrived on discussion and free thinking, whereas Finney's pedagogy was confrontational if not intimidating. This conflict ultimately caused Cox to quit his studies, and, in 1851, he and Helen left for Northeast Ohio's Western Reserve.

Settling in Warren, Cox became the area's first school superintendent, then two years later changed career paths again by becoming a lawyer. As he rose as a founder in Ohio's Republican Party, the Coxes befriended the Garfields, and both Jacob and James won Ohio Senate seats from nearby districts in 1859. As war was on the horizon, both men used their political influence to gain military commissions. Jacob was appointed brigadier general in the Ohio militia; Garfield was later commissioned as a colonel in the 42nd Ohio, which was sent to Kentucky under the command of Don Carlos Buell. Meanwhile, Cox and the Ohio volunteers went off to the Kanawha Valley under George B. McClellan, "the young Napoleon," and the future "Citizen-General" began to make his mark.

Schmiel traces Cox to the rendezvous base near Cincinnati, at Camp Dennison, describing how the brigadier general and his soldiers trained to fight and live in the army. Schmiel then follows Cox and the newly branded Kanawha Division to the mountains of western Virginia. The Ohioan and his troops faced real combat for the first time in the rugged terrain. Their learning experiences were invaluable, and, after meeting with George McClellan, Cox and the Kanawha division were given more responsibility. They were attached to the IX Corps under Jesse Reno, under the command of Ambrose Burnside's wing. He and his men were thrust onto the national stage, partaking in the strategic fighting on South Mountain in western Maryland, culminating in the Battle of Antietam in September 1862.

It had become clear to many of his superiors in the field and to politicians in Washington that Jacob Cox, although not a West Pointer, was deserving of advancement in the Army of the Potomac. The reader will find meetings with the "Young Napoleon," Ambrose Burnside, and other prominent personalities. Cox was cautiously optimistic that he would be promoted to major general of volunteers until Eastern theater battles led to the firing of his main advocates, McClellan and Burnside; their fates doomed Cox to a desk job for much of 1863. During this interregnum, which must have been painfully boring to the ambitious Cox, he did get to see Helen in person in Warren, one highlight in his tenure as a "Paper General." Finally, orders came for him to rejoin field service, this time in the Western Theater.

Vying for control of East Tennessee brought Cox back to his days campaigning in western Virginia. Yet much time there devolved into the inactivity of camp life, probably not what Cox expected, particularly after suffering through the doldrums of his former post in Cincinnati. Finally, his men were marched into Chattanooga, under William Sherman and John Schofield's XXIII Corps; the smaller unit was utilized for maneuverability, and hence flanking assignments helped in attack or stalemating Rebel advances. With Atlanta a primary Federal objective, Cox saw action in the crucial Battle at Resaca in the spring of 1864. Although the Union lost more men, Federal troops gained more ground toward their prize of the rail hub.

After Atlanta fell, it seemed that Cox would be going with Sherman on his march toward Savannah, but instead, he was sent back to Tennessee and figured prominently in the Franklin and Nashville campaigns. After its feats, the Schofield Corps, with Cox at its side, were ordered back to the Eastern Theater. While in Washington, in preparation for finishing the war in North Carolina, Cox's coveted major generalship of volunteers finally came. On his way to the Tar Heel state, Cox made sure he visited with Washington dignitaries, preparing for his transition back into politics in the postwar world.

The next chapter for him and Helen, in the political realm, would also contain many battles.

My Dearest Lilla: Civil War Letters Home from General Jacob D. Cox provides readers with the scopes of Eastern and Western Theaters, communiques with high-ranking officials, and the exploits of Cox, demonstrating that the citizen soldier could rise—it also shows that a confidant was needed in that process. Gene Schmiel writes, "Using his own experiences and his letters to Helen as a base, Cox would write extensively about the role of the citizen-soldier in his *Military Reminiscences*. He would advocate military reforms, including opening up leadership positions based on ability and not only West Point credentials, many of which would ultimately be implemented in the US armed forces." Woven into this story is Helen, as Schmiel notes, "For his part, Dolson always exhibited his love and his appreciation of the sacrifices Helen and the family had to make." Cox himself acknowledged, "I long for you very much, but this is the time for endurance and we must trust in God . . . and not flinch from the stern duty." Indeed, that duty was shared by husband and wife, one on the war front, the other at home. Although Helen was vexed that Jacob had not asked her about going off to war, it would not have mattered. Still apparently bothered in looking back on the situation years later, Helen once told a granddaughter, "He had no right to make the decision alone," but she also admitted that "I would have told him to go."

Michael P. Gray
East Stroudsburg University

Preface

Jacob Dolson Cox was an intensely private person. Nevertheless, as he was caught up in the maelstrom of nineteenth-century American history, he created a historically influential public persona. His public career included not only significant service as a general in the Civil War, but also as governor of Ohio, president of the University of Cincinnati, president of the Toledo and Wabash Railway, secretary of the interior, congressman, and dean of the Cincinnati Law School. However, his writings, including authorship of several histories of the Civil War, reviews of books, and extensive letters to family and friends, have become his historical legacy. His two-volume *Military Reminiscences of the Civil War* is one of the finest memoirs of the war and, arguably, the best by a non-professional soldier. His books *Atlanta* (1882) and *The Battle of Franklin* (1897) were the definitive studies of those Civil War–era events for nearly a century.

As typical of the era, Cox was a prolific letter writer. Those letters, along with his official reports and messages during the Civil War, were often the bases for his historical writings. Cox was intellectually well-versed in the ability to "read" people and assess their strengths and weaknesses. His letters contained in-depth analyses of contemporary people and events, their implications, and predictions of future trends which often proved accurate. His letters to his close friend, future president James A. Garfield, as well as to confidant, Salmon P. Chase, an Ohio and national political leader, contained not only analyses of battles but also extensive commentary on the politics and social changes of the era. But of all his letters, those to his wife Helen Finney Cochran Cox were by far the most important element in providing a basis for his future historical writings. They are also a means of understanding his evolution from an untried military neophyte facing the realities of war for the first time to becoming a respected skilled military leader.

During my studies at The Ohio State University in 1968 and 1969, I began research into Cox's life for my doctoral dissertation, *The Career of Jacob Dolson Cox, 1828–1900: Soldier, Scholar, Statesman*. The overwhelming majority of Cox's papers are in the Oberlin College archives, where I spent many months poring through his writings and related material. I was extremely pleased both that Cox kept a careful record of his official correspondences and, just as importantly, that he had legible handwriting!

I found that approximately ten wartime letters from Cox to his wife Helen survive—a few at Oberlin and a few in New York in the papers of their son, Kenyon, a famous artist in the nineteenth century. Those letters showed both the affection he had for Helen and his respect for her as an intellectual equal. Helen was the daughter of Charles Finney, former president of Oberlin College, where, in keeping with the "radical" nature of that institution in its admission policy, she had attended. Using her affectionate nickname, Cox usually addressed his letters to her as "My Dearest Lilla" and signed himself as "Your Loving Husband, Dolson" (his middle name).

In 2010, I began to write a biography of Cox based on my dissertation, modern scholarship, and new material which scholars or archivists had found since 1969. That book, *Citizen-General: Jacob Dolson Cox and the Civil War Era*, was published by Ohio University Press in 2014. During my research in 2012, I had returned to Oberlin College in hope that additional materials about Cox might have been acquired by the archives. Oberlin archivist Ken Grossi told me that, in 1994, his office had received from Ellen Spears, Helen's great-great-granddaughter, a typescript of his letters to Helen during the war. When he told me that there existed 213 letters in the group, which comprised over 150 pages of text, I was astounded.

I had previously seen only a few of these letters. The remainder, or copies thereof, had apparently been kept by the family until this typescript was prepared. Unfortunately, the letters were not kept in their original form and the fate of the actual letters is unknown. According to the family, Helen, with her husband's assistance, had at some point, perhaps in their retirement years in Oberlin (1897–1900), transcribed the letters' texts into what they called a "copybook." It appears that she excised those portions of the letters dealing with family matters. In at least one case, she removed references to an embarrassing family situation involving the arrest of Cox's brother-in-law for cooperating with the Confederacy.[1] It seems likely that Cox, an eminent historian, would have ensured that all matters related to his wartime experiences were included. Although unknowable, Cox's removal of anything pertinent to the war seems unlikely. At the same time, it is regrettable that Helen's wartime letters to her husband are not extant, although many of her letters to family and some prominent individuals are available in the Oberlin Archives and elsewhere.

This typescript is a treasure-trove of information, insights, and analysis. Within, the stoic, introverted Jacob Cox revealed—as he did to no one else—his inner thoughts and concerns to his beloved partner, providing her with in-depth discussions and analyses of the war, his changing life, his ambitions, and other related topics. Cox's books and other writings about the Civil War constitute an important part of the conflict's memory. He not only participated in but also objectively and skillfully recorded historical events; his works are viewed by historians as important contributions to the genre. These letters, annotated in this book to provide context and background, are another part of his historical legacy. They were clearly used by Cox when he wrote his postwar histories and they contain the first draft of his analysis of the military and the socio-political events of the day. They also create a balanced picture of a person who became a Renaissance Man in the Gilded Age as he made the transition from an unestablished military man to respected general officer.

In addition, these letters offer an inside look at many of the problems the nation had to face and resolve as it entered the unforeseen period of continent-wide civil war. From creating a mass volunteer army on the base of a tiny regular force, to dealing with the manifold political and military agendas at the national and state levels, to deciding on war objectives, from reunion to abolition, the nation underwent a massive transformation during the Civil War era.

Jacob Cox was not only part of the process of change; he was an astute observer and analyst of it. The fact that he served in both the Eastern and Western theaters, as well as in West Virginia and on administrative duty in Ohio, while working with key actors at both the state and national level, allowed him to have a more variegated window on the experience of the Civil War than most others. That too is a major element of these letters' value as we see through Cox's pen his family's and the nation's evolution and adaptation to the many new and unexpected realities and results of a continental war and enormous socio-political revolutions.

I would like to thank Ms. Ellen Spears and Mr. Ken Grossi for providing access to these letters; Hal Jespersen for his wonderful maps; and Don Richardson for his skillful editing of and advice about this book. Any mistakes I made in processing these letters or in my analysis are, of course, my own responsibility.

Editorial Decisions

Cox's letters to home were written during military campaigns and often hurriedly under difficult circumstances. Thus, although he was usually meticulous in formulating his language, these letters contain numerous abbreviations, occasional odd spelling, and colloquialisms. Also, there are occasional references to personal friends of the Coxes about whom little is known and often well-known people, e.g. General George McClellan, are only referred to in a short-hand way, e.g. "McC."

For the most part, I have let the letters speak for themselves. I left the abbreviations unchanged on the presumption that the reader can discern that, for example, "R.R." means railroad; "Tenn." means Tennessee; "hdqtrs" means headquarters; "&e" means etc.; "regt." means regiment; and "Secesh" means secessionists. I have left spellings such as "centre" and "despatches" unchanged for the same reasons. When referring to army corps in the letters, Cox uses Arabic numerals. In the descriptive narrative, I have followed the usual practice of using Roman numerals to designate corps, e.g., XXIII instead of 23.

Finally, at several places I have inserted brackets "[ ]" to provide context to the reader.

Introduction

> "So far as my personal enjoyment of life is concerned,
> I have never been more content or happier
> than during our field campaigning."
> —Jacob Dolson Cox to General John Schofield, 12 July 1866

In this 1866 letter to one of his former commanders General John Schofield, Jacob Cox expressed a feeling he could not have imagined a few years earlier. Nothing in Cox's background or upbringing indicated that he either could be or would be a military man. As Cox would write later, "I have become used to being surprised as to my own fate, and take it rather quietly, feeling a kind of third person's curiosity at looking on to see what is to become of me."[1] Yet by the end of the Civil War, he had performed so skillfully on the battlefield that in 1865, General William Tecumseh Sherman offered him a brigadier-generalship in the regular army. The book *Citizen-General: Jacob Dolson Cox and the Civil War Era* explores that process in detail. This companion book considers Cox's thinking as that process evolved during his military service, while also providing insights, through Cox's words, into many elements of the revolutionary changes in the national political, military, and social landscapes.

Jacob Dolson Cox, the first son of Jacob Dolson Cox I and Thedia Redelia Kenyon, was born on October 27, 1828, in Montreal, Canada. His mother was a direct descendant of Elder William Brewster, the religious leader on the *Mayflower*. Cox's Anglo-Saxon identity was firmly anchored in that relationship. His father, a master builder, was in charge of the construction of the church of St. Sulpice in Montreal, Canada when their first son, his namesake, was born. Afterward, the family moved to New York City.[2]

The Puritan tradition, Anglo-Saxon pride, and abolitionism were core elements of Thedia Cox's approach to raising young Dolson (as he came to be called by friends and family).[3] Perhaps not surprisingly, as a youth, Cox was shy, introverted, and bookish. As a teenager, he studied law in a local firm, and taught himself Greek, Latin, and French to prepare for college. In 1845, Dolson attended a revival in New York led by the eminent theologian and abolitionist Charles Finney, who was also president of Oberlin College in Ohio. Finney's commanding presence and fervent evangelization made him a leading actor in the ongoing Second Grand Awakening of the era.[4] On that day, he gave such a powerful sermon that Dolson decided both to give his life to God and to attend Oberlin College under Finney's tutelage to train for the ministry.

Oberlin College, founded in 1833, was an antislavery and Underground Railroad center in Ohio's abolitionist-oriented Western Reserve. A very strict moral sense pervaded the school, with a firm emphasis on religion and the Scriptures.[5] Cox, who never smoked, drank, or cursed, adapted well to the stern environment. He even looked the part of a stereotypical youthful scholar. At 6 feet tall, weighing no more than 135 pounds, he showed little ability for sports or physical activity, though he was reputedly talented at fencing. He often said his favorite activity was reading and, while at Oberlin, he soon became recognized as an intellectual.

During his sophomore year (1848–49), he and Helen Finney, Charles Finney's eldest daughter, met and fell in love. They agreed to marry in the fall of 1849 and Dolson planned to enter the theological seminary in 1850. But theirs was by no means a typical courtship, because, when they first met in Oberlin, the nineteen-year-old Helen had recently been widowed and was pregnant with her first child.

Born on June 10, 1828, in Philadelphia, Pennsylvania, Helen grew into a tall, delicate, religious, reserved, dutiful woman with a keen intellect and refined taste—exactly the kind of woman the stoic, reserved, dutiful, intellectual Dolson Cox would have wanted in a mate. In her youth, she had often traveled with her father on his revivals. As she grew older, however, she resented the stifling bounds placed on her. Few fathers, even in that era, were as strict with his children as was Charles Finney. According to Helen's son William Cochran, as a child she took every opportunity to be away from her father, for example, to visit friends so she "could indulge in games with children without fear of rebuke" from Finney. It is possible that this was one reason why in 1846, at the age of 18, she had agreed to marry an older man, Professor William Cochran of Oberlin. Even then, Finney exhibited his stern and unsympathetic nature, reportedly saying, after giving his blessing to the marriage, "Thou knowest, Oh Lord, that she is no more fit to be married than this chair," emphasizing his remark with a sharp blow on the chair."[6]

Sadly, Helen's husband died in 1847 in New York, to which they had moved. At the time, Helen was several months pregnant and she had returned to Oberlin to live with her parents. While at Oberlin, she and Dolson became very close. She gave birth to her and Cochran's son, William, in March 1848,[7] and she and Dolson were married on November 29, 1849. The Finneys went to Europe earlier that year on an evangelical tour and, for unknown reasons, did not attend the Coxes' wedding. For the next 18 months, the Coxes lived in the Finney home, caring for both Helen's son William and the Finneys' other children, while Dolson pursued his theological studies.[8]

Cox's path to a career as a minister and perhaps a professor of theology seemed preordained. But just as Helen found Charles Finney difficult, so did her husband. During his theological studies, Dolson found that he loved debate about the esoterica of religion and theology. He had an independent intellectual streak unlike most of his fellow theology students, who accepted the Oberlin rule of never questioning their professors. Not surprisingly, Finney did not condone free thinkers. In his teaching, Finney used a confrontational Socratic methodology and most students regarded him with "wholesale fear."[9] These two very different approaches to theology clashed during a class one day in 1851. After Cox had questioned a particular point, Finney reportedly angrily told him, "Dolson, you are not honest, you do not *want* to see the truth." Cox felt he had been deeply insulted. Even after another professor tried unsuccessfully to get Finney to withdraw the remark, Cox decided to cease his studies. He believed that if there could be no debate, then there was no reason to continue studying theology.[10]

Even though the families stayed on good terms, Dolson and Helen decided to move away. In 1851, they took up residence in the Western Reserve town of Warren, Ohio, where he became the region's first superintendent of schools. They would live until the end of the Civil War in Warren, where Helen would give birth to five children. Meanwhile, Dolson became a community leader and, in 1853, he changed careers to one as an attorney and was admitted to the bar. In 1854, he became one of the founders of the Republican Party of Ohio, attracted by its laissez-faire philosophy and its opposition to the expansion of slavery. At the same time, while Cox despised the institution of slavery and despite his education at Oberlin, he was not an egalitarian.

Cox remained active in Republican party leadership for the rest of the 1850s, but did not run for office until 1859 because he wanted to create a more secure economic base for his growing family. He finally decided to seek office after the so-called Wellington Rescue in 1858, when citizens from the Oberlin area prevented slavecatchers from taking freed black men to the South. At public meetings afterward that protested the arrest of the rescuers and the institution of slavery, Cox stated that any solution to the evil of slavery had to come through control of the state and national legislatures. Cox decided to run for an open Ohio Senate seat so he could more actively pursue those solutions.[11]

During the late 1850s, the Cox family had become good friends with another aspiring northeast Ohio Republican politician, James A. Garfield, and his wife Lucretia. In their first attempt to gain public office, the two men were elected to the Ohio Senate in 1859 from adjoining districts. They quickly became leaders there as fervent anti-slavery radicals.

Fearing war was possible as sectionalism worsened, Cox used his influence to get an appointment as a brigadier general in the Ohio militia.[12] He then engaged in an impromptu yet intense self-education in the history and theory of the military arts, reading relevant texts in Greek, Latin, and French. Cox and Garfield, both in their early thirties, had extensive discussions about their roles in a potential conflict with a seceding South. They agreed that because they were among the most adamant antislavery men in the Senate, it would be incongruous for them to shirk their duty and not fight. However, Garfield, who was a burly and boisterous man, told Cox that perhaps he should not join the army because, at six-feet tall and barely 140 pounds, he was too frail for the rigors of war. Ironically, Cox found the military life exhilarating and he only grew stronger physically. Garfield, by contrast, was constantly sick and left the army in 1863.[13]

When he was appointed a brigadier general of Volunteers soon after the war started, Cox the citizen-general believed he was as intellectually prepared for war as any West Pointer.[14] The question remained, of course, how he would react to the bloody and confusing realities on the battlefield.

⸻

Cox made the decision to go to war without consulting Helen, though she knew about his preparations and discussions with Garfield and was, as always, supportive. Her reaction to this decision typified the couple's strong, loving relationship. Years after the war, Helen told one granddaughter, with feigned resentment, "He had no right to make that decision alone. He left me with little children to support alone. I, not he, should have made that decision . . . but of course I would have told him to go."[15]

The firm bonds between them were also exhibited in their correspondence to others. Helen wrote to Lucretia Garfield during the war, "visiting Dolson was enough in itself to insure [sic] complete happiness."[16] On another occasion she told Mrs. Garfield, "was I not assured of my husband's loving appreciation of my work and self-denial, I should faint by the way."[17] For his part, Dolson always exhibited his love and his appreciation of the sacrifices Helen and the family had to make. In one letter, he wrote, "I fully appreciate your noble spirit, dear Lilla . . . My love for you grows very rapidly of late." In another, reflecting their strong and mutual religious beliefs, he wrote, "I long for you very much, but this is the time for endurance and we must trust in God ... and not flinch from the stern duty."[18]

Perhaps the most poignant example of their strong bonds came when their son William Brewster Cox, born on January 26, 1861, died the following September, when Dolson could not come home from the war to help her grieve. Dolson had only been able to see the baby once, and when he learned in early September that the child was seriously ill, he wrote to Helen, "My heart bleeds Lilla, when I think of you watching beside the little one's death-bed, or perhaps already following him to the grave alone." The child died on September 14, and in the copybook Helen added a note on her husband's letter of September 10, "I received this letter the very day our dear little Brewster died—H.F.C." Cox would write later in his memoirs, "I had to swallow my sorrows as well as I could ... leaving my wife uncomforted in her bereavement."[19]

In keeping with the Victorian traditions of the day, Helen accepted most of the responsibility for child-rearing. Despite her unhappiness with her father's rigorous sternness, she inter-mixed her love and admiration for Dolson and her children with strict child-rearing methods of her own. In one letter to her son William Cochran during the war, she wrote, "You know Mama's duty is to point out the errors that every child must hone so that you may be the *perfect* man she hopes to see you." In another letter, she told William, "how good you must be not to disgrace such a father."[20]

It appears that at some point in her youth Helen had held some ambitions to make more of herself than just being a traditional wife. However, perhaps after she was both widowed and gave birth before her twentieth birthday, she had accepted her role and status and put aside her own aspirations, while gaining pleasure from the achievements of her family members. In a postwar letter to their son, Kenyon, Helen wrote that she basked in the reflected glory of her family's achievements and notoriety, stating, "My ambition has always, from childhood, been for fame, and although my own life has been in the quiet domestic lines, the fame of my father, my husband, my son has been dearer than life to me."[21]

In the years leading up to the Civil War, Cox and Garfield were seen as "coming men" in the Republican Party. Both would use their service in the Ohio Senate and the war, as well as their friendship with Salmon P. Chase, as springboards to high-level political careers as the Republican Party led the successful war effort. They even roomed together during legislative sessions in a boarding house run by Republican Party chairman, W. T. Bascom; and

Cox would make Bascom's son, Gustavus, one of his military aides. In 1861, as the secession crisis worsened, Cox and Garfield were active in military drilling on the Capitol grounds. Cox continued his study of the military arts and led discussion groups among the legislators concerning military strategy and tactics. Early in 1861, Ohio Governor William Dennison asked Garfield to lead the legislative effort for war support and Cox to become his military chief of staff. In April 1861 Cox met and became friends with Ohio's first commander, General George McClellan, as they together helped prepare the state for war.

McClellan, who had a strong antipathy to volunteer soldiers, nevertheless was impressed by Cox's acumen and commitment to the war effort. In July 1861, McClellan showed his confidence in the untried Cox by giving him an autonomous command in the Kanawha River valley of Virginia. Within a few weeks, Cox proved his mettle by taking Charleston and Gauley Bridge, key steps toward the creation of the new state of West Virginia. During this period, Cox developed a well-founded reputation as a solid and reliable commander. However, he was not charismatic, and his stoic demeanor ultimately brought him the respect of his troops, but not their adulation. Especially in the first months of the war, some of his men found Cox's teetotaling, non-smoking, and strait-laced approach to life somewhat sanctimonious. Cox repeatedly assured Helen that he was slowly gaining the men's respect, signaling that his evolution as a respected military leader was a gradual one, with several missteps along the way.

In August 1862, Cox transferred to the Army of the Potomac. While he arrived too late to participate in the Second Battle of Manassas, he and his Kanawha Division would play key roles in the subsequent Maryland-Antietam campaign. His Kanawha Division took the key city of Frederick and then were the lead force in the Union victory at the Battle of South Mountain on September 14, 1862. Cox unexpectedly became commander of the IX Corps that day when General Jesse Reno was killed. Cox co-led the Union's left wing at the Battle of Antietam, for which he was promoted to Major General of Volunteers. He was then sent back to West Virginia, where he effectively stemmed a Confederate effort to re-take the incipient state later that year.

After a lengthy period in military administration, Cox marched with General William T. Sherman on the Atlanta campaign as second in command of the Army of the Ohio under General John Schofield. Cox's men cut the critical supply line to the Confederate forces in Atlanta, forcing the rebels to abandon the city in early September 1864. Cox then played an important role in the Franklin-Nashville campaign which would end the war in the West. He commanded the forces on the line at the Battle of Franklin, November 30,

1864, and, in December, he helped ensure the ultimate destruction of the Confederate Army of Tennessee at the Battle of Nashville. Cox rejoined Schofield in North Carolina and participated in the battles leading to Joseph Johnston's surrender in 1865. For a short period of time, he was Military Governor of part of that state before returning to Ohio to campaign for Governor.

Throughout the war, Cox fought actively in the "political-military wars," struggling for rank and place in the army, while gamely seeking recognition for the military contributions of "Political Generals" and citizen soldiers like himself.[22] However, Cox was often his own worst enemy in this politicized arena. Diffident and disinclined to self-promotion by nature, Cox idealistically believed when the war started that any achievements he made would by themselves gain him recognition and promotion. When he experienced disappointments and a lack of recognition in spite of his achievements, he would write bitterly to Helen in early 1864, "I went through the experience of learning that intrigue, pretense, & self puffing are surer roads to promotion than modest performance of duty. It was not a pleasant thing to learn."

In the end, his achievements did gain him some recognition, but his disinclination to self-promotion often led to his being taken for granted by the military leadership. Using his own experiences and his letters to Helen as a base, Cox would write extensively about the role of the citizen-soldier in his *Military Reminiscences*. He would advocate military reforms, including opening up leadership positions based on ability and not only West Point credentials, many of which would ultimately be implemented in the U.S. armed forces.[23]

When the war ended, Cox's political horizons seemed unlimited. Cox stepped onto the national stage in 1865 by winning the Ohio governorship. However, he proved to be an impractical politician, stubbornly standing on his principles and integrity at all times. He lacked the ability to win allies via compromise and he disdained the use of patronage and decried the spoils system, an approach which was, at the time, a fatal political flaw.

During his successful campaign for governor in 1865, Cox engaged in the national debate on Reconstruction against the advice of his party colleagues.[24] Recommending a transition period for black development, he advocated creating a *de facto* new territory along the southeast coast of the nation where freedmen would be protected and privileged. This unique but inherently impractical plan, described in what was called his "Oberlin Letter," divided him from the Radical Republicans and became a *cause célèbre* during the campaign.

His second political misstep came when he supported President Andrew Johnson's approach to Reconstruction for some time. Despite his eventual decision to disavow Johnson, Cox was seen as having "abandoned" the Republican Party at a critical time when it was moving toward a harsher Reconstruction policy. Cox's decision not to run for re-election in 1867 reflected his own and the party's unhappiness with his role in Reconstruction.

At the same time, he retained a strong reputation within the party, as evidenced by both Sherman and Grant advocating that Johnson avoid his ongoing conflict with Congress over Secretary of War Stanton's tenure by appointing Cox to replace him. Later, Grant's respect for Cox's ability led him to nominate Cox as his first Secretary of the Interior. In that office, Cox instituted the federal government's first extensive Civil Service reform program. But within 18 months, he had a falling-out with the President over his reformist ventures and resigned. When Cox opposed Grant's re-election in 1872, his national political career was effectively over. He did serve one term in the House of Representatives in the late 1870s in the hope he could help his former subordinate, President Rutherford B. Hayes, legislatively. However, he achieved little and did not run for re-election.

The last years of his life, 1879–1900, underlined why Cox was considered a Renaissance man, as he spent time as a lawyer, railroad president, congressman, Dean of the Cincinnati Law School, and president of the University of Cincinnati. In his spare time, he did scientific research and served as president of the American Microscopic Society.

His most important post-political career by far was as an influential historian and analyst of the Civil War and his writings are his enduring legacy. His book on Sherman's Atlanta campaign was the definitive study for over a hundred years. His book on the Battle of Franklin was the definitive study of that battle for many decades. His magnum opus was the two-volume *Military Reminiscences of the Civil War*, published posthumously in 1900. It is still cited by historians as a foundation for the memory of many aspects of the war. Cox's dozens of reviews of Civil War books for *Nation* magazine also played an important role in shaping contemporary thinking about the war.

Cox's wartime letters were a key foundation of his Civil War writings, serving in effect as his first draft. The letters he wrote to Helen are the most incisive and revealing of all. These in-depth missives are among the most useful collections of Civil War letters written by a self-made and not formally-trained military man. They span the entire war and describe how Cox made the voyage from untested military neophyte to highly-respected corps commander. They are the work of an intellectual "Political General" who performed well enough for Sherman to offer him a military commission at war's end.

These letters show us the missteps Cox made as he adapted his stoic and unemotional mien to training common soldiers. They illustrate his views of the rivalry between West Point-trained professional soldiers and self-made generals for position and power and how that affected his own career. We learn from the letters why even such strong critics of volunteer soldiers as George McClellan and William T. Sherman came to recognize Cox's military ability. Also, we see how one man, faced with the momentous changes wrought by the Civil War, adapted so well and so unexpectedly that, at war's end, his military career seemed to be an inevitable springboard to the heights of political power.

These letters provide both the scholar and the general reader greater understanding of how these titanic, unexpected events transformed not only one man, but an entire generation. They also illustrate the love, respect, and admiration the Coxes had for one another, as well as Jacob Cox's inclination to treat his college-educated wife as an intellectual equal. Finally, a constant theme in their letters is their firm religious faith that God would protect Dolson and bring him home to the family hearth at war's end.

1

The Making of a Soldier, 1861

> I am hearty and healthy and browning like a berry. I've foresworn shaving this week, & shall let my whole beard grow, and really believe the outdoor life will give me strength & be of lasting service to me. I don't have time to give you any notion of my life or its duties. I work like a horse and find no leisure moments.
>
> —Dolson to Helen, May 5, 1861

April 1861 was a time of growing tension within the Ohio Legislature, where Jacob Cox and James Garfield wondered if Civil War would come. For several weeks, they had pored over Cox's French and English language military books, led military drills on the Capitol grounds, and discussed their roles if war came. Both had decided that, as dedicated opponents of secession and slavery, it was their duty to fight. Then, Cox wrote later, "On Friday, the twelfth of April, 1861, a Senator exclaimed 'the telegraph announces that the secessionists are bombarding Ft. Sumter'. . . the gloomy thought that civil war had begun in our own land overshadowed everything."[1]

The next day, the Ohio Senate passed bills to enroll and organize the State's militia. With Cox acting as Governor William Dennison's military chief of staff, the legislature appropriated $450,000 for arms purchases and equipment and $500,000 to fulfill President Abraham Lincoln's request for Ohio's quota of the total of seventy-five thousand volunteers.[2]

Dennison soon afterward named Cox a brigadier general of Ohio Volunteers and convinced General George B. McClellan, who was at the time a railroad executive based in Cincinnati, to command Ohio's troops.[3] The two young men—McClellan was thirty-five, Cox thirty-three—struck up a solid friendship as they prepared Ohio for war. McClellan, a West Point graduate who normally disdained volunteer soldiers, was clearly impressed by Cox's intellectual preparation and commitment. For some time, he would treat Cox as a protégé, even telling him once that he was his best brigadier general.[4]

Ohio's war objectives in these early days of the war were focused on the northern counties of Virginia south of the Ohio River. A majority of Virginians in that region had voted against secession in a state referendum and early meetings in 1861 in Wheeling by Unionists, led by Francis Pierpont, were actively discussing separation from Virginia and the creation of a new, pro-Union state. McClellan perceived rightly that the opportunity was ripe to take advantage of pro-Union sentiment via early military moves into the region.[5]

McClellan and Cox prepared schedules and estimates of the needs of Ohio's ten thousand troops to be sent into the field, and McClellan ordered Cox to explore possible training camp sites. On April 29, 1861, Brigadier-General Cox left Columbus with half of the 3rd Ohio Regiment and the 11th Ohio Regiment—with which he would be associated for much of the war's early years—for Camp Dennison, near Cincinnati. This base lacked everything necessary for a military camp, from tents to sanitary facilities. So just as the unprepared national government was "making it up as it went along," Cox's first job was one for which none of his military reading could have prepared him.[6]

At the camp, the new troops had to be taught every aspect of military life, from drill and tactics and unquestioningly following orders to how to make requisitions for equipment. Untrained cooks prepared many an unpalatable meal. Volunteers who had never been far from home contracted new diseases like measles, so hospitals and infirmaries had to be created. In a harbinger of how the war would provide the foundation for modern American nursing, a group of Cincinnati nuns volunteered at Camp Dennison as nurses and performed yeoman duty.

The intellectual, aloof, and stoic Cox too was learning new lessons in the military arts. He had to manage many young men who were not always ready for the strict discipline he demanded of them. His frequent reassurances to Helen over the next months that he was making progress in his relations with his men probably indicated that things were not going as well as he hoped. Ultimately, however, especially as his men realized that he was always committed to their welfare, Cox gained their respect, but never their admiration or love in the way McClellan would.[7]

On April 30, one day after his arrival, Cox wrote his first letter from the camp to Helen—the first found in the typescript—as he began to muse about his new reality and the significant responsibilities he had been given.

The Making of a Soldier, 1861

Camp Dennison, Tues. 30th April 1861

My second day of camp life. I came down yesterday morning with 1300 men and began camp here. Rough lumber was waiting for us, our engineers had staked off the ground, and about 2 past one we arrived here and went at it.

By dark about half the huts enough for the men were up. I took up my quarters at an old school-house, bringing with me my aid-de-camp Mr. [Gustavus] Bascom.[8] We brought down a cot apiece and a comforter, beside our overcoats & shawls—also some articles for housekeeping, such a half dozen tin plates, iron knives & forks, etc., also a ration box of cold victuals. A telegraph office is established here also, so that my orders come through to me readily.

We managed to get a candle after dark, and when the men crept into their sheds or under piles of lumber, for the huts were not completed, I threw off my uniform coat, put on my overcoat, wrapped my shawl about me, and went off into the land of nod.

Shortly after midnight we had a fierce storm of wind & rain which blew through the broken windows over me at a terrible rate, but as I slept with my cap on it did not trouble me or give me a cold.

Today the men are still at their huts trying to get them finished. The weather is variable, bright and warm when the sun is out, cold & blustering when the clouds are over us. But little else can be done but build till tomorrow, when drill will commence and things take a more soldierly form. The responsibility of this new position weighs heavily on one sometimes.

> In his next letter Cox expanded on his adaptation to military life, including, like many others, that he was beginning to grow a beard and that, perhaps to his surprise, military life was making him physically stronger.

Camp Dennison 5th May 1861

In the hurry and the turmoil of the camp I found no opportunity to write on Thurs. as I intended and how many minutes I may get today is hard to tell. I am living in the same manner as when I wrote on Tues. and as we shall be constantly receiving troops for some days to come I see little chance of bettering myself immediately.

The weather here has not been good this week. One or two days have been fair, but we have had several very wet muddy days & have begun at the worst end of camp life. I think every day will make matters better.

I am hearty and healthy and browning like a berry. I've foresworn shaving this week, & shall let my whole beard grow, and really believe the outdoor life will give me strength & be of lasting service to me. I don't have time to give you any notion of my life or its duties. I work like a horse and find no leisure moments.

The next letters dealt with many organizational issues as the Union created a mass citizens' army. Calling upon his teaching experience in Warren, Cox made sure each man got instruction in drill, tactics, and discipline in the temporary "schools." Cox also had to convince the ninety-day men to sign up for a longer period, a task made easier when many leaders from home towns visited the camps to encourage the men to do their duty.

Another issue which would be a major problem for the Union army was the administration's decision to allow newly-recruited military units to elect their leaders. This rewarded the men who raised the volunteer companies, but it also led, in Cox's view, as stated in his *Military Reminiscences*, to "hosts of charlatans and incompetents" being put in command and to major problems on the battlefields. One incident in particular galled Cox when Garfield was not chosen as Colonel of the 7th Regiment. The victor, E.B. Tyler, would be a thorn in Cox's side later. Cox too was concerned by delays in his confirmation as a brigadier general of Volunteers. These letters also discuss personal matters, including that Helen (then pregnant with their fifth child) visited him that May. They also detail Cox's relations with senior commanders, especially McClellan.

Camp Dennison 7th May 1861

I hoped to have written in time for the mail today, but the constant hurry & drive of work has prevented, and besides, as I still continue to quarter in the school-house, I can get no such solitude as I like when writing home. The Telegraph and Express offices are both in this little room, and every body crowds in, so that privacy during the day is a sheer impossibility.

When night comes I am little better off, having four or five persons constantly about me until bed-time. The weather has been villainous most of the week past, and the mud terrible. The men have been forced to work in the rain getting their huts built, and our new arrivals of troops have been badly exposed till they could get some shelter for themselves.

When the fourth regiment came they bivouacked, building campfires and laying boards against the fence for shelter, and they would have done nicely but for the drenching rain which set-in about midnight and soon made mire of the ground around them.

The Warren boys came yesterday with the 7th regt. and, as usual, with our arrivals, in the midst of a falling deluge. We had a few huts up for them and they managed to get some shelter, and were all bright as larks this morning, and went to work to complete their quarters. . . .

The 7th elected officers this P.M and I hoped Garfield would be Col. but he was defeated by sharp maneuvering and Tyler of Ravenna elected.

Our life has not been very military, for hut-building and rainy weather have sadly interfered with drill, but we hope for better things now.

My hopes of being relieved and allowed a chance to go home have been baffled thus far, but I continue to hope. I am left alone in command of the camp, our Maj. Gen. [McClellan] having his hands full elsewhere. We shall expect him every day until he arrives however, and then we will see what can be done. I hope it may continue bright, for wet weather is emphatically lost time here. Every hour ought to be improved in drilling and learning duty, for we can't tell how soon we may be ordered off.

Camp Dennison May 25th 1861

The week has slipped away in cares and hurry and I have been hindered from writing until now, & now can only begin a letter.

On Mon Gen. [William] Rosecrans[9] took command, but all that day and Tues. we were crowded together in the little school-house, with no room for either of us to do anything. On Wed. I got my new shanty quarters, and right glad I am to be here. On Thurs. we began having our own mess, and we enjoy this also very much.

Our family consists of my Brigade Major [Henri] De Villiers [a Frenchman] and Bascom. The situation of my quarters is delightful, and during the fine weather we are having, we all enjoy it hugely. It is very hard to believe that you have come and gone.

Sun 26th The question of the enlistment for three years or the war is before our men and they must settle it today or tomorrow. Most of them will go, and the places of those that refuse will be made up by companies lately formed. It is settled that Ohio will have 21 regiments. Garfield will undoubtedly get one. The Generals will have to be reappointed by the President, but Gov. Dennison does not anticipate any difficulty in the way of those whom he has already appointed.

Yesterday about 3 P.M. Gen. Rosecrans sent orders to have our Brigades on parade for inspection as soon as possible. De Villiers, my Brigade Major, jumped on a horse & made him fly almost, as he conveyed the order, and we had our whole line formed in less than ten minutes, and far in advance of the other Brigades. We got high compliments on our promptness.

Today Gov. Dennison, Gen. McClellan and the Governor's staff have been in consultation with us as to the longer enlistment, and the more perfect organization of the Army. My time has been fully taken up, and although for two days it has been hot enough to roast eggs we have been busy as bees, sweating under the sun at a terrible rate, but I keep hearty as ever.

It is daily becoming more uncertain how long we shall be here, the late little battle in Virginia [a minor skirmish at Sewell's Point, near Norfolk, VA] is quite likely to be the prelude to more stirring things. I doubt if we shall keep snug in our new quarters long after the men are clothed and a little better drilled.

I make myself no promises now as to the future—every day brings so many duties & so many uncertainties that I am tired of cheating myself with hopes of seeing the little ones, which come to naught after all.

Camp Dennison June 2nd 1861
Your friend brought the box safely, and I find it a very nice thing. The articles in it are all very nice and very welcome. The shirts I like very much. Bascom sends his thanks to Nelly[10] [Cox's daughter Helen, age 11] for the needle books, and I send her a good kiss for mine.

An Oberlin Professor is here today using his influence with the Oberlin Company to keep the ranks full. Most of them who go in for the three years have a furlough to go home and start tomorrow. They will have a grand reception at home & will create quite a sensation in their new uniforms.

We are still all mixed up with the question of the enlistment for the war, and shall be embarrassed unless the three months' men are soon taken off our hands....

A hard rain the other night nearly drove me from my quarters. The board roof of my hut leaked in all directions, and after various movings of my cot, I was forced at last to sleep under the oil-cloth covering, & let the water trickle down and off again....

My days are so occupied and I am so constantly in the presence of others that I get very little opportunity to write & you must pardon me, if I am somewhat irregular. Perhaps I may be able to make a better system of it before long. At any rate I will try.

I cannot add more tonight, but will try to do so in the morning. Remember me kindly to all our friends. I am gratified to know that they show their sympathy with you in my absence. Heaven bless them for it.

Camp Dennison 14th June, 1861
We are busy today getting rid of the three months men, and a very few

days will put the regiments upon the permanent three years footing. It will be a great relief to us when it is done, for the mixture of organizations has been a perfect nuisance, and until we are settled we feel that our time is wasted, for the troops are to elect new officers and it is a hopeless task to attempt much in the way of drill & discipline when the officers feel that they are dependent upon the caprice of the men for their continuance in their position. When however the three years organization is complete all this will be changed. As it is, the changing process has spoiled more than two weeks work for us.

I see no immediate prospect of getting home. I cannot leave while we are unsettled, for it needs constant care & work to preserve decent order & prevent total disorganization. Afterward there is no telling how soon we may be ordered away.

The weather has been oppressively hot for a week past. I think I never felt it more so. It makes us look with longing eyes toward the Virginia mountains, & hope we may be sent up the valley of the Great Kanawha, as it is rumored a force is to be sent there, to act on a line parallel to that of the troops now at Grafton and Philippi. . . .

The day before yesterday I felt some bad effects of riding in the sun at midday without my havelock, but was entirely over it next day.

I get no official notice of my reappointment by the President as yet, though I hear from a dozen sources that it is determined. I am also uncertain, if appointed, who my staff officers will be, for appointment of all but an aid-de-camp will be made at Washington, and the aid, I shall have to select from officers elected in the line. I shall try to keep De Villiers, who is a soldier, every inch of him.[11]

Camp Dennison, 19th June, 1861

We look for marching orders soon. One of my regiments will probably be ordered off within a couple of days, but I get no orders for myself personally, nor do I know whether I shall be re-appointed. I am very anxious to have it settled.

I do not court the responsibility. If there are experienced & qualified military men who can do the duties better, I will cheerfully yield them my place, but one way or the other it ought to be decided. The influences at Washington are such that my expectations of the appointment are not very sanguine. But appointed or not, there is a month of my present commission remaining and we are likely to find enough to do in that time.

The change in the regiments will be completed in a day or two & the reorganization done with. Major DeVilliers has been elected Major of the 8th Regt. and as my keeping my command is uncertain, I have advised him to take it. If we are ordered into Va., we do not anticipate being kept there a great while, but look for being recalled to form a more important movement south: but this is the merest conjecture.

I continue very well & very hearty. The work here agrees with me, but I look with longing eyes to my books and the quiet of home. Still it would be impossible to be content there, with the country all on fire with excitement. We must see the war through, and if God spares my life to see an honorable peace, after the establishment of the authority of constitutional government I shall go back to my studies and my profession with new zest.

> In the next letters, Cox wrote that he finally received his commission as a brigadier general with the help of Secretary of the Treasury Salmon P. Chase. In response to Helen's concerns, these two letters also contain significant introspection about his fate and the future, as well as Cox's oft-stated reliance on the Almighty.

Camp Dennison 22nd June 1861

My commission for the three years service has come from Washington. Sec. Chase enclosed it with a very friendly letter from himself. So it seems I am well looked upon there, though in all this matter the weight of the responsibility has weighed heavy upon me, & it has been a question of duty rather than desire for promotion.

I trust that in all circumstances of danger God will give me such prudence, wisdom & courage, that you & the children will never have occasion to be ashamed of me. I have no marching orders yet, but am on the look-out for them.

Camp Dennison, 26th June, 1861

I am still here, and am still uncertain as ever how long I shall remain. Two of my regiments are gone & two remain to be completed by the addition of new companies, and armed with better weapons. I fear it will be a fortnight before this last can be done. Meanwhile what orders I shall receive are entirely uncertain.

I was ordered to report by letter to Gen. Scott [General-in-Chief Winfield Scott] for orders, and have done so, but it will be several days before anything further could be heard from him, and I do not expect to hear anything except that I shall continue under Gen. McClellan's command. But there is time enough.

This matter will not be finished in a month, and I bide my time. I have always done so before, and have had no cause to regret it, so that although

I suspect there was a little crafty management by which Gen. [Newton] Schleich [one of McClellan's other brigadiers] was the first ordered away, I console myself with "l'homme propose, mais Dieu dispose."[12]

Major DeVilliers has been elected Lieut. Col. of the 8th and will leave me. I shall miss him much, for I have taken a great liking to the impetuous little Frenchman, & his attachment to me is unbounded. He would stay on my staff with only a Capt's rank now, if I should say the word, and he declares he prefers it. But I have a duty to do to his family & the regiment, & so I tell him to take his promotion. Bascom will probably get a position in a Co. in the regular Army, if so, I shall have a new aid, & must look around for a good military man.

I send with this a letter from Gov. Dennison & one from Mr. Chase in regard to my appointment which you may file away. Perhaps they will have an interest to the children twenty years hence. Every thing about my position seems to me like a dream sometimes. I don't realize what it is generally, but go along about my duties until something occurs which forces my attention to the position I am actually in, and then I have a fit of astonishment at it.

When I ask myself what the future will be, I am equally perplexed, and give up all attempt to imagine. If I escape the chances of war, I picture to myself a quiet home again, with my books & the pleasant shade of our quiet village street, & I love the dream, though I know well enough that I am embarked on a public career which circumstances will determine quite differently from my dreams.

I am amused at the way in which you speak of my stay here. You show that you share my impatience to be where the danger is to be braved, & the duty done, yet you also dread the danger and almost wish me out of the service altogether. It is natural that you feel so, but I hope you will cultivate the feeling that whether in the field or at home, the same Divine Wisdom controls all forces & all lives, and that it does not become us to fret at the possibilities of danger, since "not a sparrow falls to the ground without our Father."

Stephen Cole [Helen's nephew] left with his regiment yesterday, I saw him with his musket and knapsack, marching at the head of the company as they filed past me in marching to the cars from the camp, and he bade me a cheerful good bye, full of vigor and hope.

Nothing has touched me more than the universal expression of the unwillingness of my regiments to go into the field without me. They insist that they will be satisfied with no other commander, and their last words as they waved an adieu from the cars was that they should hope to see me head the column in a few days.

In his last two letters from Camp Dennison, Cox exhibited both his nervous tension as he contemplated his first assignment and his confidence that he would succeed. Paralleling an advance to the east by Rosecrans, McClellan had ordered Cox to take some twenty-five hundred men up (south) on the Kanawha River to Charleston and Gauley Bridge. McClellan believed these offensives would be a key to reinforcing Union sentiment in northern Virginia (the future West Virginia). He also saw them as establishing a bridgehead for an advance on Richmond. The fact that he gave Cox greater autonomy than he did to West Point graduate Rosecrans led Cox to admit to Helen both his pride and his concern about being capable of his upcoming responsibilities.[13]

Camp Dennison 3rd July, 1861

My rather wearisome stay here is at last ended, and I have marching orders for Virginia. The delay has not been particularly disadvantageous to me for I go now in command of a movement of considerable importance, and as I shall be for some time at least separate from other troops, it is one in which I shall hope to do some notable service.

I take three regiments from here, which with a company of cavalry and battery of artillery, and another regt of foot now at Gallipolis will give me a force of nearly 4,000 men. We go into Va. at the mouth of the Great Kanawha river, and for the present will occupy the vicinity for a dozen miles or so above the Ohio. My orders will prevent me from any decisive forward movement till Gen. McClellan is ready to cooperate.

My HQ will be near Point Pleasant, Va. to which place you had better direct your letters. I will make arrangements to get whatever is sent there, and let you know in time any change we may make.

I do not regard the service we now go on as likely to lead to any collision with the enemy very soon, for when the rebel forces at Charleston find themselves in danger of attack by front and rear, they will run or disperse, unless they are in greater force & better armed than we have reason to suppose them. Our caution however will be sufficient to keep us from any overconfidence, and make us act carefully. Our men are all very impatient to get away, & the only unpleasant feature of the thing is that I have to take regiments which do not belong to any Brigade—I am to have 2 Ken. regiments & the 12th & 21st Ohio.

I would prefer that you should say as little as possible in regard to my movements, for too much of our operations gets into the newspapers. As soon as our forces are ready to act together we shall make a clean sweep in

The Making of a Soldier, 1861

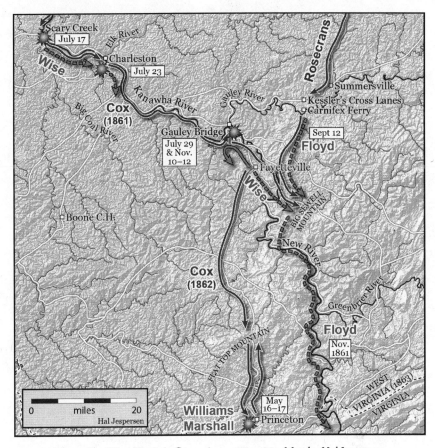

Map 1. The West Virginia Campaigns, 1861–1862. Map by Hal Jespersen.

Western Va. and then see what there is on the other side of the mountains. My hope is that the large rebel army near Richmond may be signally defeated and so destroy the prestige and moral power of the rebellion. I think it will be comparatively easy work after that.

It would be very sweet to see you and the little ones once more before starting, but since I can't, there is nothing for it but to go ahead where duty calls, and trust God for a quick end to the war. You must excuse me for not writing much for my hands are full of work till we get off. Tomorrow two regiments will start, and I shall go with the third the day after.

Camp Dennison 7th July 1861

The delay of the R.R. Co. in furnishing transportation has hindered my getting off as soon as I expected. One regt. went last night, one is already at Gallipolis, and another goes today, & I go with it. Two more follow in a day or two.

My attention to my duties has been rewarded by the most independent & responsible command given to any of the Brigadiers. Shall I not give every day & hour to it, & so try to command success? All my staff have gone, and we are staying here in the most unsettled condition—worse than camp confusion is about us.

2

Baptism of Fire

THE HILLS OF (WEST) VIRGINIA

> Military men are held responsible for success without much question being made as to the means given them to secure it, & I sometimes fear that the embarrassments & delays occasioned by my not having the kind of assistance in cavalry & artillery, & in good weapons which was expected, will make my expedition here seem less energetic & successful than it should be. But whatever blame may come, I shall do my duty as well as I know how & leave the rest with Providence as calmly as I can.
>
> —Dolson to Helen, July 22, 1861

The parallel movements into northwestern Virginia by McClellan's troops under Rosecrans and Cox had both military and political objectives. Union control there would solidify political support against secession and provide crucial reinforcement to a nascent movement by regional leaders to create a new, loyal state. Military success would create bases for campaigns to be launched to the east toward Richmond and to the south toward Kentucky and Tennessee. Further, these campaigns would be an essential element of the Union ensuring control of the Baltimore and Ohio (B&O) railroad, the key rail link from Washington and Baltimore to the Midwest, which ran along Virginia's northern border.[1]

West Virginia's rugged, forested, mountainous countryside with few serviceable (and all perennially-muddy) roads presented numerous barriers to armies and their supply trains in the Civil War years. Also, all movement of forces would necessarily be funneled through narrow valleys and defiles surrounded by high peaks, making them easy to defend against attacking forces. Cox would adapt to these difficult conditions, but he never found them palatable. On the other hand, he frequently took the time to describe in some detail for Helen the flora and fauna of the regions where he campaigned.[2]

On May 26, Confederate forces had made the first move to solidify their control, occupying the B&O Railroad at Grafton, Virginia. On May 27, McClellan sent some Ohio militia troops over the Ohio River to link up with two Unionist Virginia regiments to re-take Grafton. The Confederates retreated in a panic toward Philippi and on to Beverly on June 3. McClellan's report, which he sent to Washington using a new tool in war, the wire telegraph, made it seem like a major triumph. Northern newspapers colorfully trumpeted the victory of the "Young Napoleon."[3]

Reacting to McClellan's success, Robert E. Lee, then Jefferson Davis's military adviser in Richmond, was ordered to lead a military response, sending forty-five hundred men under his adjutant, General Robert Garnett, to block the passes from Beverly and Grafton. He ordered a separate force under former Virginia governor General Henry A. Wise to the Kanawha River valley to block Cox's advance.[4]

While McClellan was hopeful that Cox would do well in his initial assignment, it seems clear that he was worried that the untried amateur soldier might fail. As a result, he had sent Cox detailed instructions about every aspect of preparing for the campaign. Also he limited Cox's responsibility at first only to hold off Wise until he and Rosecrans finished off Garnett in the east, at which point both armies would attack Wise.[5] Early in July Cox took the 11th Ohio and the 1st and 2nd Kentucky Regiments to Gallipolis, Ohio. There, he was to pick up the 21st Ohio and head for Point Pleasant—near the mouth of the Kanawha River where it joined the Ohio River—and begin his first military campaign. Cox noted in his memoirs that he was pleased to have this autonomous command, a privilege which few generals, political or professional, had early in the war.

When Cox arrived at Gallipolis, he found that McClellan had changed his orders. Cox was now to make an offensive march to Charleston and Gauley Bridge and, if possible, drive out Wise. Cox began his movement from Point Pleasant on July 11, riding upriver (south) on river steamboats. Cox's description of his travel underlined both his writing ability and the wonderment (as well as a bit of naïveté) a neophyte soldier was likely feeling at that critical moment.

Cox's next four letters described the inevitable problems in the first days of a campaign involving green troops and officers on both sides:

Gallipolis 10th July 1861

Having a moment's leisure before the embarkation of troops for Point Pleasant, I will try to improve it by writing to you, though what success I shall have depends upon the number of interruptions I may be subjected to. I find my command a good deal extended by Gen. McClellan's order.

He has made for me a military district of the Kanawha, extending from Parkersburg to Guyandotte inclusive, & running back till we meet. I shall have 8 regts. under my orders and a good deal of separate responsibility.

I have been hard at work ever since I came. Rode yesterday on horseback nearly thirty miles, got soaked twice by heavy showers, and am here hearty & strong as need be.

I have a command that means work, & Gen. McClellan in a very kind letter speaks of it as the most important detachment yet made. God grant I may do my duty well and successfully. Three regiments are in this place, & I take them into Virginia today. We shall go about five miles in steamers. After that I will keep you posted as to our movements.

Headquarters Dist. of the Kanawha, 12th July 1861

I have just returned from an expedition thirteen miles up the Kanawha where I took two regts yesterday. I go back today with parts of two more.

My yesterday's trip was a very pleasant one. I sent scouting parties out in the morning to see that the way was clear, & we followed on starting about three o'clock.

The P.M. was a lovely one, the troops filled three steamers crowding them full as hives, and as we went up the romantic river, between the high wooded hills, passing here & there a farm or a little hamlet, opening into new reaches of the river, our flags flying, band playing, the pageant was certainly an imposing one.

We reached 12 mile creek just about sunset. The advanced guard had possession of the village and the two brass rifled cannon were gleaming from the top of the high hill beyond the houses. The tents were carried up the heights, & the last rays of the sun shown upon as lovely a scene as ever was pictured. The three boats lay in the narrow river below, the hillsides were covered with the soldiers and the tents and cannon above stood out in bold relief.

About 10 o'clock a countryman came in a panic, with information that Gen. [Henry] Wise & 400 men were coming down upon us; but we have learned to doubt rumors, so we quietly kept out our scouts & pickets, occupied the passes, & went to sleep, ready to spring to arms at a moment's notice: but confident there was no force in Western Va. that would dare attack us.

The morning dawned as beautifully as if there were no such thing as war, & the camp being peaceful and undisturbed, I came back to this place to arrange for forwarding the remainder of my army. I am confident that we shall have no general engagement with the enemy for some time to come. They will probably retreat before us as far as Gauley River, and there, if at all, we may have some fighting.

Of course I am as cautious as though the enemy were bolder & more enterprising, for I do not wish to make any mistakes, but you need have no apprehensions of danger at present. They have been all around here, & the Union men have been leaving in scores, but they keep retreating as we advance.

Red House Va. 14th July 1861

We have now come some thirty two miles up the Kanawha through the most romantic scenery, the romance being heightened by the fact that we have an enemy in front who might make serious use of the mountains & defiles.

Until yesterday the general order of march was to have a strong scouting party in advance on each side of the river, and have the steamers follow up with most of the troops & baggage. Yesterday morning one of our boats got aground in a narrow rocky channel & we did not know but we were to be shipwrecked. The delay separated us a little from the advance guard, and we had hardly got off when we heard a cannon shot from our own artillery ahead, & a man in a skiff shouted to us that a general engagement had begun. We knew it could not be very general till we got in, & so we steamed ahead, threw out a regiment on one side with the artillery & four companies on the other, pushing ahead with skirmishers in advance.

We found that a party of the enemy's horsemen had fired upon our ordnance guard from the opposite side of the river, but they scampered as if the old Nick [Satan] was after them when our rifled cannon threw a shot among them. Once or twice beside we have done a little skirmishing and this is all we have seen of the enemy who retires steadily before us. We have very little prospect of any serious resistance before reaching Charleston, which is some 25 miles above us. Perhaps not even then. We are to remain here a day or so, waiting for a better concentration of our forces. I hope to date my next letter from Charleston.

Mouth of the Pocatalico 16 July 1861

We are not yet at Charleston as I had hoped to be before writing again, but one must get accustomed to see his plans fail in some particulars of time etc. The last days march was in the face of continued skirmishing, which amounted to very little however, for the rascals opposed to us took such good pains to keep out of danger, that their own shot had very little effect.

One of our men was pretty badly wounded. I am now encamped here awaiting the rest of my artillery, tents, cavalry, etc. I may be kept here two or three days.

Charleston is a day's march ahead & Gen. Wise is there in full force. His army is variously estimated, but I suppose it is about 5,000 men of all arms. Our lack of cavalry hinders us from reconnoitering as fully as we would like to do.

Gen. McClellan's victory [Battle of Rich Mountain, July 11] will dampen their courage and we do not anticipate serious trouble from them unless they get very strong entrenched positions.

There has been a singular enchantment about this expedition up the Kanawha. The spice of danger has added to the enjoyment, and until yesterday the weather was charming. The mixture of horseback riding and steamboat sailing has been just the thing, and very little has occurred to mar the pleasure.

Sunday night we had rumors of an attack, & what little sleep I got was on the ground, rolled in my blanket: we had no attack however, and are confident the enemy dare not make one. Had my artillery and cavalry been with me I am sure we should have been beyond Charleston before this. We are now about forty miles from the Ohio, and considering all circumstances we have done pretty well.

> As he advanced, Cox received an encouraging message from McClellan, urging him to "win your spurs by capturing Wise & occupying Gauley Bridge. I impatiently wait to hear from you that my expectations are justified. Do not fail me but push straight on & complete the first act of our drama."[6] But Cox's first military action would not turn out as he and McClellan had hoped.
>
> At the Battle of Scary Creek on July 17, Cox's forward forces acted impetuously after initially driving back the Confederates. The rebels had then returned in force and killed 10 Union men and wounded 35 others, leading ultimately to a standoff. McClellan criticized Cox for what he thought was a failure and, in his next two letters, Cox complained to Helen that he was being unjustly judged, noting his lack of cavalry and promised equipment. Cox told Helen that ultimately Scary Creek would be seen as a success, but he admitted his mistakes and said he would accept his fate.

Mouth of Poca Creek, 20 July 1861

You must not complain if my letters are very short, for I feel obliged to be out about camp every hour when not necessarily engaged in official business at my desk. The responsibility makes me uneasy unless I myself see what is going on. I am concentrating my force here which is about as high up the river as we can go without some decisive measure of strength with the hostile force. It is principally encamped about five miles from us.

I am without cavalry, having less than forty mounted men, and these undrilled & next to worthless. I was to have had two companies of about 70 each. I was to have had six rifled cannon, but have only two, so that in these very important branches of the service, especially for this country, I am very poorly provided. This makes it necessary for me to move slowly, & I incline to the opinion that it may be well to bring in another force in behind them, but I will not bore you with such matters.

The 12th Regt. had a little battle on the 17th [Battle of Scary Creek], having been sent out to reconnoiter, they found a battery of the enemy in a strong position and attacked it. They were fairly victorious, when their ammunition gave out and the enemy received reinforcements, & they retired. There was no need of their doing so, as they might have sustained themselves till I could reinforce them, but the Colonel of the regt. lacked judgement, & the men were not led as they deserved to be—the rebels sustained a loss eight times as large as ours, besides losing a cannon destroyed. They were so severely handled that their small parties now keep very shy of us.

Our lack of cavalry prevents our getting information. We cannot send footmen far, by reason of their liability to be cut off, & we are left to guess. The force opposed to us is generally spoken of by the residents here as being five or six thousand—but I don't believe they have more than three thousand. Still we have to be very careful lest we should find ourselves largely out-numbered.

When we get our cavalry & artillery increased, if at all, we shall be in a condition to advance again. I am somewhat embarrassed by the folly of two of my Colonels, with two or three other officers, who going out to reconnoiter, without leave, got so far out as to be taken prisoners. Col. De Villiers was one of them.

It is only a question of time, how soon we shall clear the rebels out of this valley. We have plenty of force to do it in Gen. McClellan's army, & in a few days it can be easily concentrated.

The weather & the scenery is delightful, but the people are scared away from their homes & the country is desolate. We can buy nothing, find nothing, learn nothing. The Union men have been violently driven out or so cowed that they dare not say their souls are their own, & the secessionists are away as we approach. We have to depend upon the river for our supplies.

I sleep in my tent, but take my meals & keep my office on a steamboat which lies under the bluff bank of the river. The greatest personal discomfort is the lack of sleep, for I wake quickly when any noise occurs at night and find out the meaning of it, so that I may be ready for any attack or disturbance.

I hope the success of Gen. McClellan has inaugurated a speedy triumph of the cause & that it will not be many months before I shall be again at liberty to return to my family & my books.

My own progress thus far has been completely successful. The affair of the 12th regt. may be called a disaster by some but it is not so. It accomplished a necessary military object, & in the encounter our troops were proven superior, though they committed the fault of neglecting to take sufficient ammunition, & of retiring too far when they had to check their progress. A few days will show that the plan of operations is a good one, & will be successfully carried out.

Poca, 22nd July 1861

We are still here where we have been for four days, waiting for the proper time of moving forward. Gen. McClellan is moving his forces southward to cut off the retreat of the enemy & I hope the whole force will be captured.

Military men are held responsible for success without much question being made as to the means given them to secure it, & I sometimes fear that the embarrassments & delays occasioned by my not having the kind of assistance in cavalry & artillery, & in good weapons which was expected, will make my expedition here seem less energetic & successful than it should be. But whatever blame may come, I shall do my duty as well as I know how & leave the rest with Providence as calmly as I can.

I had hoped before this to be far up the river, at least as high as Gauley Bridge. I think Gen. McClellan expected it also, but divers [sic] hindrances have occurred, & I am still here.

On July 22, McClellan telegraphed Cox that after the Union defeat at the First Battle of Bull Run, he had been called to Washington to take command and was being replaced in the region by Rosecrans. Still showing that he had confidence in Cox, McClellan reiterated that he hoped to hear imminently that Cox had taken Charleston and Gauley Bridge.[7]

Still unsure of his men and his own abilities, Cox moved slowly toward Charleston. He was assisted by intelligence gathered by a Union spy who had interviewed a Confederate Colonel, George Patton.[8] Using a flanking maneuver on July 23, Cox forced the inexperienced Confederates to flee in panic from their posts. The forceful offensive movement continued on July 24 and, the next day, Charleston's mayor surrendered the city. Cox then announced a new counter-insurgency policy, in direct contrast to what he called the "profane and disorderly behavior of the rebel army."[9] That approach helped gain further support for the Union, and Cox over-optimistically told Helen that the army had achieved its objectives and the entire region was now pro-Union. The next two letters discuss Cox's concern that his victory had been almost too easy, even as he hoped it would help ease the pain of the Union defeat at Bull Run and McClellan's criticism. He also continued to describe the region in almost poetic terms.

Charleston VA 25th July 1861

We have had a couple of days of excitement, chasing & skirmishing with the enemy, but no hard fights. We have marched through a country of precipitous hills & deep defiles, where several batteries had been placed, but I managed to take a direction to turn the flank of the batteries and they abandoned them, & ran in such haste, that our men found their supper on the tables in the quarters of the rebels.

We made a detour from the river and came in above a steamboat used by them, having several hundred of them on board, & towing flat-boats loaded with wheat. As we came in just where their own men had been a few moments before, they supposed we were their party, & as we had boats coming up the river with our men we did not know but they were ours, but we soon made out the secession flag, & I ordered our rifled cannon to throw a shell into her, when they landed in double quick time, set her on fire & made for the hills.

Today the whole army is in full retreat, & we marched to this town in triumph. Wise and his vandals signalized their departure last night by partly destroying the fine suspension bridge here. They burned the timber part at one end & nearly cut-off one of the large wire cables upon which the roadway hangs. Our engineer company will manage to secure it, & we shall march our teams & artillery over it in the morning, when we will continue the chase.

Ten miles above here navigation ceases, & we shall have to rely upon our baggage trains for everything. The country grows more & more romantic, but every day I am compelled to wonder how they permit us to go through a land which in every mile has passes which a hundred men could hold against a regiment.

The news of the defeat of our army in the East [First Battle of Bull Run, July 21] was rec'd here yesterday, but I have a good deal of faith that the worst has been heard first, & that whatever reverse has happened will soon be retrieved.

Kanawha River 11 miles below Gauley Bridge, 28th July 1861

We are camping in the most romantic spot we have yet seen. The mountains rise on each side of the river close from the banks, & as the stream winds along, every mile has its peculiar amphitheatre of wood-crowned cliffs. The sides are quite precipitous, the rocks jutting out from the mountain sides more and more frequently as we progress further.

We are now beyond the place where our boats can reach us, & we are reduced to regular army transportation by wagons, of which we have more than two hundred in one train. We start early in the morning, march along some twelve or fifteen miles, with occasional rests for the men, & then camp for the night. The regiments have their place assigned them, their wagons are parked near the tents, a site is selected for my Hd. Qts., our wagons drive up, our servants pitch our tents, & get us something to eat & a cup of coffee (without milk) our cots are spread, we take our camp stools, & from the door of the tents issue our orders, & arrange matters for the night & the next day's march, & then to sleep.

One night last week our march was a hurried one, and as we had a bit of a brush with the enemy we were late getting ready to camp, & we all bivouacked, i.e. we wrapped ourselves in our blankets & lay side by side on a hill with nothing but the blue above us. We all remarked in the morning that we never had slept so sweetly.

I have with me now, the Rev. Mr. Brown of Cleveland, Chaplain of the 7th. He came a long adventurous journey on horseback to meet us & find where we were, & I have kept him until we meet his regiment, as I hope to do before long. He is an admirable man, & adds greatly to our happiness.

This evening we took a stroll up the river toward our advance guard, & when we got away from the camp, we had an hour of exquisite enjoyment of the scenery, & of one of the most gorgeous of mountain sunsets.

We have had no hard fighting—just enough to get me a little used to the whistling of bullets, the roar of the balls from our rifled cannon. Wise has been in full retreat from the evening we turned the flank of his batteries at the place where we slept on the hill-side.

Tomorrow will bring us to the place where it has been expected he would make his final stand: Gauley Bridge. The river there runs through a gorge with the Gauley river entering it from the left through a deep cleft in the hills. The rocks being precipitous on all sides, as they are described to me. The rebels have burned the bridge, but I do not expect to find them in any great force: their number has been rapidly diminishing by desertion, & those who were the most active secessionists in the valley are cursing Wise for the barbarous course he has been taking.

When we have possessed Gauley we shall have accomplished the task assigned to us, & shall await further orders. We have been a week longer about it than I had hoped when we started, but have taken no more time than was necessary to do it properly and safely.

The whole of Western Va. is now free from the secessionists, and we think will soon quiet down into a permanent & willing recognition of the U.S. Government. I have adopted a most lenient course with the rebels, giving leave to all to remain quiet in their homes who choose, and asking no questions as to opinions or conduct heretofore. The result has been that very many who supposed we came on a revengeful mission to harm and destroy, & were induced to take up arms, have laid them down again & promised never to oppose the U.S. Government.

> On July 28, Cox moved rapidly south against a fleeing Wise toward Gauley Bridge, a key outpost 40 miles south of Charleston, which sits astride the Kanawha and New rivers. Wise put up little resistance and Cox easily took possession of Gauley Bridge on July 29. McClellan's congratulations and Rosecrans's plaudits helped relieve the sting of the incident at Scary Creek.[10]
>
> Wise blamed his defeat on his belief that, after Scary Creek, Cox was heavily reinforced, reporting that "Ohio has sent thousands of gallons [of whisky] over the border, doubtless to demoralize the camp"—which of course the teetotaling Cox would never have permitted. Wise also complained that Cox's counter-insurgency policy was working, writing, "The Kanawha Valley is disaffected and traitorous . . . You cannot persuade these people that we can or will ever reconquer the northwest, and they are submitting, subdued, and debased." The "debased" people voted overwhelmingly on October 24 in favor of statehood.[11]
>
> The next two letters describe Cox's military successes to date, his pleasure that his efforts were being recognized by the Union command, his interest in the flora and fauna of western Virginia, and his relief that he was finally able to take a bath—in the Gauley River:

Gauley Bridge, 30th July, 1861

I reached here yesterday noon, pursuing Wise's flying army, found the bridge burned, some property destroyed, but a considerable quantity of arms & ammunition left behind in his hurried retreat. This completes with success the work laid out for me when I left Camp Dennison & I now await further orders.

At this point the Kanawha is formed by the junction of the Gauley & New rivers, & from Charleston up, is wildly grand in its scenery. The road runs through the narrow valley, the rocks rising in perpendicular overhanging cliffs, in some places hundreds of feet high. The bridge here was some 700 feet long, upon several heavy stone piers, beneath which the blackened timbers are now floating.

The people of the valley are loud in their curses of Wise's vandalism in the destruction of public improvements, & declare they have no wish to hear of him or his cause again. I cannot conjecture what work will be next laid out for us, though it is quite probably we may co-operate with Gen. Rosecrans in concentrating our forces on Staunton or Covington where Wise will perhaps try to rally.

There are three or four houses at this place. My Hd. Qs. are in an old two story frame house, rather dilapidated. I have a large room on the right of the hall for my office & etc., & my cot occupies the front right hand corner. Col [Charles] Whittlesey of Cleveland, my Chief of Engineers, sleeps in the room overhead, & the rest of the staff & servants sleep in four tents pitched in the door-yard.

Fine locust trees shade the door, & the Gauley river is just across the road as we face the East, the mountains rising steep & high just across the stream. Thus you will see that I am a little to the left of the point where the rivers meet, having turned off a few yards up the Gauley.

We went this morning about sunrise a little way out of camp along a glen covered with luxuriant foliage, & came upon a little cascade falling into a basin of rock about 15 yards across & waist deep. Here we had a glorious bath & came back treading springingly as deer. It was a rich treat.

There would be no limit to my enjoyment of this scenery were it not that our warlike mission casts a certain air of sternness and gloom over the whole. In peaceful times, with no rude army to pollute the scene, it would be a trip full of delight, & when peace comes I shall hope to take you over the route again.

I wish every day that I had with me my own brigade as it was organized at Camp Dennison. In discipline, good order & efficiency it would be far ahead of this. I am sure I should have been here several days earlier with them.

My health continues good. I am in the saddle much of every day, & with such exercise, such scenery, & good company, I can't be otherwise than well, notwithstanding we are reduced to hard soldiers' fare. I am grateful to all who have wished me success.

Gauley Bridge 6th August 1861

The last paper I got was dated 1st inst. and it gave me the interesting information that the Senate had the question of my confirmation under consideration. They have had time enough to decide it surely, & it would be satisfactory to learn how. The noise and confusion in the newspapers about the appointments has been such as to make me very indifferent whether the appointment is confirmed or not. If confirmed, I shall probably remain here sometime, fortifying & preparing the situation for defense, with a view to holding all of Western Va. that has been gained.

My taking this place has called out congratulations from Gen. McClellan, Gov. [Francis H.] Pierpont[12] & others. It was thought I might be unwilling to remain after the expiration of three months unless the three years question was settled, & Gen. Rosecrans, who is my senior, telegraphed me that Gen. Scott wished me to remain in command of this force, & that he himself strongly desired that I should do so.

Yesterday I went with a reconnoitering party up the river about ten miles to the 'Hawks Nest,' a most romantic place. The road is a gradual ascent all the way, running along the river bank, & giving beautiful little bits of scenery, as the woods open now and then. At the Hawk's Nest a path turns to the right, & in a few yards brings you out upon the edge of a stupendous cliff hanging over the valley at the height of a thousand feet. It juts out like a promontory, so that right & left & before you, you have a clear view. The river at this point is bent toward you, nearly like a horseshoe. Looking toward the left, you see it for a couple of miles threading through the mountains, which open a way for it as regular as to seem almost like a giant's trench dug with engineering skill. To the right the valley is more irregular & you can see but half a mile or so, the hills are abrupt, & the river foams & dashes over the rocks with wild confusion & loud roar.

Looking over the dizzy edge, the tree tops are far down below, & the river seems just under your feet, yet we tried in vain to throw a stone in it. Around the horizon the mountains tower up higher & higher needing only to change their wooded summits into rocky ones to make the scenery Alpine.

I have made an acquaintance here which is interesting and rather peculiar. Col. [Christopher Q.] Tompkins[13] of the rebel forces, is a former U.S.A. officer! He left the Army however, some fifteen years ago. He is wealthy & has a country seat on a mountain two miles from camp, besides a house in Richmond. He has been looked upon as the leading military man in the valley, & when Wise retreated could not move his family well, & so he left them, sending me a letter in which he asked me as a gentleman to see that they were not molested. I have been very particular in placing a guard at the house to protect the family & keep them from annoyance.

One day last week I called to learn how my instructions were obeyed & to pay my respects to Mrs. T. in person. I found her a very ladylike woman of forty or thereabouts, lively, intelligent, & well-bred. She is a Baltimore lady, & does not sympathize very fully with the rebels. She made me stay to dinner, which was an excellent one & was every way very polite & kind. We talked laughingly over the relative positions we occupied, softening the evils of war as far as possible by personal politeness. It has been gratifying to me that I have been able to quiet her fears, both as to her own safety, & that of her family, as well as in regard to the treatment her husband might expect, should he at any time be taken prisoner by our troops.

I shall probably know whether I am to remain a soldier before I write again. If I am relieved, the delights of home will more than make up for the poverty we must expect for awhile, and if I am retained here, we will hope for a speedy & glorious termination of the conflict. We will hope and pray for this, either way, but our hopes and prayers will doubtless gain some strength, if our own re-union is dependent upon the fulfillment.

>For the next two weeks, Cox stayed put, presuming he would join Rosecrans to meet any new threat. He heard rumors that Robert E. Lee, even then reputed to be the Confederacy's best general, was coming to the region personally to push back the Union advance. While he waited, Cox dealt with several unique problems. First, some junior officers had come to him at Charleston and told him the army should not advance without their consent since they had as much military experience as he did. The calm and stoic Cox told them that they were committing mutiny and they backed down quickly. Colonel Tyler was likely one of these malcontents. Cox did not mention this incident to Helen at the time, but he later would vent his anger in a letter to her.

>On another occasion, some newspapermen asked to accompany Cox's army with military rank. At the time, many generals were agreeing to such proposals as a means of gaining publicity for themselves. Cox was not a self-promoter and he refused to give the reporters rank in his army. He told the reporters that only Washington could give them a rank and that, while they were welcome to accompany the troops, he would have to review their dispatches to ensure that the Confederates did not gain useful information. The journalists

refused. They proceeded to write damning commentaries, alleging Cox was incompetent and his troops were demoralized and undisciplined drunkards. Fortunately for Cox, these slanders were published alongside the news of Cox's success in taking Charleston and Gauley Bridge. Still, Cox was concerned that it might harm his chances for promotion.[14]

In his next two letters, Cox discussed his concerns regarding Robert E. Lee and described the incident with the newspapermen and the resultant press criticism with a touch of anger:

Gauley Bridge 11th Aug 1861

I have written to [William T.] Spear [one of Cox's law partners and a future Ohio Supreme Court Justice] in regard to the personal attack upon me, and as I have not time to reiterate the same things, I will ask you to get that letter from him. It had never occurred to me that such a mode of warfare would be attempted. After the first anger was over, I really felt that duty did not call me to sacrifice home and family, when I was to be followed with that sort of malice; but since I have received news of the confirmation of my appointment, of course I dismiss all that & go at my work again.

The order you saw in the papers, & which gave you some trouble, was only the usual order announcing the close of the three months' service under my appointment from Gov. Dennison; the appointment from the Prest. Not being complete till confirmed in the Senate. I have satisfactory evidence that all the superior officers are satisfied that the expedition has been a complete success, & whatever drawbacks there were in the Scarry [Scary Creek] affair being the result of the condition of the troops, & circumstances beyond my control.

My chief sorrow is that pain has been given to dear friends when there was no occasion for it. As to the wound to my pride though rather sore, I take it as a lesson I need to learn & which I hope will do me good.

I am as sorry as you that we couldn't catch Wise, but if he wouldn't fight, & would burn the bridges & drop trees across the road, must I be responsible for that too? We ran into these defiles & gorges faster than was prudent according to military rule, as it was. My chief regret in regard to the composition of my force has been that I could not have had my own brigade with me. They would have had a pride & esprit-de-corps which would have kept them from any such meanness as others have been guilty of.

As for the 'disgusting' man in the NY Herald, I have to say that Gen. McClellan telegraphed his congratulations to me from Washington upon the news of my reaching this place, busy as he was with his new position.

Gauley Bridge 16th Aug. 1861

I seize a moment to write you a line, though my time is occupied with matters, which so burden my mind that it is almost impossible to get my pen for any other than official business.

My orders are to hold this place, but I have been worried with the conviction that those in command over me have not sufficiently arranged for guarding my line of communications down the river. All that we have gained would be so much loss if our supply of food etc. should be stopped, for the country will not support a regiment.

We have a large force of the enemy accumulating in front of us, & the air is full of rumors of their expectation of being able to cut us off. Gen. [Robert E.] Lee is their leader and he is an educated soldier; one of their best. Their number is reckoned at all sorts of figures, but never less than several times our own.

We can only employ ourselves as actively as possible in perfecting our defenses & getting ready for any result, so that we may hold our post if our communication should not be interrupted, or fight our way out somewhere if they should.

I saw in the Cin. [Cincinnati] Commercial of the 15th I think a letter from Clarksburg, giving further evidence that my course has been approved at head quarters. Did you see it? I am not as sensitive on the matter as I was at first. I have made up my mind to take calmly what comes, hoping only that God will give success to the good cause, whatever becomes of us who are fighting for it.

Gauley Bridge 18th Aug 1861

We have been living for several days in the midst of rumors of immediate attack and don't know what hour it may come.

The 'Times' & 'Tribune' you sent also came safely. The letters in them I think I can trace to their source. I wish I had time to detail to you the facts to show how some of the [lies] are entirely without foundation. The truth is that extreme caution in scouting & picketing has been the characteristic of my movement all the way. That I was sent with extremely raw & undisciplined troops is true, but notwithstanding I have lacked support from some regimental commanders, who are really responsible for everything pertaining to discipline, I have been assured by regular army officers that for good order & soldierly appearance, our camp compares favorably with all the volunteer camps.

Don't let it trouble you. It will be right some day. If I fall, I believe enough know the truth who will give me my just character & share of praise or blame impartially. If I survive, I can wear out such criticism & in the long run win the confidence of officers & men—but I start with great disadvantages I admit.

When the malicious criticisms first made their appearance I was a good deal depressed & felt that it would be good if a stray ball would rid me of the responsibility and the attacks of such enemies at once but since then I have overcome the temptation to gloom, & acquired a faith that as part of the discipline of life it will have a good affect in making my character a really better one if I hear it rightly. If I am to help honorably in a cause which I firmly believe to be God's cause of truth & freedom & good government, I shall be thankful, & even if I am to fail & perhaps be thought an injury to the cause itself, I must be content to have that so too, if I am sure, as I am, that I have striven to do nothing but my duty in the matter.

I have told you of the supposed intent of the enemy to get around us in our rear & stop our supplies. I am not sure that they will attempt this, but nearly every one believes they will. Here however my orders & my judgement keep me, & I will hold my post as long as possible. I cannot give any particulars of affairs for I do not feel that my letters are entirely safe. The time will come for that. If we are attacked here I trust we shall give a good account of ourselves.

On September 18, 1861, the *New York Times* wrote, "Nowhere else in the war has the Union army so well sustained their cause as in western Virginia. General Cox enjoys the unquestioned honor of winning the important valley of the Kanawha for the Union."[15] That article, in a paper which had viciously criticized him earlier, reflected a consequential month during which Cox and Rosecrans united their forces and defeated the Confederates at the Battle of Carnifex Ferry on September 10.

That success, however, was preceded by a near-disaster for Cox in late August when Colonel Tyler was overwhelmed by a Confederate force led by another former Virginia governor, John Floyd. Tyler's retreat was stopped when another Colonel, Jack Casement—later builder of the Union Pacific Railroad—came to his rescue. Casement and Cox would eventually become close friends.

Cox and Rosecrans's success at Carnifex Ferry was made easier because of dissension in the Confederate ranks. Former Governors Wise and Floyd, who were supposed to cooperate against the Union forces, refused to do so, each demanding that the other subordinate himself.[16] Lee tried to persuade his generals to work together, but he failed. On September 9, Rosecrans advanced on Floyd at Carnifex Ferry and soon afterward Cox attacked Wise, causing both Confederate forces to withdraw. On September 13, the two retreating Confederate armies were encamped near one another (but not united) on Big Sewell Mountain.

On September 17, Rosecrans met with all of his commanders to go over strategy. It was at this point, with their forces united, that Cox's autonomous responsibilities ended. It had been a difficult, but mostly successful introduction to military life. He had established a leadership style which would remain consistent for most of his military career. While he lacked the ability to "fire up" his men because of his lack of a "common touch," he always had his men's respect and his forces always had high morale. As will be seen, the only occasion in his career when he did "fire up" his men came at a critical moment in the 1864 Battle of Franklin and, even then, he retained his *sang-froid*.[17]

Cox's next letters summarize his pride in his achievements and the recognition he had gotten from his military peers. He also wrote about the attempted "mutiny" and his belief that he gradually was gaining the respect of all of his men. The letters dated September 10 and 17 are particularly poignant examples of the love and strong bonds between Helen and Dolson as they dealt with the death of their infant son, William Brewster.

Gauley Bridge 26th Aug 1861

I can only say I am well but greatly hurried with work. Col. Tyler's regt. near Summerville 27 miles from here was beaten early this morning by an overwhelming force of the enemy, working in where I have informed the powers that be that it was rumored they were intending to, yet I don't think many were killed, but cannot tell. The force opposed to them was about five thousand, moving in toward Gen. Rosecrans line, with a view perhaps to get behind us. They were driven into the woods & scattered.

We are pretty well prepared for a defense, & I doubt if we shall get an attack in front. If they can get around us they will.

Keep good courage & faith. Our Heavenly Father rules yet, & here or hereafter we shall see that it is all right.

Col. Tyler's regt. was in that position by positive orders from Gen. Rosecrans, & his misfortune cannot be helped.

Gauley Bridge 29th Aug. 1861

We have been seated here among the hills, strengthening our position, condemned to a sort of garrison duty, its monotony only varied by the excitement of occasional skirmishes or rumors of attack.

The defeat of the 7th [Tyler's regiment] does not turn out nearly so bad as at first reported, & one hundred will probably cover all the missing, of which only fifteen are killed. I suppose that Stephen Cole is a prisoner, but have learned that he was not hurt. If so he is in no danger and will be decently treated. Another company is safe I understand at Charleston, where about four hundred made good their retreat under Major Casement.

The regt. feels chagrined at the result, quite as much because they feel that the surprise was chiefly their own fault, as on account of the defeat itself. Their orders were explicit that if at any time they found themselves in face of a superior force they were to see that they were so placed that they could not be surrounded or their retreat cut off. These commands they had received direct from Gen. Rosecrans, and I had reiterated them, but they slept quite carelessly within two miles of the enemy, with picket fires burning, contrary to every military rule & the orders of their Col. & so the rebels knew every point of their position & arranged the attack at their leisure. They knew they were occupying an advance post nearly equi-distant between Gen. Rosecrans & myself & to secure their retreat in case of attack by a superior force was the first duty of such a detachment.

But I am glad it is no worse. Another thing has caused me annoyance. One of my captains shot a mutinous soldier yesterday. He was too hasty in doing it, and raised an excitement in the 2nd Kentucky regt, which gave me & the regimental officers some trouble to quell. The work in the trenches and defenses has been hard, and when called upon to do some more duty of the sort, a party of men refused & this one, being the ringleader, was very violent when ordered by the Capt. to fall into his place & obey orders. The captain finally drew a pistol and told the man to obey or he would shoot him, but the man defied him & he shot him down.

I disapproved the act because I thought the arrest of the man might have been made, and I therefore ordered the Capt. under arrest to await a court martial, though the man was undoubtedly guilty of mutiny.

Judging by past experience you will probably see some strange exaggerations of the occurrence in print, but the above is the literal fact as I have had it from disinterested eye-witnesses. I arrived at the spot immediately after the shot was fired.

I think the coming week must bring matters to a crisis between us and the enemy. They have been boasting that they would surround and overwhelm my little command, but I trust they will find it harder to do than talk of. I have begged for a force sufficient to keep our communications safe beyond peradventure, but could not get it. Do not be alarmed however if you learn that we are entirely cut off from communications with Ohio. A week or two might show them that it was a case of biter bit.

Still I am sorry that our Ohio troops have been sent away to the far West, when four or five thousand have been greatly needed in Western Virginia. My orders are to hold my post at all hazards, & my feelings are in accordance with the order.

Gauley Bridge 4th Sept 1861

We have had several exciting days. Attacks & skirmishes on all sides. Yesterday we were attacked on two sides at once, but drove the enemy off without much trouble or loss to us. They are not very well inclined to attack us in our position here, but seem to be striving to get around us, stop our supply trains, etc.

We are anxiously looking for the day when we shall have such reinforcements as will enable us to take the offensive in earnest, but at present our work seems confined to beating off the swarms which surround us. We have reason to hope that another week will change all this.

I cannot stop to explain my views or experience in army discipline nor to tell you the history of the jealousies & disappointments that made a clique of officers reduce misrepresentation to a system & insubordination to a fine art. I have faith now as formerly in time to test my plans & do me justice. So you must be patient.

I have had to laugh to notice one paper trying to hold me responsible for Tyler's surprise, the basis of it being that both he & I were acting in regard to his movement under explicit orders from Gen. Rosecrans.

Don't suffer yourself to be uneasy about me. My only trouble in regard to safety is that we are not likely to have an enemy bold enough to drive right at our position here. We are rather anxious to have them try, but they have not as yet gained an advantage over our outposts.

If they should succeed in cutting off our communication with Ohio, still you must not be troubled for we can maintain ourselves three or four weeks, & by that time the way can be opened again from without. We ought to have three or four thousand more men in the valley, but as it is they must come to do some hard fighting if they want to get Gauley Bridge again.

Gauley Bridge 10th Sept 1861

We are passing through a critical point in our affairs here. A day or two will either effect a junction with Gen. Rosecrans & put us in a position to drive the rebels out of the valley, or will give us hard work. We have been subject to frequent attacks and alarms of attacks, but my position is a strong one, & I have felt no doubt of being able to hold it easily, even if quite surrounded by a superior force.

The disposition of the officers towards me has undergone a marked change in the three weeks past, & I see the proof that my course in going firmly and steadily on my way, not making a sensation by the show of power, but quietly and gradually bringing the reins tighter has been the correct course. Some of the officers who were very much prejudiced have volunteered the most frank acknowledgments within a few days, & have assured me that the general tone of the Brigade has greatly changed. This will enable me to perfect discipline & make the command far more effective.

I see the papers too are changing their tone. So let us bide our time. We are not only anxious about Gen. Rosecrans movements, but we are expecting news of a great battle near Washington. God grant it may be decisively in favor of the Government, & against the rebels as to be an end of the conflict in the vicinity of the Capitol. If this were so, & the victory at Hatteras is followed up by like expeditions to other parts of the coast, the tide will turn. The rebels will no longer be able to concentrate great armies, & the column of our forces may push forward rapidly.

In that event I should hope to spend the Winter in Tennessee or even further south, & to see the Spring open upon the restoration of peace. On the other hand, another great reverse would throw us back upon an obstinate determination to perfect our military discipline until our Army shall be a fine representative of the real superiority of the North.

Every skirmish that we have demonstrates to me that we have the best men. The enemy have had the advantage in preparation, & it will take us six months to catch up in this respect: We may beat them before & I trust will, but after that I cannot look upon it as doubtful.

I am very sorry to hear of little Brewster's [their infant son William] illness. Does he seem to have a chronic difficulty with his throat? I long very much to see him, for he is a little stranger to me as yet. I can form no idea of his looks from the appearance of a little one-day-old.

By the way let me tell you an incident which gave me much comfort the other day. It was Sunday—I was resting for a moment—& took up the Bible, & by mere accident opened to the 41st chapter of Isaiah—I had been feeling somewhat anxious about our position here, & gloomy at the fact that our labor had been so little known & appreciated, & the chapter came to me like a prophecy indeed, inspiring hope & courage. I had hardly read it when scouts came in reporting distant cannonading, which we received as proof of the real advance of Gen. Rosecrans' column, then the enemy was reported to be keeping more shy of our lines. This was followed up by the acknowledgments of the officers I have been speaking of and the assurance of the content & devotion of the troops to me, & this by several papers containing favorable comments. So that I was greatly cheered & encouraged. You will see that from the 8th verse onward there is a singular aptitude in the same circumstances & all.

Write regularly as you can, & don't be alarmed about me. We are in God's hand, & only his will can happen to us.

[On the typescript following this letter, Helen wrote the following: "I received this letter the very day our dear little Brewster died,—the 14th of Sept.—H.F.C."]

Spy Rock 17th Sept 1861

I am here twenty one miles above Gauley Bridge, the enemy retreating before us & Gen. Rosecrans column following, so that we are now the advance guard of the whole army, and pushing forward. On Sunday I went over to Cross Lanes near Summerville and met Gen. Rosecrans, who called all his Brigadiers together to consult us as to the future prosecution of the campaign.

While there I got your telegram of the day before notifying me of the critical condition of the baby. I still try to hope that better news will come, but I dare not think much about it, for the impossibility of leaving my command only aggravates my distress in regard to the little one & you. I cannot but be thankful for my own sake that it is not either of the other children that is in such danger, for little Brewster is so much of a stranger to me that it is not possible his hold on my heart-strings should be quite like that of the others. Having seen him but a day, it is hard for me sometimes to realize his existence at all, and thus that which has seemed a misfortune to me, may be after all a blessing, since I fear I should be unfitted for my duties if I had learned to love him as I do the rest.

With you however it is very different, my heart bleeds Lilla, when I think of you watching beside the little one's death-bed, or perhaps already following him to the grave alone. God help us all & give us strength for these trials. I see no probability of my getting away from the Army until some decisive action occurs, which will determine the character of the Fall campaign.

Indeed till the war ends, I can promise myself but little leisure. I have very strong hope that a few days will put a very different face upon our affairs and open a clear road for our Army in Eastern Virginia to move southward. In that event our column will cooperate with that, & the result of the war put beyond peradventure. Each day brings its active duty, and from morning till night our unceasing round of labor calls for my attention.

My visit to Gen. Rosecrans' camp was in many respects very gratifying to me. The manifest cordiality & respect with which I was received was the best proof I could have that among military men my military career thus far is regarded as a creditable one. My views with regard to the movements to be made were received with even greater weight that I could ask and they informed me that they had satisfactory evidence that the enemy held me in a respect quite as great as I could ask, if not so cordial.

The press too is taking a different tone, & items coming from authoritative sources near head-quarters give me some assurance that I do well to wait patiently the result—doing my duty as heretofore. I have strong hope that in God's good providence the Spring will see peace restored upon the basis of the supremacy of the Constitution, and the complete restriction of slavery extension. It will then be but a short time before the system itself will die, & the hopes of the world in regard to our institutions will be fulfilled. If the war is protracted, the abolition of slavery may be accomplished by more direct & positive methods, but in either case the same result is sooner or later inevitable.

This forward movement of ours may be continued to Lewisburg which will bring us close up to the Alleghenies & within ten miles of the White Sulphur Springs. It must result also in the better appreciation of the Great Kanawha line as an important line of operations, and if Gen McClellan is successful in the East, will soon be followed by the opening of communication with him direct. The next few days are big with important events.

Kiss all the dear little ones for me, and if our little Brewster still survives hug the dear babe close to your breast till papa's return gives him still more love. If he has gone to heaven may God comfort you, & give us both strong faith in His loving providence.

> While both sides were waiting for action near Big Sewell Mountain, Lee finally had Wise transferred from the region and ordered all Confederate forces united under Floyd.[18] However, Lee was unable to act with the united forces because Mother Nature and hunger intervened. It had been raining most of the year, but now the storms got worse and any movement in the omnipresent mud seemed impossible. Separately, Rosecrans decided on October 5 to make a general retreat to Gauley Bridge to re-group and shorten his supply lines, a decision which Cox reluctantly accepted. Floyd took advantage of the retreat, moving his forces slowly toward Gauley and re-gaining some of the lost territory.[19]
>
> Cox's next letters display his unhappiness with the withdrawal, but also his commitment to follow orders religiously. He also noted

with understated pride that his stoicism in the face of danger helped him deal with the enemy's threats. These letters make frequent reference to the muddy conditions all around them and how that reality often became so dreadful that he could only laugh at the ridiculous situations it caused the army.

Camp Sewell 25th Sept 1861

I am here thirty-five miles above Gauley Bridge. The enemy is in plain sight, but my orders keep me from an attack until Gen. Rosecrans comes up. His column has been delayed waiting for transportation of stores & baggage. I have been almost two weeks on the road, & yet have made but three days march.

Yesterday we had a lively skirmish, the advance guard keeping up a straggling fire three or four hours, and the enemy throwing shells & cannon-balls almost constantly. The range was too great for any damage to us, & was probably only intended to hold back our advance guard. We replied with a few long range shells from our rifled cannon & dismounted a howitzer for them, & killed some of their cannoniers. I hope two or three days more will be all that will be needed to bring up the whole column, & then something more vigorous may be done.

Spear spoke of some newspaper correspondents giving extracts from dispatches from me to Col. Tyler. I don't quite understand it, and would like to know in what papers any such thing appeared. It would be a gross offense against military discipline to allow any person to have copies of the dispatches sent. I would like to know it especially if they garbled them.

Camp Lookout 8th Oct 1861

The past two weeks we have spent at Sewell mountain 13 miles in advance of this. When I arrived there I believe a fair opportunity was open for a complete victory over Wise, who was in advance, but Gen. R. feared we were not strong enough, & sent imperative orders not to attack till he came up. By the time he came the opportunity was gone. The enemy had been reinforced largely, & fortified their position in a mountain gorge so strongly that attack was deemed impossible, & on receipt of news of still further reinforcements under Lee reaching them, we were ordered to make a night march back.

The army will be encamped for some weeks at Hawk's Nest, ten miles below here, & I doubt if we have any very active service this Fall. The rains are making these mountain roads impassable, & neither army will be able to venture far from its head of steamboat or railroad transportation. This at least is the present appearance of things. Many things of this last fortnight's experience I should be glad to tell you, & must try to make room for it in my next.

One thing I think is certain, that by being brought into contact with other brigadiers, I have lost nothing. I find my regts. Very anxious lest they be should be detached from my command, instead of desiring the separation, & I find regts. Of other brigades earnestly striving to be attached to mine. This will please you I know, & I could give you hosts of items of amusing & interesting kinds if I had time.

You cannot appreciate the beauties of tent life in the driving, drenching, howling storms we have had lately. We live in a sea of mud and an atmosphere of water—cold water at that.

Camp Tompkins 17 Oct 1861

I am back again almost at Gauley. Indeed most of my command is there or below. It is doubtful whether much more will be done here before we go into Winter quarters. I have some hope that my Hd. Qs. May soon be placed at Charleston where the communication with the civilian world will be by steamboat direct. If the enemy shows no disposition to follow us up, our advance guard will be left to keep the ground we have gained and the mass of the troops will be put where provisions can be easily transported to them, & better shelter than tents provided for the Winter.

We had terribly rough weather on Sewell mountain. Numbers of horses died from the exposure, & I feared many of the men would, but we came out better than we had reason to expect. I had a contrivance which made my tent very comfortable. The mountain is covered with loose flat stone like flag-stone. I had a furnace made of these in the back of the tent by digging a square trench, setting up the stone on edge with others on the top, plastering the cracks with mud, & leading the trench out of the back of the tent, letting it end in a stone chimney topped with a cracker barrel. It drew beautifully, & the heavy stones when once hot keep warm a long while.

If we go into Winter quarters I shall first have to get my brigade reorganized, the vacancies in officers filled, the companies recruited up to their full numbers, & a system of drill & instruction put in operation. After that, if this part of the country remains quiet, I may possibly get leave of absence to visit home.

It is not worthwhile for me to comment on the military movements of our army since Gen. Rosecrans joined us with his column. We marched to Sewell Mountain, & marched back again. Gen. R. has been very severely criticized for the small accomplishment of the movement. His order to me not to fight when we first reached the mountain gave great dissatisfaction to the force under my command, for all believe we should have been victorious, & driven Wise & Floyd to Lewisburg before Lee could have helped them.

I had the post of honor both in the advance & the retreat, being nearest the enemy & in the only place of danger, my brigade being the advance guard as we went out, & the rear-guard as we came back. Our march back from Sewell was for a while an exciting one. The enemy were in plain sight as we faced each other on opposite hills, where our tents were plainly visible by day, & our campfires by night. There was danger that we might be attacked as soon as the retrograde movement began, and unless the rear-guard was reliable & steady a Bull Run panic might ensue.

The order was given to strike tents at ten o'clock P.M. The baggage train was to move in advance, & at half past twelve the troops were to follow. The condition of the roads was such that the wagons moved very slowly. It was half past one when the head of my brigade filed out of the camp ground into the narrow road leading down the mountain, & which for a mile & a half is deep rocky gorge with sides too steep to climb. I kept a few pickets back to give notice of any attack on the enemy's part, but it was broad daylight before we had accomplished that mile & a half, being some four hours in the defile, kept back by the impossibility of getting the train forward faster.

During all that time I sat on my horse at the extreme rear of the column revolving in my mind the predicament we should be in if the rebels should have discovered our movement & make a vigorous attack upon us. And as day began to dawn before we were out of it, and it became evident that they would at once become aware of our retreat while we were still in that pass, I was very thankful l that I was not a nervous man, & that I could sit there with apparent sang-froid. At no moment of the last half of those four hours would a volley of musketry from the rocks over our heads have surprised me. The rebels fell in my estimation for lacking the courage & enterprise to take advantage of our situation.

Gauley Mount 29th Oct 1861

I had also the pleasure of having Henry Ranney [a family friend from Warren] spend a day with me last week. It seemed very strange and strangely pleasant to see home faces again. I rode with Ranney & a couple of his friends who were with him to Hawk's nest. He enjoyed the ride wonderfully, & could not tire of expressing his admiration of the mountain scenery about us here.

I find however that one's admiration of mountain country is considerably modified when he has to make it the theatre of military operations. The tourist's eye & the soldier's are very different. Still I find myself treasuring up the scenes for future use, & have no doubt that if I return safely at the close of the war, the remembrance of these scenes will be so sifted that I may enjoy the scenery in retrospect with a zeal greater than the present vivid sense of hard roads, difficult transportation & inaccessible positions permit to me.

Once in a while we have a feast, & such a one we had yesterday—Monday. It was given by some of the officers of my brigade in honor of my birthday. I went down to Gauley Bridge to be present. About twenty sat down to as fine a dinner as one often sees. It was doubly gratifying to me as an evidence of the change in the sentiment of many of my officers. The dinner was prepared at the house of a lady who though a secessionist by family connection has always been very kind to me. A Colonel presided, & in proposing my health after dinner spoke very handsomely of the way in which acquaintance had begotten friendship for me as a man, and full confidence as a soldier and leader.

Besides the hostess we had two ladies present—the wife of one of our surgeons and of a Major of the 1st Kentucky. The latter by the way is a very nice little lady, born and brought up at Newburg on the Hudson where her father is a clergyman of fifty years standing. She has been married some three years and left her boy baby with her father while she came up the Kanawha to visit her husband who has been ailing somewhat. Her presence made us all think of home, & when I proposed the health of those we'd left behind us, it was drunk with an earnest feeling which spoke for itself.

Our future is yet uncertain. There is some force of the enemy in the country the other side of the river. We shall probably have a rap at them before we go into Winter quarters, if we go to such quarters at all.

> Robert E. Lee left the region in late October, his efforts to stop the Union advance an abject failure. This was the lowest point of his military career. The southern press castigated him as "Granny Lee" and "Evacuating Lee," and the *Richmond Examiner* pronounced him "outwitted, outmaneuvered, and outgeneraled."[20] Floyd would, however, advance north and, on November 1, surprise a neglectful Rosecrans at Gauley Bridge. In response, Rosecrans instituted an ultimately successful plan which would not only push Floyd back, but also surround the Confederates by swift flanking moves.[21]
>
> This series of events would underline for Cox the divisions between West Pointers and Civilian Generals. Cox's role was to keep the Confederates' attention on their front while another brigadier, H. W. Benham, who had graduated first in his class at West Point, moved around the rear. Cox quickly secured his position, but Benham dawdled long enough that Floyd was able to retreat on November 12, just hours before he could have been surrounded. By November 19, he was all

the way to New Bern, no longer a threat to the Union forces. Benham was one of those generals who had allowed the press to report what they wished, in return for positive mentions of himself. *The New York Times* even reported on November 24 that Benham was responsible for this victory. In fact, Rosecrans had Benham arrested for neglect of duty. (He was not convicted; he was arrested again later in the war and again not convicted; and eventually obtained a significant position in the Army of the Potomac under General Joe Hooker.) In his report, Rosecrans stated that "General Cox is the only reliable man here."[22]

With Floyd's retreat, Cox wrote, "The line of the Alleghenies became the northern frontier of the Confederacy in Virginia, and was never again seriously broken."[23] On November 19, Rosecrans ordered the army into winter quarters. Cox was now put in charge of the Department of the Kanawha, with headquarters at Charleston, while Rosecrans set up his command at Wheeling.[24] To his disappointment, Cox would still be in Charleston when the spring of 1862 arrived. Despite several requests from Washington, Rosecrans refused to allow him to be transferred elsewhere, so confident was he of Cox's reliability.

Cox's next letters discuss these campaigns, life in the muddy backwoods, his distaste for men like Benham, and his planning for winter quarters. During this period, Helen visited him for three weeks, so there are no letters between December 30, 1861 and February 20 of the next year.

Gauley Bridge 6th Nov 1861

Since the approach of Winter has made it evident that we could do little more in the way of active operations, Floyd has been trying hard to annoy us in regard to our transportation, so as to force Gen. Rosecrans to fall back below the Gauley. On the first inst. he succeeded in getting several pieces of cannon in position on the mountains opposite the camp here at Gauley, & they have been pelting away [at] us with shot & shell every day since. Their object has been to destroy the ferry over the Gauley & to make the road along the river too hot for our wagons, & cut off the supplies of the army above the Gauley River.

I was at Hd. Qs. at Gauley Mount when the fire opened, but by Gen. R's permission came down here immediately & took command. The river here is so rapid & rocky & our boats so few & inefficient that it is a desperate enterprise to cross & scale the cliffs to where the guns are, so we have to keep up an artillery duel with the enemy, till other places for surrounding the scamps can be matured.

Today they are quiet, but for the five days past the whizzing of the balls & explosion of the shell have been very familiar music. Strange to say no one has been hurt among us. This is chiefly owing to the fact that the enemy's position is so high that their shot are all 'plunging' & good aim is almost impossible when they have to depress their cannon so much.

The day I came down from Hd. Qrts. the rebels had posted a company of riflemen along the river bank at a narrow gorge where the road is under a bluff rock, & from the opposite side made it very unsafe to pass the road. Accordingly I took a path over the hills with my aidedecamp, & sending back my horse by a dragoon when I could take him no further, we clambered over the peak & started down the mountain side to the Gauley. The side of the mountain I had slashed in Sept, & the trees lay over each other in a dense entanglement of trunks & branches. The mountain side is very steep, the rocks rising perpendicular in many places. We thought however our shortest way was to thread along through the entanglement straight down the side.

After a hard scramble we found ourselves at the foot of the wooded part, but between us & the water was a perpendicular rock some twenty feet down. To jump on the rock below would be to break our legs or necks, so we first tried to clamber along the brink to some place where there was a practicable descent, but the rocks & fallen trees soon proved to us that this was impracticable even with our utmost exertions. So there was nothing left but to clamber up again & follow the ridge to where the timber had not been felled. We started, but if the descent had been hard, you may imagine what it was to retrace our steps. I never experienced such exhausting labor. I had on a heavy over-coat, sword, pistol, reconnoitering glass, & it was raining hard. We pulled ourselves up over logs, through branches & brambles, panting & soaking. Several times we stopped through sheer exhaustion, but finally reached the top & passed along with comparative ease to a place where we could slip, slide & run down to the river. We then came down along the bank until we were met by a skiff from this side of the Gauley.

The men in camp were delighted to have me among them again, but a more completely exhausted pair of mortals than we were it would be hard to find. Our clothes soaked from within & without, by rain & perspiration, & our legs trembling under us, our trousers nearly torn off us, our only satisfaction was in knowing that we made the abatis in Sept. a very good one, & that no enemy would be likely to get through it.

Gauley Bridge 15th Nov 1861

After being hammered at by the enemy's cannon for a week & a half

The Hills of (West) Virginia

waiting for Gen. Benham to make his loudly promised move to Floyd's rear, which was to 'bag' that traitor, to use the language of the papers, I became tired of artillery practice, (you know one will tire even of a good thing) and sent over detachments of my own brigade, & after a brisk skirmishing fight over the mountains which lasted most of two days, we drove the rebels out of their position & opened the road to Fayette C.H. which they had occupied.

Gen. Benham not having yet had time to make his march 'to the rear,' marched back again from his position five miles below, & out on the road we had opened, & has been pursuing the enemy without the most remote chance of catching him, or being harmed: and so ends the 'bagging of Floyd' by the 'regular army officer,' which exploit the papers all said was to end up making Gen. B. a Major Gen. Vive la bagatelle—anglaise 'humbug' [Here Cox mocks Benham as a "bagatelle," i.e. a nothing or a "humbug"]

Having had the little affair with Floyd which I anticipated and driven him out of this region, the question of Winter quarters is again mooted, but is no nearer a settlement than before, except that as we are a few weeks later in the season, we must be nearer the end of all things & questions, that one not excepted. The landing of the fleet at Port Royal gives me hopes that the war will be carried into interior, & if it is the signal for a general & vigorous movement southward I shall rejoice, even if it involves the necessity of a winter in the field, & the postponement of all plans and prospects of seeing the dear ones at home.

A strong determined & successful winter campaign & the rebellion crushed before next Summer would be a consummation worth praying for. God grant it may come. I have feared we could not hope for much progress till we are ready to carry freedom to the slave as we go: but I think the relations between the war & the slave system have been seen better by all concerned for a little while past, & that the system is doomed.

Gauley Bridge 24th Nov 1861

You ask how Floyd happened to get away. The simple & truthful answer is that a General who boasts of being a West Pointer & a regular Army officer of nearly thirty years standing took twelve days to get ready to do what ought to have been done in forty eight hours, & didn't do it after all, but marched up in the rear of my command after we had driven Floyd from his position by an attack in front, whereas he ought to have opened the ball a week earlier by an attack on Floyd's rear, which it was loudly trumpeted over the country he was going to make.

Yet he has somehow procured the most fulsome puffs in the papers and is actually trying to make capital to secure a Major Generalship by reason of what every energetic man in the army regards as a most disgraceful failure to do a plain & easy duty, & which he could only have failed to do through lack of nerve.

More than a week ago I had orders from Washington to take three regts. of my brigade to Kentucky, but the order came to me direct instead of going to Gen. Rosecrans, & he as commandant of the Dept. objected to their ordering his forces away in that manner: the order was declared to be a mistake & the choice of eight regiments to go out of Va. into Ken. left to him.

I fear this condemns me to remain here, for Gen R. is complimentary enough to say he would much rather spare the others than to spare me & my brigade. All of which though very kind & complimentary, & intended in very best of spirit is very like killing with kindness.

Gauley Bridge 2nd Dec. 1861

I expect to be in Charleston in the course of three days, & will report from there as soon as I can get at all settled. Gen. Rosecrans leaves the valley going to Wheeling, & I shall consequently be once more in command of all the troops in this valley. In fact I am the only General officer now in it, Gen. Schenck being at home sick, & Gen. Benham under arrest to await a court martial in regard to his recent exploit in not 'bagging Floyd.'

Gen. McClellan promised Gov. Dennison to try to arrange it so that I should get into a different field. As to my own position I have made up my mind to be contented & 'bide my time' as heretofore. My brigade greatly needs an opportunity of drill & if I can get it by going into Winter quarters I shall be glad, knowing that we shall be better fitted for work & have more chance of doing our duty creditably in the Spring. I tried to go to Kentucky & having failed, I would fain console myself with the belief that it all for the best.

Charleston 11th Dec. 1861

I have been so busy for the week past, moving troops to this post & arranging the preliminary business here, that I have failed to get a moment for writing to you. I am more comfortably situated than I expected to be, though the town is a terrible mud-hole in consequence of the late flood.

My boarding & lodging place is at a very pleasant place—an old brick mansion with large door-yard filled with evergreens. The family besides myself and staff, consists of only a young married couple & their servants. I go to my Adjutant Generals office every morning, & usually ride through the camps in the P.M. How long I shall remain is entirely uncertain.

Hd. Qrs. Div. of the Kanawha Charleston 22 Dec 1861

I have been excessively busy since writing last. My brigade as such, is broken up & I am assigned to the command of the whole Div, including the forces in this valley & down to the Kentucky line, still however subject to Gen. Rosecrans orders, he remaining in command of the Dept.

Garfield is in Eastern Ken. & as Sen. Col. in his command has a brigade whose field of operations is directly adjoining mine, so that we may yet act together. Col. Tyler caused me some vexation. His regiment is removed from my brigade & ordered to Kentucky and it is generally thought he procured it to be done by urgent solicitation to Gen. R. feeling unwilling to remain in my brigade after having attacked me. All the officers (except himself) of the regt. united in a letter to me before they left, expressing their chagrin at the change which took them out of my command, & implying their disapprobation of the means by which it was done.

I find daily proof that to do one's duty as manfully as one can without stopping to fret about reputation, not only carries its reward with it, but in the long run is the surest way to retaliate upon malingers. Day before yesterday I had a painful duty to do, in superintending the execution of a man condemned to death by a court martial for desertion & mutinous conduct. He was executed in the presence of all the troops at this post.

Charleston 30th Dec 1861

Gen. Rosecrans has gone to Wheeling & I presume it cannot be many days before I shall be aware of the shape matters will take in regard to the Court Martial & which may be the occasion of my being summoned there.

My command has taken substantially the shape it had when I entered the valley. It is called the Dist. of the Kanawha instead of Div. as I stated in my last. We are emphatically waiting to see what will 'turn up,' hoping we may be ordered to join some great moving column, instead of being kept here as a police force for Western Virginia.

I see more of the people here, & of their feelings & sentiments than I could when further up the valley, & the duty of glancing over letters which persons wish to send through the lines to relatives & friends in the rebel army, has forced upon my attention much that is very painful. They have been worse off than we, for wives here whose husbands are fighting against us have very rare opportunities of sending a line across the debatable ground between the armies.

Nearly all the wealthy, well educated & influential families here are secessionists—not originally perhaps, but became so on the silly plea that they must go out of the Union because Old Virginia had done so. The ladies remaining in the houses keep very close, we seldom see them in the streets, & avoid all sight of us as far as possible. It is fashionable with them to affect contempt of the 'Feds'.

For myself, I am treated with the greatest personal respect, for which of course I am indebted to my station & the power I wield but I avoid society, having neither the time nor disposition for it at present. My mornings I spend with orders, correspondence, dispatches etc. in my Adjt. Gens. Office, & in the reception of officers, & others calling on business. We dine at one o'clock. The P.M. I spend in the saddle visiting the regimental camps, inspecting them, criticizing their drill, &e. The evenings go partly like the morning, & sometimes I get a little time for reading some military work.

This P.M. I was with my staff & a troop of cavalry for escort four miles up the Elk river where I made a call on Mrs. Wright, a widow lady, sister to Mrs. A.B. Lyman of our town. The road is a most romantic one, under the mountains along the river bank, & as the P.M. was a fine one we enjoyed it to the full. I can hardly conceive of a finer sight than our cavalcade made when at sharp turns of the road the whole troop was seen trotting along in single file on the narrow path with rocks and trees above and the blue river below.

The first four months of 1862 would be frustrating times for Cox. He had proven himself on the battlefield, yet as the weeks went by and several of his regiments were sent to other regions, he stayed put. Separately, he wrote to Garfield that within his "command there had gradually grown up a very different feeling in regard to" himself.[25] One officer who agreed was a young Colonel in the 23rd regiment, future president Rutherford B. Hayes. Hayes wrote to his wife, "General Cox is a great favorite, deservedly I think, with his men." Later, he wrote in his diary, "visited General Cox; a good talker, a sound man, excellent sense. I wish he commanded our brigade."[26]

It was also during this period that, after having to deal with Benham, Cox first began to exhibit his frustration with the rivalries between professional military men and self-made men like himself. He wrote to Garfield that, although he was spoken of in Washington as one of the best civilian brigadier-generals, unnamed West Pointers like Benham were getting all the good publicity and best commands "while doing nothing."[27] Meanwhile, he was literally and figuratively stuck in the mud of western Virginia.

While waiting, Cox focused his attention on training the new forces being sent to the region. Also, in another new experience for a "Citizen

General," Cox had to supervise several courts-martial "to try offenders of all grades, including worthless officers who were driven from the service and negligent ones disciplined."[28] He also had to deal with sporadic guerrilla attacks on his forces, but in his letters to Helen, he was dismissive of that danger. At one point, he would tell her that he felt like a "spider in the web," watching for threats but able to deal with them effectively.[29]

In late March, Cox heard rumors that he might be part of a new command, the "Mountain Department," under John C. Fremont, which was created in part because of McClellan's inaction in moving out of Washington.[30] In early April, Fremont replaced Rosecrans, and Cox was given command of the ten thousand men stationed along the Kanawha and Ohio Rivers. Fremont's objective was to move south from West Virginia to take control of east Tennessee, a strong loyalist region. Cox was pleased with Fremont's appointment because he hoped it presaged a more active campaign. Cox's letters leading up to the Fremont campaign illustrate how unhappy he was until this opportunity, in which he would again have an autonomous command.

Wheeling Va. 20th Feb 1862

I am detained here waiting for a boat, & now expect to leave this P.M. at 3 o'clock. It is yet uncertain how we shall be employed this Spring, though unless events take us out of Va. entirely, it is probable we shall make some further advance up the Kanawha valley.

Charleston 25th Feb. 1862

I arrived here on Sat. evg. [evening] last. All seemed very glad to see us again even the townspeople, and I verily believe that notwithstanding their disloyalty many of the Charlestonians have quite an attachment to me personally.

I chafe at being kept here when such glorious work is being done in Tenn. At Wheeling I could learn of no definite plans for action in this Dept. and fear we shall be condemned to inaction till late in the Spring. The victory at Ft. Donelson I have regarded as breaking the back of the rebellion, & do not think they can recover from the disastrous effect of the loss of important positions and the destruction of the morale of their troops.

We are having today a most lovely Spring day. The air is as balmy as May, & I sit in my window writing, the smoldering fire in the grate being hardly necessary to temper the air. Spring will soon be here and God grant that as the weeks roll around that bring the Summer, they may give us an opportunity to help the reestablishment of the lawful government in the South at so early a day that the work may be practically finished before the heat of the dog days comes with its pestilence. I hope we shall not wait many days before we get news of activity on the Potomac, & of the destruction or scattering of the rebel army at Manassas.

Charleston 4th March 1862

I intended to have written at some length, but the press of business prevents me. I am presiding at a board of examiners to test the competency of officers, & my day is so filled with this & the necessary work connected with Hd. Qrs. duties that you will have to be put off with a very short note this time.

There still seems to be no opening by which I am likely to get away from the Kanawha valley before some decisive action takes place at the East. But there is no use fretting about it. I have done what seemed right to secure a transfer & must now patiently await the course of events.

Charleston 9th March 1862

I am looking anxiously toward the Potomac, expecting to hear before long of a retreat of the rebels there. There may be some fighting at Winchester, but the unopposed occupation of Leesburg which the telegraph announced last night makes me doubt even that.

I know that a majority perhaps of the rebel politicians in their Congress are urging aggressive action on their part, but it is easier for their politicians to urge this than for their army to take the initiative, demoralized as they must be by their recent reverses.

I look for the first of April to find them on the move Southward & then & hardly till then, I shall expect some marching orders for my command.

I have just returned from a ride—the first since you left. We went up to the cemetery, then along the hill tops toward the 12th regt. encampment, then down the hill-sides, back by the road to Elk river, up the river past the deep bend in the road & home again. The air is charming. If it would only continue such weather a little while the roads would be greatly improved. I was frequently reminded of our last ride up that road together. The view today from the turn in the cemetery road where we look off toward the camp & the river was exquisite, the atmosphere was warm enough to make a smokey haze in the distance, & the further hills looked as lovely as you can imagine. They miss you here I think, and all desire to be very kindly remembered to you.

Charleston 16th March 1862

I suppose you have noticed that my prophecy of there being no fight on the Potomac has turned out true so far. We have had some expectations of the rebels trying to force their way through here, & indeed I have information that a pretty heavy column had almost reached Lewisburg when they were turned back on receipt of news of the advance of the Potomac army, & the retreat of that at Manassas. If the roads were a little less impassable, we should be on our way over the mountains.

The news of Fremont's assignment to command us came very unexpectedly, but most of us hail it with pleasure in the belief that it means work & that we shall not be left idle. He has not yet assumed command, & we do not know where his Hd.Qrs. will be nor what changes he will make in the organization.

23 March 1862

I have faith in our being set to do something, & that the circumstances will bring the inglorious rest of this Winter to an end. The condition of the roads is not promising. We have had almost constant rains, growing colder of late & mixed with snow, so that we seem to be going back to Winter instead of forward to Spring. But this can't last forever, & either the roads must dry up, or we must go forward as they are.

The expectation is that considerable reinforcements will be brought in the department, & that Fremont will take the field in person. This is what I hope. The preparations will probably take a week or two yet, & if Spring does not fairly open up by that time, we may be still longer delayed. [General Don Carlos] Buell is not in our Dept. It only includes the Eastern part of Ken. where Garfield is, & I hear he is ordered out, but do not yet credit the rumor.

Charleston 13th April 1862

The week past has been a continuous storm, excepting only one day. The plans I had formed to make some movements have been delayed by this for transportation of supplies is impossible till the roads become settled. I am as much in the dark as to the plan of the campaign as ever, & get as yet no information in regard to it from Gen. Fremont, who I suspect is embarrassed by not being able to get the troops & supplies which he has expected. The news from Corinth & the Mississippi encourages the belief that the war may yet be decided before Midsummer. As soon as a vigorous blow is struck at the Eastern Va. army I shall look for a general forward movement of our lines as well.

Charleston 20 April 1862

The unending rains have put our roads in as desperate a condition as at any time last Winter. Movements to any considerable extent are still out of the question, though I have made some preliminary changes and have been getting my regiments concentrated more at the front. Expeditions right &

left have been sent out after bushwhackers, and all the troops have had something to do.

Orders from Gen. Fremont's Hd. Qrs. indicate that his plan is to keep us quiet till the other portions of his forces come further down the valley of Va. toward us. But the elements are stronger masters now, & it would be utterly impossible to provide our men with stores in a forward movement until some settled good weather mends the roads. We have had scarcely five bright days in more that two months: nothing of consequence can be done under a fortnight, even with fair weather.

It is very distressing to think of the agony of suspense of our dear friends in Warren in regard to the [Battle of] Shiloh fight. I suppose Garfield was not there, & I trust Lucy Opdyke [wife of Cox's friend Emerson Opdycke] has been happily relieved of fear before this.

If I ever again have the chance of meeting the enemy, you may rely on my letting you have telegraphic news of my safety, if I survive—and if I fall, some of my staff will be ordered to transmit the news at once, for I agree with you that on the whole, the worst of truth is preferable to suspense.

Charleston 27 April 1862

I fully expect that this will be the last letter I shall date at C. for sometime. If the good weather continues, I shall probably be off by Sat. next at latest.

Where my Hd.Qrs. will be, I cannot be sure, but shall press forward towards Princeton as soon as possible. My route will be along the South side of New River till I pass into Mercer & Giles counties. What we shall find there we don't exactly know, but we go to look for the enemy, & if we find him, I feel quite confident of a good result. Two or three thousand rebels are now in that vicinity, & the problem is whether they will run away, or be reinforced & make a stand.

This P.M. I took a ride on the old route, & the fresh green of the trees & the bright emerald of the grass give to the landscape a new charm. The valley is becoming lovely again. I wish you could see it now.

Charleston 4th May/62

My arrangements are made for leaving here tomorrow A.M. and I shall push forward as fast as possible. My advance guard had a brush with the rebels near Princeton on the 1st but I doubt if we shall get any sharp fighting before we reach the railroad. Your acquaintances here send very kind remembrances.

We have had three fine days again, & I begin to hope for settled weather. As our campaign must now go on in earnest it is a matter of great importance to us. The horrible condition of the roads will make weeks of fine weather necessary to put them in passable order.

    Fremont's plan was to have Cox move south toward Princeton while he paralleled that advance by taking the Shenandoah Valley. Cox faced very little opposition at first, but would be hit very hard at Princeton in mid-May. He was almost surrounded at one point, requiring a 3 a.m. retreat on May 17. Eventually, he would retreat back to Flat Top Mountain, though there he was able to ensure continued Union control of the region. For his part, Fremont would fail in the Shenandoah campaign, being outwitted and outfought over the next few weeks by Thomas "Stonewall" Jackson.[31]

    Cox's next letters describe his activities in some detail, admitting that he had made some errors and escaped a potential rout by his early morning retreat at Princeton. These letters also discuss a phenomenon which he found somewhat puzzling—that the women in Confederate areas were more virulently anti-Union than the men. Finally, in consonance with his optimism that McClellan would take Richmond, these letters repeat his almost constant refrain—a desire that the war end soon so he could return to his family and his books.

Fayette C.H. 6 May 1862
    You see I am pretty well up the country already. The altitude is considerably above the Kanawha valley. We left the trees in full foliage along the river, & here in twelve miles we have gone up until the climate is so much cooler that the trees are only just beginning to bud. It is like passing from June back to April. There it was too warm for fires & one sat with open windows, & covered ourselves lightly at night.
    Here we are sitting about a fire, & will pull our blankets over us carefully. We are making Hd.Qrs. at a deserted 'secesh' house and Bascom has just got out his travelling desk, which enables me to scribble a line. Two & a half regts. Are here, besides artillery. They are mostly Germans constituting our German brigade, but are fine, soldierly, well drilled men.
    The regimental band of the 28th has been serenading me for an hour. It numbers twenty-four performers, and is the best band I have heard here. They played some very sweet, & some very fine things . . . We came up on the steamboat as far as Soap Creek. I greatly wished you could have been along. It was the finest view of the river scenery we have had, & the weather the beautiful day & everything combined to make it a most delightful trip. You would have appreciated the mountain scenery of the Kanawha.

The road from Gauley Bridge up here is the roughest and wildest I know of in all this region. I shall stay over tomorrow here, & then go on to Raleigh Court House. We are waiting for more horses & wagons which are absolutely necessary to much further progress of the army. My advance guard had a very brilliant little action with the rebels near Princeton the other day, in which the rebels were completely routed.

Raleigh C.H. 9th May 1862

We reached here last evening after a most delightful ride of twenty-five miles. The country is very high, but less broken than near the river. The backwardness of vegetation is very striking, coming as we have from the valley where the trees are full foliage. The days are warm but the nights are quite cold, & in spite of blankets one gets rather chilly in a tent toward daybreak.

We are getting down to our regular camp life now, travelling & pitching our tents in the old familiar style. Military matters are being pushed through, yet I am greatly cramped for want of the necessary transportation. I am moving most of my troops without their tents, till we can spare wagons to send back after them. You would be astonished could you see the tremendous trains it takes to keep even a small army supplied.

The news from the upper part of Gen. Fremont's dept looks as if we were to have some of the work in our dept. If I had my wagons a single week would accomplish the portion of the labor assigned to me. If we get a good chance to do anything you may be sure you will hear a good report of us. I have some matters now in train which I will not commit to paper, but which you may hear of before this reaches you. We are all very well & in the finest spirits.

Princeton 15th May 1862

I am spending two or three days here getting up supplies etc. & then I shall move forward again in the hope of getting a rap at the rebels who are reported to be waiting for us in considerable force.

You must not suffer yourself to look upon my campaign life as a great hardship. In itself it is quite the contrary. The exposure is a tonic, & strengthens the system so that hard fare & hard lodging, & hard riding, seem easy and pleasant.

My military family is nearly the same as when you were in Charleston. We have good servants. Monroe is still with us, & is a most faithful, useful fellow in the field. Joseph is one of our cooks. [This is one of the few times when Cox names his black servants] You can scarcely conceive anything more picturesque than the group now sitting on camp stools chatting around the crackling camp fire between the rows of tents before me as I am writing tonight.

The night is dark, & it has been rainy for a couple of days, but we are as cheerful as crickets. The hardest meal I have eaten was on my way from Raleigh to Flat-Top. We had outridden the wagons, & stopped at a farm house at noon to try to get something to eat. They excused themselves by saying the rebel army had nearly eaten the country up, but would give us what they had, so they put before us a corn 'pone,' made of coarse meal & water baked in a thick oval loaf, a cup of coffee without milk, sweetened with very dark dirty looking sugar, & a little piece of fried pork. This without butter or anything else whatever was my dinner, but after a twenty mile ride my appetite mastered enough of it to keep me from hunger till we went into camp in the evening.

Again when we came into Princeton we had a rough time. The wagons were again delayed & were not likely to arrive till midnight, but we had some biscuits & sliced cold meat & a box of sardines along, & a couple of our servants had me in one of the ambulances, bringing our blankets & some ground coffee, so we found an empty room in a deserted house, one of two or three not burned by the rebels when they destroyed the town on their retreat, hunted up a rough board table—our boys borrowed a sheet iron camp kettle & some tin cups from the soldiers, & made us some coffee, & so without chairs, plates, knives or forks we used our fingers, made our suppers, & then rolled in our blankets, seven of us slept on the bare floor, two slept in the ambulance, & another made a pen of rails stretched a rubber blanket over its top put another on the ground, & rolled in their blankets slept comfortably through a night without taking cold or complaining in the morning.

These little variations are only when we are hurrying a march. Ordinarily in camp we live in a very snug way. Our tents are neat, our cots comfortable, our mess chest well supplied with crockery & glass, & our cooks get us up very good meals. To be sure we never see milk, & butter is a rarity, but those are trifles one soon learns to dispense with in campaigning.

Battle near Princeton, May 20th 1862

We have had a few days of most exciting and wearing work. The enemy learning of our advance toward the railroad, threw in reinforcements from Eastern VA, till their troops more than doubled our numbers according to the best information, & tried very hard to trap us as we advanced. I have completely foiled them, & although prudential reasons made it best to draw in my lines somewhat, as they were getting too long for my means of supply, I have lost nothing of advantage.

I have a splendid position here, where I can defy almost any force, & can sweep down in either of two directions whenever opportunity offers. With the troops I believe I have gained reputation & influence by my handling of them under difficult circumstances.

Gen. Fremont warmly approves my conduct, & so although I have not done precisely what I intended, I have every reason to be satisfied: for we have secured a large portion of this country the rebels controlled before, but which I am sure they cannot again deprive me of.

By means of a circuitous road, & before we were informed of the increase of the enemy's force some three thousand of them attacked Princeton where my Hd.Qrs. were, & where there was only a small detachment of about two hundred men at the time. I had sent forward most of the troops about fifteen miles intending to attack the principal position of the enemy the next day when I should be with them, & remained behind waiting for the telegraph wire which was to meet me there on Fri. Evg. About two o'clock the advance guard of the enemy came toward the crest of some hills on our right, and were met by outposts of ours some five mile out. They gradually pushed on till I got out the whole of the little force to resist them, but it soon became evident that it was not a small detachment we were dealing with, & about 5 o'clock I was satisfied that there were enough of them to take the place.

This of course would cut the line of our communications, stop our trains with supplies & play the mischief generally. I accordingly gave orders to send back & stop a train on the road, & directed the officer in command of the detachment to hold the place as long as possible, had our Hd. Qrs. baggage & papers etc. put in our wagons, & sent out of danger: then mounted my horse again & with the staff road forward to where the bulk of the troops were. The road was a horrid one, & it was almost dark when we started. I reached them about half past eight P.M., immediately ordered in the detachments which were guarding the roads in different directions, took fifteen hundred of the troops already there & marched back to Princeton.

As the men were cooking the next day's rations when I got there, I let them complete that, & then we started. You can scarcely imagine gorges so black & deep as those that mountain road ran through. We proceeded cautiously, marched all night, & at daybreak entered the town, driving the enemy before us. They hardly waited for us giving ground at once, & retiring to the mountains skirting the town, where they had their artillery put in masked battery. We drove them from the heights nearest us, and a warm skirmishing engagement was kept up all day. They found we were inferior in number & tried to drive us back again, but we declined being driven.

Toward evening the remainder of my command came up, & I expected to give battle in the morning (Sun) to their whole combined force, for as soon as my reinforcements came up they were pretty closely followed by those who had been in front of them before. By this time we had felt of the enemy enough to be pretty sure of his superiority in numbers, but were confident of our ability to cope with him if the attack was made in front.

We carefully stationed our outposts & sentries, & while the men slept on their arms, I was busy receiving reports, issuing orders, examining persons coming with information etc. About eleven o'clock I received information from the outposts that the enemy's cannon on our right was being moved off on a road leading parallel to that coming behind us, & coming into it some eight or ten miles in our rear, or going by another fork far behind us into the Guyandotte valley, whence they might reach Charleston & the Kanawha.

On this I called the principal officers together and all agreed in advising that we should retire to a position from which we could quickly go or send help to any point that might be threatened, & so frustrate the enemy's plan of trapping us. Information continued to accumulate showing that troops had been pushed in by railroad in great numbers and that we could only hold our own by getting strong positions & being very active.

At two o'clock Sat. night we decided to move before day-light and at three marched in perfect order, the rear-guard and myself leaving the town just as it began to be broad day. The difficulty of accomplishing this when we had our wagons, baggage, ammunition etc. to carry, no one can imagine who has not had experience in such matters.

My Hd. Qrs. are twenty miles from where we were before, we are a hundred and ten miles from Charleston, & seventy or seventy five mile from Gauley. So much for what was done. The endurance was a thing not to be forgotten. After an ordinary day's work wound up by the excitement of a sudden battle sleep is usually welcome, but instead of getting it I rode all night, having eaten nothing since noon.

The whole of the next day was spent in moving troops, fighting & skirmishing, & the next night again spent without sleep as stated above, so that it was not till the end of the third day that I got any rest. I had no regular meal after noon the first day, & during the whole time ate but two crackers, and drunk some coffee without milk three or four times. The lack of food however I did not apparently feel, for the loss of sleep deprived me of all appetite, & my mind was to intensely occupied most of the time to think much of any physical want which did not make itself imperatively felt.

As soon as my movements were such that I felt confident no superiority of force could take me at a disadvantage, and I got a night's rest, my appetite returned and I was at once all right.

The responsibility for the lives of thousands of men in a critical situation is a tremendous burden, but now that I have gone through it, & know that the army itself & Gen. Fremont acknowledge that I have acted wisely and coolly, & have saved my troops by judicious generalship, I am of course far from sorry that I have gone through it.

We are now preparing to accommodate our action to what we learn of the enemy's force and position, & feel that we have every strategic advantage.

Gen. Fremont is demanding more troops for my command, & we hope to go to the railroad very soon not withstanding the rebel reinforcements.

There was a portion of the time on Sat. morning before we drove the enemy out of Princeton, when I fully expected that was to be my last day on earth. The rebels were in our rear and it was imperatively necessary that they should be routed. The boldness of their movements proved that they were in heavy force, for they are never enterprising unless they are more than double our numbers. I therefore expected a desperate fight, & should have most certainly [been] in the thick of it. Their quick retiring from the place as we entered, saved us probably a good deal of loss, as it unquestionably saved them more and as it also gave me a longer lease of life.

I presume you will not quarrel with them for not standing their ground better. Had my movement not been successful, I should not wish to have survived the others.

Summit of Flat Top 24th May 1862

We are still pushing forward and our line is becoming a long one. We are now three hundred miles from the Ohio river, & almost upon the border of Eastern Va. As yet we have had no fighting that has been severe, though we have had a couple of brisk little combats in which our advance guard was engaged. A week will show whether the enemy will make a decisive stand this side of the Tenn. railroad.

I am having an exciting little campaign here this season, and am full of hope as to its good result. I have just received news of the decided victory of my 3rd brigade at Lewisburg, over three thousand of the enemy, capturing four cannon, two hundred small arms, one hundred prisoners, &e. This is one of the results of our combinations & I have others in preparation from which I think you'll be hearing before long.

I shall not remain here longer than will be necessary to complete my arrangements for the subsistence of my command. As soon as I am on the move again I will write, & keep you well-informed, so that you need indulge no anxiety. We are moving with fewer facilities for transportation than common this season, & consequently have rather more privations to endure, but we do so cheerfully, making sport of hardship.

You can hardly imagine how easy it is to accommodate oneself to a nomadic life in tents. It would seem as if the blood of the patriarchs would tell at a distance of forty centuries, & that the old nature stirs within us very easily.

It is a rainy day today, & the cool upper region of the mountain is completely cloud-wrapt, but I sit on my cot with the front of my tent open, a good camp fire burning a little in front, my overcoat on, as comfortable as you please. In fair weather this mountain commands one of the magnificent views in the country, stretching across intermediate ranges for thirty or forty miles, you have a panorama of height on height the dim blue backs of the Alleghenies closing up the distance.

My health continues perfect, & I have every reason to be thankful that my life of exposure agrees so well with me. For amusement we have the re-hash of the stories & rumors down the river. They had a report at Charleston the other day that I was captured & my whole force cut to pieces, & the town was in a terrible ferment. They thought they were to be taken by the 'Secesh' at once, & it is said many people went out in the hills to sleep, for fear of an immediate attack on the place. 'Wars alarms' are very queer things, & based upon very queer foundations too.

Flat Top 29th May/62

I am still here on top of the mountain, & our future movements depend so much on what is done in other parts of the state that I cannot predict how long we shall be here. The news of Gen. [Nathaniel] Banks's [one of Fremont's subordinates] retreat puts upon us the necessity of looking out for ourselves, for a way is left open by which our little column might be cut off.

I am hopeful however that a few days will recover all that has been lost, & see McClellan in Richmond. When that is done we shall be in a better condition for moving. I am not desirous of prolonging our stay here more than is necessary, for not only am I anxious to see the whole army, my division included, pressing forward to the heart of rebeldom & to the close of the campaign, but I am anxious to get my troops down to a less elevated region. The cold nights on this mountain, following very warm days, predispose the men to dysenteries etc. & the result upon their health is not good.

Flat Top 2d June/62

The concentration of rebel forces along the line of the railroad & the retreat of Banks has necessarily reduced us to a stand still, and until affairs are brought back to their former position in the Shenandoah valley, it is doubtful whether much activity will be manifested here, unless we are attacked.

We are looking every day & hour for news from McClellan. As soon as the contest at Richmond is determined we shall expect to see more clearly the indications of what the next move must be. The chief question being will the rebels retreat by way of Danville and North Carolina, or by the Tenn. R.R.

Keep the little ones in heart about papa's return. We are full of hope that this week will be the turning point of the war, & that the rebellion will then go down rapidly & certainly.

When once it becomes certain that the fire is conquered, & we have only the embers to quench, it will seem but a little while till we are at home again, since the definite end of our service being in view we shall be free from the anxiety of uncertainty, & the great dread of unfortunate results.

Flat Top Mountain 8th June 1862

I see by the papers that what you say of the new excitement in Warren is true of the whole country. Everywhere the people seem to be roused to new determination to do everything that could be asked to sustain the administration. If the government could only take the decisive step of proclaiming liberty to the slaves in the rebellious states, I am sure it would not only be sustained by the Northern states, but the danger of foreign intervention would be greatly diminished.

I see that Fremont has recovered most of the lost ground in the Shenandoah valley, & we are hopeful that the enemy in that region will be vigorously pushed until our advancing columns there may be brought within communicating distance of my own command. Till then we shall be kept on the defensive here, unless accident should give us the opportunity of assuming the aggressive.

We have been enduring a cold rain-storm nearly all the past week, & on this mountain it has been far from comfortable. Today the sun is trying to shine occasionally, though the wind is chilly enough for October. The concentration of our forces so that we may move into a more genial climate twill be decidedly welcome to us, though we may wish for the mountains again, if we get into real Southern weather.

We have been a good deal amused at the conduct of the people in Charleston, or rather of the secession women there, since our affair of the 17th. Their first reports were that we were all captured & used up, nearly all the staff killed, wounded or missing. The rebels then expected the Confederate army down in a jiffy, & it is said some of the women cooked suppers for the soldiers of rebeldom so expected. This continued a day or two, & they began to be 'down in the mouth' at hearing the other side. Then the prisoners taken at

Lewisburg, & on this line were sent down & they got up a lugubrious excitement over them.

Many of the women behave ridiculously, showing that they are ready to do all the mischief they dare, & would seize any opportunity on a reverse of ours to stimulate the men to open rebellion again, if there seemed the slightest chance of escaping severe consequences.

Flat Top 12th June/62

This is the first really pleasant day we have seen for a long time. The rain has been almost constant & the winds so bleak that we have actually expected snow part of the time. Pretty weather for the 'sunny south' isn't it? We shall get the heat however in time no doubt.

Matters are progressing so with Gen. Fremont's column that we shall very soon expect to be on the move again & beyond these mountain ranges. I presume we shall find heat enough to make us wish ourselves back again.

I don't think you need fear that the heroism of the women at home is unappreciated in the army. Those who think much are ready at all times to acknowledge it in the fullest manner. Indeed as a general rule, I do not regard danger & hardship as painful things to endure at all. The only thing which ever weighs upon me is the responsibility for that part of the cause committed to me, & the men under my command.

To be actually & personally in danger sometimes is often a relief. It is when pondering upon the condition of affairs, weighing probabilities as to position, force, and plans of the enemy, & in determining what we ourselves are to do that I feel the need of fortitude & strength.

I am sometimes very weary of my position. For a year I have had a very important command with always an inadequate force for the work, & have been obliged to feel my way along gaining mile by mile, never free from the peril of being overwhelmed by a superior force, since the railroad communication of the rebels enables them at very short notice to concentrate troops heavily anywhere between Staunton & the Tenn. line.

Perhaps the day may come when I can indulge in 'brilliant movements' without compromising the valley entrusted to me, but if it don't I shall continue to use prudent caution, & as heretofore endeavor to do the best thing, without inquiring whether it looks bold or timid. I think as you do that the great armies might have been moved with more speed and decisive results, but to run my little command into a trap & be caught, I must not do it.

Flat Top, June 15th/62

The date of my letter shows you that I am still here, & though we are keeping the keenest lookout for the opportunity to make an effective movement, it is a question of much doubt whether we shall be able to move very soon.

By looking at the map you will see the great Va. & Tenn. R.R. running from Charlottesville through Lynchburg into Tenn. passing in front of us & about sixty miles distant from my present camp. From Lynchburg you will see another road running East to Petersburg on the other side of Richmond. From Richmond you will see two roads running North (which are now said to be cut by McClellan) & two running South, one to Petersburg & the other to Danville. These railroads are the base of operations for the rebels, enabling them to concentrate their troops rapidly upon any point along their routes. From Charlottesville Va. to Chattanooga, near the Georgia line they can concentrate forces at any intermediate point in twenty-four hours.

My advance sometime ago was made as an experiment to see whether they had the troops which they could spare for this kind of concentration between us & the railroad, & the result was that they did so, & after driving them back some forty miles they were able to send in additional troops in such numbers as to make further advance suicidal, & I fell back accordingly to this position.

Fremont is now advancing with what I hope will prove a sufficiently strong column to push his way to Charlottesville or even Lynchburg. At the latter point he could cut all communication by rail between Richmond & the West, & this would leave the forces now scattered in the rebel camps along West Va. and East Tenn. without chance of reinforcement. We would then have the advantage & by concentrating forces could feel confident of driving them out—or destroying them. From this you can see the importance of Fremont's advance to make an advance proper for us & how it is that a small column here may be obliged to remain inactive till matters progress to a certain extent elsewhere.

Accident may give the opportunity of striking a blow sooner, but if the enemy are prudent & wary they can delay the campaign. My position is a delicate one, & I cannot afford to take great risks in the hope of brilliant results. The slightest rumor of a reverse here sends a panic all the way to Cincinnati for the loss of my force leaves the way open to the Ohio. I am here nearly two hundred miles from the Ohio & have all the long line behind me & a sweep of country nearly as wide right & left to protect with my division. These circumstances fix my duty, as they have done from the time I entered the valley, & impose upon me the cautious, gradually progressing policy of gaining step by step the country & holding it.

I look most eagerly for the time when Gen. F. will get far enough forward to unite us with the rest of his command, & then we hope for an opportunity to change our strategy and show what we can do in the way of dash. To do so sooner would be to prove myself a poor soldier, as everyone is who would risk important results & interests for the sake of mere éclat.

It should be remembered however that although our warfare has not been on the large scale, there has been no section of country where the enemy has been more active or collisions with him more frequent. Every step of our advance from the mouth of the Kanawha has been contested & whatever merit there is in acquiring the valley to the Union belongs to my division. I have gone this fully into my position in order to enable you to understand the kind of necessity which attends my movements and that you may not be disappointed in regard to them.

There is one contingency which may give us more to do than we want. If the rebels should see that Fremont's advance threatens to cut off their way of retreat into East Tenn. & Ga. they may evacuate Richmond and precipitate their whole army upon Western Va. I don't believe they will try this, although it has been loudly threatened, for there are two sides even to that question.

A large army will starve, where a small one can subsist, & this fact alone will probably prevent the bulk of their force from going far from Richmond. Still if retreat from Richmond becomes necessary, one may see a larger part of them than we would care to make the acquaintance of in the present state of our numbers in this quarter.

We are having some fine warm days now, almost the first of the season. My health is very good indeed.

Flat Top 19th June 1862

Yesterday I had a ride of forty miles on horseback to the New River and back to examine a crossing. I was a little ailing when I started & the exertion of the ride has given me just that feeling of languor today which follows a fit of sick headache.

The dragging way in which the campaign in the East progresses still throws doubt over our prospects for movement. The opportunity may occur any day, & then I shall take advantage of it. I weary greatly of this forced inaction. I burn to have the war rightly ended.

A year from one's home, family, books, & accustomed thoughts & studies is enough. The second year will I fear drag awfully. If Richmond were taken, and our armies pressing forward concentrating & rapidly pushing everything before them, the prospect of a speedy end would satisfy us, but when affairs go so slowly we tire of it, especially while under the nervous depression which follows a fit of headache.

My great wish has been that Fremont would push forward rapidly with his whole command & move onward. I feel most contented and am in a much easier position when acting with other troops, for trammeled as I necessarily am, with a force kept at the minimum that will do for the position, the advantages of a separate command are all nominal, & the disadvantages real.

The battles between Jackson & our troops appear to have been far from decisive. Jackson evidently had more troops than was reckoned on. I presume by this time however the concentration of our forces there must be such as to give them the proper preponderance & I must earnestly pray they may be able to give a quick decisive close to the campaign.

But I ought to avoid military subjects when I am not in a hopeful mood. What a pleasure it would be to drop in upon you this afternoon! I wonder what you are doing, & how the house & the village are looking. It is two years since I have seen Warren in its greenery, for I left in the Winter, & two Winters & nearly two Summers have passed since then, out of which two poor days are all I have spent there.

Well the longest lane has some turning & the war can't last forever. It seems to me as it seemed last month, that a very few days—weeks at the farthest—must be decisive. Although the disbanding of the army would not probably follow immediately upon the restoration of peace, there would at least be some little chance for temporary absence.

Flat Top 22nd June/62

In my position the suspense of awaiting uniting for the movement East & North & South which must precede any very decided or permanent advance on my part keeps me in that expectant, anxious state which is not favorable to letter-writing.

From my mode of speaking you perhaps think that nothing goes on in my district, but this would be a misapprehension. Let me enumerate some of the items of work going forward. Col. [George] Crook[32] thinks he has a chance to hit effectively the part of Gen. [Henry] Heth's force that he defeated a month ago, & is after him, a march of thirty miles away from this camping ground. A party of bushwhackers nearly two hundred in number have cut the telegraph line some forty miles North of Gauley Bridge, & I have ordered a detachment after them. Another party has been committing depredations down near the Ken. line, & I have sent another party after them. Still another detachment is out to the front watching the rebels there & gathering information of their present position & forces.

Then the orders to be given in the Quarter Master's dept, & commissary's, the moving of troops for benefit of health from one locality to another, & the ordinary routine of army work all contribute to make something to do, but because we look toward Richmond, & circumstances do not favor our movement thitherward, we say we are idle, & become restless.

I wish Jute [nickname of Julia, Helen Cox's sister] & you could have stood with me yesterday morning a little after sunrise, on the crest of the mountain just above my camp. The dense fog which covered every river & stream in the landscape below us filled up the smaller valleys, & the mountain ridges stood out of it like islands out of a milky sea. The upper surface of the fog was as well defined & smooth as satin at first, but after awhile it began to break into waves, & then to lift, & finally to move off in clouds. Meanwhile the upper air was as pure & clear as could be, & the high ranges in the distance, twenty or thirty miles away were so sharp & clear-cut that our glasses enabled us to distinguish the open spots on their sides & even some fence lines. I enjoy these things very much, but as I have before said, the surroundings and associations are not such as to favor such enjoyment to the utmost.

I can remember hours at home in which I have lain by the banks of the Mahoning looking out on the quiet landscape, watching the children playing in the water's edge, with a keen zest in the enjoyment of nature which I cannot have when looking even at the grandeur of these scenes, so long as white tents & rattling drums fill the atmosphere with thoughts of war instead of peace.

The hope that the decisive campaign of the war would be over in May was one so cherished that the disappointment at the lingering of affairs before Richmond is very great. June was to have seen McClellan's army in North Carolina, my own command united to Fremont's & probably in East Tenn. The rebel army was to have been irretrievably broken, & only the occupation & quieting of the country to be done. My faith is strong that the end is only postponed, but one cannot help but find it very tiresome waiting, when home & friends are separated by so long a lapse of time as well as space.

Cox's next letter responded to Helen's query about his daily life:

Flat-top mountain 26th June/62
Your inquiries as to the personal matters of every day life here are natural, but there is little of interest to be said in reply.

We have not had the variety in food we would wish, yet we have no reason to complain. Our meats are good. We have first rate hams which we order from Cin. & our fresh beef is as good as could be desired, much better indeed than you generally get in the Warren market. White beans are our chief reliance as a vegetable. Rice we have at all times, & during the Spring we had potatoes, though we have seen none now for a month.

We are now getting most of our bread from the post twenty miles behind us, & it is very good and light, though not very white. When we fail to get it we usually have flour & our cooks make soda bread & biscuits, though you know I am not at all fond of bread made in this way. Our constant life in the open air keeps us in good appetite and our solid food, plain & unvarying as it is, is eaten with good relish.

If we were in a country where some vegetables could be got we should be better pleased, but nothing is raised here—in fact scarce anybody lives here, & so we are as absolutely dependent upon what we import from Ohio, as if we were on the sea.

Living in tents is not in itself a hardship except in bad weather. When the ground is soaked with rain & you cannot step beyond the front of your tent without getting into deep mud, it is not at all pleasant. At such times neither riding nor walking is pleasant, & if the air is chilly as it usually is during storms on these mountain tops, you may stand in the smoke of your campfire, & let the rain run off your back without being more comfortable than is consistent with proper appreciation of the vanity of mundane things.[33]

> As Fremont's initiative faltered, the war news also began to turn for the worse elsewhere for the Union, which would lead to a major change in policy. In the West, Union advances stalled at both Vicksburg and Corinth and, in September, Confederate generals Braxton Bragg and Kirby Smith advanced into Kentucky. In the East, McClellan's Peninsula campaign to take Richmond came to naught. Behind the scenes Lincoln's support for a conciliatory approach was waning and, on July 13, Lincoln told Secretary of State Seward he was committed to issuing an Emancipation Proclamation. The "hard hand of war," including taking Southerners' "property" (those enslaved) was about to become a core element of Union policy.[34]
>
> Lincoln replaced Fremont with General John Pope and named him commander of the new Army of Virginia. Pope's objective was to move between Washington and Richmond both to protect the capital and to cooperate in a new offensive against Richmond. He was, at first, to cooperate with McClellan's Army of the Potomac and Ambrose Burnside's forces, which had been ordered to come up from eastern Virginia.
>
> An anxious Cox, tired of being stuck in the mud of West Virginia, telegraphed Pope on July 3: "In view of the report that disciplined troops are wanted at the East, I call your attention to the fact that my

division is among the best seasoned and oldest troops in the field, and for discipline and drill will compare favorably with any."[35] He got no answer for several days, and then was left waiting for orders for several weeks, which enhanced his frustration.

The next letters underlined Cox's concern that he was being forgotten as he languished in the muddy crags and defiles of West Virginia. While he expressed doubts about Pope's abilities,[36] Cox wanted nevertheless to be involved in active duty, even as he used his leisure time in ways most generals did not, i.e. re-reading the works of Baron Jomini. Helen obviously was just as exasperated, especially because Cox was again being attacked in the press for not moving, despite his lack of orders. He told her that he would try to deal with it and advised her, "Take it coolly, Helen."

Flat-top 28th June/62
The rumors that Gen. Pope has been assigned to command the united forces of Fremont, McDowell & Banks puts us in great doubt—what is to become of us? Indeed I seem to be almost out of the world, for not withstanding my almost daily dispatches to Gen. Fremont's HdQrs I have not a single syllable from him in regard to the campaign since the first of June—now four weeks!

The necessity of uniting the forces in the valley of Virginia is so palpable that no one can for a moment doubt the wisdom of it, but I was of the opinion that the command should be given to Fremont.

Pope has been very fortunate, but he has never had a severe battle, & for a large independent command is an untried man. My personal acquaintance with him, which however was very slight, did not impress me favorably. But I hope for the best, & wait.

You must try to keep up good heart, & hope in regard to the progress of affairs. It is entirely out of the question for me to think of resigning in the present condition of things. Unless I get dismissed or killed I must see the war through however laborious & wearisome my part of the task may be.

The Richmond siege must end some day, & that will open a new act in the drama with a chance of a more lively movement. I must believe God will [not] permit us to fail in a contest which all admit must settle the fate of human slavery on this continent. And yet looking at it from his stand-point, one cannot say confidently what deeper wisdom or more sure progress might be worked out in another way.

One thing is sure: the war has not been without results even if it should stop here. The federal government has at length been cut loose from slavery both in the territories & in the Dist. of Columbia the public mind has been rapidly educated to see how the infernal system is necessarily at war with a truly republican government & that the permanence of our institutions demands its overthrow.

Even an acknowledgment of the independence of the South could not now seriously weaken the union of the loyal states, whereas a year ago, their independence acknowledged without a war would have split the country into fragments.

The telegraph brings news that Fremont is suspended. I wonder if they will think to enquire what has become of my division.

Flat Top 2 July/62

I write this morning in the midst of our perplexity in regard to the news from Richmond, Of course that subject is uppermost in my mind. We have only brief telegraphic dispatches of a rather inconsistent character, claiming great & advantageous results to our arms, yet admitting that McClellan's right wing made a retrograde movement saying Richmond must fall, yet ominously referring to the present shape of affairs.

Before this reaches you the whole will be known & the suspense ended. I do not like the tone of the dispatches, & fear results which will produce more delays, more danger of foreign intervention.

I cannot think there is any danger of a rout of McClellan's army. Even if forced to retreat, I believe it will do so in decent order & soon find a position it can successfully hold. But the contemplation of any such possibility is very unpleasant & I wait for this P.M.'s news with great impatience.

The past twenty four hours there has been a continuous cold rain, driving and beating like a Nov. storm. Except for the chilliness my tent is quite comfortable. I have floored it with long boards of heavy oak bark stripped from the trees of right length & flatness so that it makes a sweet and quite neat looking covering for the smooth worn ground. Still a storm which makes out-door duty a wet & slippery task, & which keeps the atmosphere within a tent damp & clammy is only to be endured, not enjoyed.

Flat-Top 10th July 1862

One of the results of the reverse at Richmond is to infuse new energy into the administration. McClellan is being very heavily reinforced & I hope will be able to take Richmond before the return steamer can bring ambassadors to propose European mediation. To do this he must have the city before the close of the month in my opinion. If he does not, I anticipate trouble with England & France.

Gen. Pope is expected to move forward so that my army can either cooperate with him, or be carried around by way of Wheeling to join him. I am in telegraphic communication with him, & two or three days will decide the plan. You ask whether Gen. Schenck's assumption of command at Middleton will not conflict with my claim of rank. No, because my force is not attached to his, but is entirely independent, reporting direct to Gen. Pope.

Thank you for the mignonette. The odor is plain enough, but it is not what I have always expected from its reputation. I enclose in return flowers of the large and small laurel, from which you can see the contrast in part.

Flat-Top 17th July 1862

The past two weeks have been the most distressingly full of suspense of any this year. I have been anticipating the announcement of a definite policy from Gen. Pope, with perhaps the moving of my command into Eastern Va. & the supplying its place by new levies.

Day after day has slid away & yet strangely I get no decision. Telegram after telegram is unanswered. There seems to be great difficulty in determining what to do & meanwhile the rebels are having their time of action.

The raids into Ken. & Tenn. will throw the West into a flutter again, & make people swear because troops have been sent East to reinforce McClellan, who I fear has a position he will find abundantly embarrassing before he is out of it. From this time till the new troops are enlisted & in the field will be a troubled time for the Administration, for the people will be demanding everything of them at once, when in fact one thing will be all they can well do, i.e. look after Richmond.

The forced quiet of matters here is likely to continue till Gen Pope's plans are announced, unless some Stonewall Jackson tries his hand in this part of the mountain region, where he would receive a pretty warm welcome. The soldiers' peculiar passion is change, anything for a change.

I fear McClellan finds such difficulties in approaching Richmond by the river that a long delay is inevitable, however full of political perils it may be. The question of the new levies is not free from difficulty, though I hope it will be solved favorably. The raising of three hundred thousand men is not to be done in a day, and if volunteering is being depended on I fear it will go but slowly.

There have been no days for a year past more full of doubt, & serious thought than these. The next month must take us past the crisis in some way.

The abusive correspondent in the Gazette is someone in the employ of a Col. who is under charges for violating an order from Gen. Fremont's hd.

qrs. & who takes the usual method of revenge practiced by mean men. The reason why I have been anxious to have my command ordered East is that in an active field & in competition with others I have no fear of relatively losing ground.

I never gained faster than when Gen. Rosecrans had three or four brigades here last Summer, & mine was only in competition with those. Now every ill-natured person holds me responsible for delays & inaction necessarily incident to our position or directly under orders from hd. qrs. Of course such abuse may injure one, does injure one, in a certain kind of public reputation, & the fact that malicious lying or lying puffery can make or mar such a reputation to a great extent is a reason why sensible people despise the whole thing of public life.

Duty is the only motive that keeps me in a day. Time & opportunity may make these things straight, but if the opportunity does not come & one is condemned to a tedious & inactive role to the end of war, he must swallow his pride, & let the insects have it their own way with his military reputation as the public get it. Take it coolly Helen.

Flat-Top 20th July 1862

Gen. Pope's reticence of information & instructions to me is becoming very strange. It is now three weeks that he has been in command & after inquiring about my force & giving intimations that some speedy announcement would be made of a plan in which we were to have a part he subsides into silence, & I can get nothing whatever from him, not the first hint or word, good or bad.

It is now almost two months since I have had any instructions, information as to plans on my right or left, or anything whatever which could help me to mature anything here, or cooperate with anybody else. I venture to say that never before in the history of modern warfare was an instance known in which so important a div. of an army was ignored at headquarters. My despatches go day after day & week after week & yet I do not get even an acknowledgment of their receipt.

If they are unable to form plans at hd. qrs, one would suppose they might at least say that until further orders I shall simply maintain my position, & then have the grace to acknowledge receipt of my messages.

I thought yesterday P.M. that a chance for a battle had come. I received word that the enemy in front had concentrated on Col. Crook near Lewisburg, & I was preparing to move instanter when better information proved the first report to be "bogus."

I sit down like a spider in the center of a web watching for some false move along my front which may give me a chance to make a move with probable success.

Flat-Top 24th July 1862

The news from Kentucky which disturbed you is not likely to prove a very serious matter. We have been rather inclined to laugh at it than otherwise & have quite commonly held the opinion that it was a God-send for the recruiting service in the northern states. If it is not the means of provoking an uprising in Ken. it will do good by proving that the South has no strong hold on the people of that state, & that they are determined to abide by the Union.

We have had a fresh irruption of bushwhackers & guerrillas near us, but beyond capturing couple of soldiers who had strayed six or eight miles from camp, they have done us no mischief, & we are hunting them out of the country again.

Heard the news this P.M. that [General Henry] Halleck is made commander-in-chief. The army needs a head badly enough, I have a good deal of faith in Halleck's intellectual ability. Still I don't like a commander-in-chief hundreds of miles away from the army.

I get no orders as to my command. The other day a Wash. correspondent telegraphed one of the Cin papers that my division was to quickly take an active part in Pope's army. The newspapers are the only medium through which I get any inkling of plans now. A pretty condition of things, isn't it!

Flat-Top 27th July 1862

The 'delightful news' that I have a prospect of leaving this valley continues only a prospect, & looks quite as distant as when I first mentioned it to you. Indeed I see so little that looks like a promising plan of a campaign at the East that I feel quite indifferent about moving away from here, where we have at least a mountain climate & a healthy one, which is better than sweltering in the valleys of the Eastern part of the state doing nothing but get sick.

The extraordinary neglect to give me any orders or information continues. I have begun to think that Gen. Halleck in assuming the command in chief might separate this army from Gen Pope's command & let me receive instructions directly from Wash. The experience of the past two months is certainly proof that it should be done.

I have been so long away from any place where quiet is to be found that it seems strange even to hear of it as abundant anywhere. This is now the second year of absence from civilization & home, the second year of tents and soldier's rations in a country where we are dependent upon the subsistence stores furnished by the government & where nothing else is to be got for love or money. We do manage however by sending a servant fifteen miles to the rear to get a little butter and a Lieut. who was down at Charleston last week brought up a few potatoes, onions & string beans, so that we are living high for a day or two.

The rebels have been a little more active since the raid into Ken. but we have kept them from mischief in our vicinity. I learn however that they attacked Summerville, a post up the Gauley river from here about seventy miles, a few days since, & took about a hundred prisoners, the garrison being manifestly negligent & taken by surprise. This created some excitement about Gauley Bridge very naturally, & made it necessary for me to move some troops to positions to protect that post & look after guerillas.

Flat-top 31st July/62

We are having a dull stormy day. The rain has been pouring down since last evening & I have been sitting in my tent this morning with my overcoat on, reading & thinking, with but little business to attend to.

The news of Casement I am glad to get. I was wondering whether he was going into the service again.

I fear the Government has committed an almost fatal blunder in attempting to raise a large force by volunteering. The true course was, I think, to order a draft, & assign the recruits to the old regiments, filling them up to fifteen or sixteen hundred men each. Then with a careful scrutiny of the officers, thinning out the inefficient ones & promoting freely those who show ability, the army would be worth much more than it can be now.

Two evils seem now to threaten. First, the requisite number cannot be got by volunteering, or if got at all will be obtained so slowly as to make it too late to accomplish what is desired, & second, the bounty from private funds offered to the new recruits for new regiments will ruin recruiting for the old regiments, & these last will remain mere skeletons, as many of them are now. I have no heart to say anything about the conduct of the war. It seems to be the merest hap-hazard, without plan or consistency.

Flat-top 4 August 1862

I notice that drafting will be resorted to in Ohio about the middle of the month. That is just a month too late. It should have been done in the middle of last month, & the new levies distributed to the old regiments by this time.

So far as health is concerned my troops are better off perhaps than any others in the service, & if the army is to be still during the hot weather, we

The Hills of (West) Virginia

may as well be here as elsewhere. Here at least we have cool nights & can sleep well, & are free from the plagues of mosquitos & gnats which worry the troops encamped in lower regions.

My leisure I spend in the study of Jomini [French writer and military historian Antoine-Henri], & think I am likely to have use for all the military science I can obtain. The war is not over yet, & we seem likely to serve out our three years.

Flat-top 5th Aug. 1862

The rebs [rebels] have been active about me this week, carrying on their system of attempted raids in every direction. A cavalry raid fifty miles to the right, an attack at the river on my left with three regts & a battery of artillery. They have been driven off at all points & we continue to hold our own anxiously waiting for the development from hd. qrs. of a plan in which we may have a part.

The weather has been awfully hot for a few days. Notwithstanding our altitude we have been scorched. How I pity the poor fellows in the low-land valleys! We get occasionally a thunder storm that makes everything snap about us. The bolts fall in our camp in every direction, riving trees, knocking men over, & playing the mischief generally. We have had eight men struck senseless by the electricity, but they were all brought to by speedy application of remedies. So much for being up among the clouds.

Flat-top 11th Aug. 1862

Matters have been lively in our vicinity for a week past. We have had at least five different skirmishes with the rebels. They attempted a raid in [Confederate General John] Morgan's style through part of my territory, intending to go down the Guyandotte river to the Ohio. The party consisted of nearly three hundred cavalry but they were met by attachments of my force in Wyoming & Logan counties & were routed & utterly scattered, many of them leaving their horses & taking to the mountains, running off by twos & threes in little squads. The Col. who commanded them & his second in command were both desperately wounded & their loss heavy. We had a Major badly wounded. I have not yet received the full accounts of casualties in the ranks.

The rebels do not succeed in getting around me very well. The only thing which has turned out badly was the surprise at Summerville where a small detachment by carelessness was routed.

Matters looked like a movement to join Pope a few days ago, but are in doubt again. We cannot be spared from this country, for it will be overrun if we go out of it, yet the exigencies elsewhere may so determine it.

Gen. Pope's communications have indicated a purpose to have us join him by way of Staunton, but this will be impracticable so long as the rebels hold Gordonsville. It is only within a few days that I have had any communication with him since very early in July. It would be a very great relief to me to be joined to a large command where I would have my division together & be rid of the responsibility for the safety of a large district of country, without being in a situation to do anything decisive.

On August 8, Cox and the Kanawha Division finally received orders from Pope to join him outside Washington. On August 14, with his advance forces already on their way down the Kanawha River (north) toward Ohio, Cox left Flat-top Mountain. On August 15, he briefed his deputy, Colonel Joseph Lightburn, who was to take command of the district in his absence, and he made arrangements with the B&O Railroad to carry his men. He was finally on his way, as he told Helen, to "do some real soldiering."[37] Unfortunately, the Confederates had learned, via a raid by J. E. B. "Jeb" Stuart's cavalry, that Cox was leaving and, in response, Lee ordered a new campaign to re-take West Virginia while Cox was absent. As Cox had predicted in a letter to Helen, all that he had gained was soon at risk.[38]

As Pope retreated toward Washington and the events leading to the Battle of Second Manassas were unfolding in late August, two of Cox's regiments, the 30th and 36th Ohio, under Colonels George Crook and Hugh Ewing,[39] arrived first in Washington. They reached Pope's headquarters in Warrenton, Virginia, on August 23. The 11th and 12th Ohio reached Washington on August 24, but were only sent to Alexandria because of problems with transportation. The remainder, including Hayes's 23rd, and Cox himself, reached Washington on August 24, when Cox reported to Secretary of War Stanton.

Cox's next letters describe his pleasure at being assigned to a major command in the Army of the Potomac and his anticipation that he would soon have an opportunity to play a key role in defeating the rebellion.

Gauley Bridge 16th Aug. 1862

The date will surprise you. I am actually moving with part of my command to join Gen. Pope. My first orders were to send half of my command & stay here myself. This put me awfully down at the heel. Another Winter of mere defensive mountain duty stared me in the face. I strongly urged him to change the order & he did so. The members of the staff are jubilant over it. Now for some active service in a large column!

The risks are greater perhaps, but the opportunities are also greater, & I shall have an opportunity to do some real soldiering. My experience has been that I have always gained in standing when acting in conjunction with other brigades & divisions, & when all the vexations, delays & other multiform dissatisfactions growing out of the necessities of trying to hold this mountain region with forces too small for aggressive movements, are not heaped upon my shoulders.

On preparing to move, I rode on in advance of my troops, & made the distance from Flat-top here, sixty miles, in twenty-four hours, coming last evening, a little saddle weary of course. My coming in advance was necessary to prepare transportation etc., & I had previously ordered up Col [Joseph] Lightburn whom I leave in command of the valley.

Your letter of the 10th met me at Fayette C.H. yesterday. Don't be down hearted. We who are in the field must take soldier's chances, but now that we have a chance at service with a larger column in more open country, we are all as lively as crickets. All the members of the staff send kindest regards to you.

I have a good deal of faith in Halleck's planning, & think you will find matters moving better with him at the head in Washington than if he were in the field with the army. He has undoubted military knowledge, & yet may lack the almost reckless executive energy which tells in carrying plans out. McClellan will act with more vigor, when he is partially responsible for the plans, so will Pope, so will [General Ulysses S.] Grant and [General Don Carlos] Buell and I am hopeful we shall see more speed made.

Steamer Marmora, 20 Aug, 1862

Whatever may be the fun of 'sailing down the river Ohio,' sailing up the river when the water is only about two ft on the bars is rather slow. We are just now backing & filling at the Falls'.

The steamboat Capt. & my Quartermaster are shouting at a man with a yawl who proposes to help steamers over the rapids by means of a warp line fastened above, which he rents so much a trip for helping boats over. Just now he seems afraid our boat is too heavy for his line & don't come near enough to enable us to hitch on. We run up to the swift water & swing back, then try it again. The fellow would like to have us force our own way through the swiftest, & then lend us the line when we don't need it. This is vexatious, & I have just ordered them to send a yawl & take his line, will he nill he [willy-nilly].

Once in a while something very like a 'cuss word' escapes the Capt. or his mate forward, but on the whole, they are very correct in their language & deportment. We've been out for awhile watching the process. We have got the warp line aboard, & are winding the boat up through the shoal by the 'nigger' as they call the stern capstan. The old fellow who owns the line paid his compliments to me, said he was only waiting till we got into a position where he could bring his line aboard, & is very civil. The water is very low indeed, & both here & in the Kanawha navigation is difficult, & even a little dangerous to the boats.

We came down the Kanawha with colors flying, & rounded to at Charleston, the brass-band playing the popular air 'Ain't you glad to get out of the wilderness.' Many people expressed their regret that I was leaving the valley, & the feeling seemed to be sincere. We know we shall have a less healthy climate, less pleasant camps, & more risk from disease & casualty where we are going, but the weariness at the necessary slow defensive policy we have been forced to play, & the natural desire to be where armies are acting on a large scale, makes it seem a very happy change to us.

We expect to reach Parkersburg sometime tonight, & thence we go by rail to Washington & on to Culpepper C.H. I presume we shall pass straight through Wash. & have no time to stop there.

Parkersburg Va. 22 Aug. 1862

I got here last evening. The low water in the river detained us fully twenty four hours longer than we otherwise would have been. The troops are being shipped as fast as possible. We go through Wash. expect to leave here this eve. I dread the ride from here by cars; the weather is dry & we shall be smothered in the dust & heat more than in marching afoot.

Washington 24th Aug 1862

I reached here about noon today. Expect to be off again sometime tomorrow. Two of my regts. are probably at Manassas, two are at Alexandria, two more are expected here tonight, & the artillery, & cavalry, & wagon trains are on the way. Another day will I hope see us more nearly together again. Precisely what our course will be after that I cannot now tell. I expect to join [General Franz] Sigel's corps & have a hand in whatever is done. A great concentration of force is making camp here, & the general expectation is that a great battle will be fought somewhere near Pope's position before long.

I trust the Kanawha Div. will have the opportunity & the fortune to distinguish itself, & trust in God the rebels will receive a sound drubbing, which shall put the legitimate government permanently in the ascendant again.

The rail-car ride from Parkersburg here, has tired me less than such rides usually do. If my command were together I should be quite content.

Met Gov. Dennison here. Have seen Gen. Halleck. Shall call this morning on the Secy. of War [Stanton] & Secy. Chase.

Keep up your courage in these stirring times, & trust God that we shall soon bring the war to a satisfactory conclusion. Then for home & a long reign of peace.

Washington 27th Aug/62

The delays in getting forward my train of wagons keep me still here, but I am expecting to leave for Warrenton this morning. Part of my command has gone ahead & I am uneasy at the scattering which the rush & crush of troops here has caused.

Nearly the whole of McClellan's army has been passing through, & the united forces in front must be nearly or quite equal to the numbers of the great Army of the Potomac a year ago. This junction of troops has removed the probability of further aggressive movements of the rebels in force & a few days will I suppose be devoted to getting the army more thoroughly organized for united action.

3

On the National Stage

THE ANTIETAM CAMPAIGN

> The only criticism I feel like making on the conduct of the battle [Antietam] is that we were not supported on the left by part at least of Fitz John Porter's Corps which was near us & was not brought into the engagement. With its aid, after we had carried the stone bridge by desperate fighting, & driven the enemy from the hills above the Antietam, we could have made the victory decisive & cut the enemy's line in two. This would have driven his two wings back on the Potomac by different lines, & probably in a panic rout. Not to seize the moment to throw his fresh reserves into the scale seems to have been McClellan's error, & the result is that we shall have to follow up the enemy & fight him again, when it seemed possible to have crushed the Southern army so that it never could have reorganized.
>
> —Dolson to Helen, September 22, 1862

Cox arrived in Washington at an extremely difficult time for the Union army. McClellan had moved slowly in sending his forces from Richmond to aid Pope's army, which was beleaguered by an active campaign by Lee, concluding with the Union defeat at Second Manassas. Separately, 1862 had seen months of political infighting between McClellan and the Lincoln administration, punctuated by intense congressional Republican criticism of McClellan and other Democratic generals for their battlefield failures. The criticism intensified in late August as McClellan dragged his feet and made excuses for not sending reinforcements to Pope.

On August 27, Cox was surprised to meet McClellan in Alexandria. As both waited to see what would happen to Pope, the old friends had daily conversations, during which McClellan complained about his status but promised that he would fully support Pope. The question as to whether he did so continues to be debated by historians. In any case, Pope's poor leadership was the key factor leading to the defeat at Second Manassas, but McClellan's inaction played an important role. Cox's letters to Helen included discussion of the rumors at the time about McClellan's alleged perfidy. At the time, Cox gave his good friend McClellan the benefit of the doubt, but that judgment would change over time, beginning after the Battle of Antietam. There Cox would come to realize, soon after the battle, that McClellan was not the great military leader Cox had imagined.

The defeat at Manassas opened the way for McClellan to resume command and for Cox to become part of the Army of the Potomac. When McClellan met with Cox on September 2, he said, "Well, General, I am in command again!" Cox congratulated him with "hearty earnestness, for I was personally rejoiced at it."[1] Meanwhile, Lee took advantage of Union disarray by moving North, crossing the Potomac into Maryland on September 4. By September 6, Lee's army was in Frederick and, on September 8, Lee issued an address to the people of Maryland, stating he had come to "aid you in throwing off this foreign yoke." The appeal fell on deaf ears in that pro-Union region, a rare piece of good news for the Union at the time.[2]

Lincoln ordered McClellan to follow Lee and stop his advance. Along the route north, McClellan divided his army of some eighty-five thousand into three wings. Cox's Kanawha Division was placed in the IX Corps under General Jesse Reno, which was part of General Ambrose Burnside's wing, consisting of the I and IX Corps. A West Point graduate, Burnside had established a solid record in the war; and Lincoln, frustrated with McClellan, had even offered Burnside the role as commander of the Army of the Potomac. He had declined, opining that his good friend McClellan was far more capable. On September 6, as the campaign began, Cox and Burnside met for the first time. They would soon become fast friends, and unexpectedly, nine days later, Cox would become his key deputy.[3]

Cox, on good terms with McClellan and Burnside, was about to enter his first major campaign. He would play a key role in the major battles of South Mountain and Antietam; and he would utilize that experience and the window that he now had into the tumultuous political maneuverings in the army and the administration in his postwar historical writings. His letters to Helen over the next few weeks would be the first draft of that analysis.

As the campaign began, Cox's Kanawha Division took the advance of the IX Corps into Maryland. Cox and his volunteers had come to Washington with something akin to an inferiority complex from their long service in the backwater of the war, western Virginia. They soon learned that the reality was quite different. They had strong legs from their mountain duty and Cox proudly noted that he had no stragglers along the way. Hayes wrote that by comparison, "The Grand Army of the Potomac appeared to bad advantage by the side of our troops. Men were lost from their regiments; officers left their commands to rest in the shade, to feed on fruit; thousands were straggling; confusion and disorder everywhere . . . discipline gone or greatly relaxed."[4]

Cox and the other Union forces moved northwest slowly and deliberately, approximately six miles a day, on a thirty-mile-wide arc during September 8–11. Clearly from his letters to Helen, he was extremely happy to be out of western Virginia and where he would finally have a chance to prove himself on a major campaign.

Upton's Hill, 8 miles from Washington, Aug 30, 62

The chaos in which matters seemed involved a few days ago is not yet entirely reduced to order but affairs are greatly improved.

I believe I wrote last on Wed. I was then expecting to go forward immediately with the whole of my command to Gen. Pope. Two of the regts. which first arrived had been sent through on the same cars they came on from Parkersburg. Two more were at Alexandria, & news coming of a rebel raid near Manassas were sent forward in the night to Bull Run bridge. Two more were with me at Wash. & all our wagons, horses, Hd.qrs. baggage was still behind.

On receiving news that the two regiments were ordered forward I took the remaining two & without waiting for anything marched to Alexandria, expecting to get cars there & join the advance. There I saw Gen. McClellan who had arrived & part of whose army, [General Samuel] Heintzelman's & [General Fitz-John] Porter's Corps., were already with Gen. Pope.

The news from the front being squally & indicating that the enemy were between us & Pope in considerable force, the General ordered me to put my two regts. with me in a position on the road to Bull Run about three miles out of Alexandria. We marched out, reaching here about eleven o'clock P.M. & here we are bivouacked by the road-side not having a tent with the whole command.

On Thursday we remained there waiting for our wagons with supplies & orders from Gen. McClellan who had been put in command of the combined army. It was a hot dusty day, & we were enveloped in clouds of dust raised by the troops of [General Edwin] Sumner's & [General William] Franklin's Corps. which were landing and going into camp just in advance of us. Interminable streams of four horse & six mule wagons, long columns of infantry, battery after battery of artillery kept the road alive and the air thick enough to cut.

About noon the 11th & 12th Ohio with Col. [Eliakim] Scammon, which had been up to Bull Run returned, having had a sharp engagement, in which they won golden opinions, & repulsed [Confederate General James] Longstreet & Jackson with a heavy rebel force between us & Pope, & apparently maneuvering to crush the wings of our army before they could be united.

In the evening before sunset we had a tremendous gale & thunderstorm. We took refuge in a piazza of a small house occupied by some ladies of officers, & slept there in our blankets that night. We managed to get one cooked meal each day, & the rest we made up with crackers & cheese.

Friday morning Gen. McClellan sent for me, & gave me orders to bring my four regiments with my artillery & cavalry to this position. Our tents & wagons had by this time come up, & we were soon on the road. The General's view of the case was that the outcome of the enemy's movement was doubtful, that they might succeed in crushing Pope's army & in that case would make an immediate advance on Wash. Then this would be the key of the whole position.

It is in advance of the original line of fortifications about the city held last year, is on the Leesburg turnpike, West of Washington. Upton's, Munson's, & Perkin's Hills are the principal eminences, & each is crowned with a small fort. Some heavy artillery & some more cavalry were added to my command with a promise of more infantry, & I was ordered in case of attack to hold my position to the last.

We came up as I said on Fri. & soon got to living in our usual camp style which seemed very comfortable after two such days as those preceding. My two regts., which first went forward on the cars are with Pope, & there is no prospect of their rejoining us till the concentration of the army again.

A great battle has been going on for two days between Pope & the enemy in our hearing. All day yesterday the roar of distant artillery was incessant. We hear it again this A.M., but more distant apparently. Communication with Pope has been re-opened & we hope the rebels will be thoroughly beaten. Heavy reinforcements from McClellan's command are pushing forward.

We are impatient at being here instead of at the front, for our fight could only come in case Pope is beaten, which is not likely to occur. Reports reach us that constant fighting has been going on between Pope & the rebels for ten days. We are hoping that the army of Longstreet & Jackson will be crushed, & that our combined force will then move forward chasing up the enemy 'to the wall.'

A great victory on our side was claimed last night but I am not sure of it. The condition of things is critical, & I shall be satisfied if we get the whole force united without more loss than we inflict on the enemy.

McClellan received me with the old cordiality & confidence.

I have not been able to learn enough of the source & the reasons of recent movements to know who's responsible for the condition of affairs. On one side it is claimed that McC delayed moving his force several days after orders were given him to evacuate the peninsula, & that this caused the hitch in affairs which gave the rebels the opportunity to turn Pope's flank. On the other it is claimed that the whole movement out of the Peninsula was rash, that Pope should have been reinforced by the new troops till strong enough to advance, & then McC could 'pitch in' to Richmond.

If we whip them now it will not matter for 'all's well that ends well,' but if Pope gets used up, there will be some bickering over it. The thing tried to be done, i.e. the concentration of the army, is in my judgement right, whether the manner & means of doing it is right, may be doubtful.

The more I see of other troops, the better I like my own. They have none better here.

Did I tell you of my interview with Stanton & Chase & their flattering reception? It satisfied me that my troops & myself stood well with the administration.

Upton's Hill 2 Sept. 1862

As I wrote on Saturday the 'great victory' will probably be followed by the question 'who's responsible'? There's no blinking the fact that Pope has been whipped. I fear badly whipped, & the army will do all that can be expected of it, if it gets into a strong defensive position near Wash. & organizes the new lines to create a new army.

I have many reasons for thinking that Pope's selection as commander of a great army was a most unfortunate one, but he had been lucky & that was taken for proof of ability. It is now manifest that all the best military men of his command lost confidence in him very early.

We shall see what we shall see, & meanwhile my position has become one of much importance, though my force is very inadequate to the work we must have if Pope's retreat continues.

I am sorry Garfield continues unwell—we want him. Matters look rather blue—but my courage rises with adversity, I think, & I am cheerful & hopeful.

Upton's Hill, 4th Sept, 1862

The grand army is once more on the old ground of last Winter, & present operations again assume the nature of a defense of Wash. Day before yesterday the retreat from Centreville was made, & the Corps d'Armee filed by different roads to positions where they have the protection of the fortifications. Gen. Pope himself with McDowell's Corps filed by my position here, & occupied in the rear of my command.

McClellan is again in command of the great army, but the demoralization consequent upon the recent battles is such that time must be used in reorganizing.

The general sentiment in regard to the late battles is one of supreme disgust. Most of the officers I have seen say we had men enough to 'eat-up' the rebels, but they were not brought into action as they should be. Misbehavior is charged upon McDowell, & want of capacity upon Pope. But the principal fact is that we have been beaten, & that we must organize the new troops & try again.

The determination to raise as much as possible of the new troops by volunteering is objectionable on account of the mode of organizing the volunteers. We have suffered from the start from the lack of discipline & efficiency in volunteer regiments, growing out of the relations between officers & men. When the troops have in great part the selections of their officers the latter are in too many cases prevented by fear or favor from enforcing discipline, & to say nothing of the many bad selections of officers made, the service suffers extremely from the cause I have named.

I expected to find troops here very superior to mine. I have yet seen none equal to them.

The news from the West is bad also. Everywhere we seem to have reverses, & must apparently take the defensive & hurry forward the new troops. If these were new levies coming to regts. already well officered, & full of the proper esprit & confidence of veterans, I should be confident the tide would soon turn, but I am not satisfied with the condition of affairs within the army.

The rebels are supposed to be moving toward our right with a purpose of crossing the Potomac. It is a hazardous move for them, but they hope to gain both supplies & recruits from Maryland. If they succeed in crossing, I trust such disposition will be made that they will never come back.

In some of the papers are maps of the environs of Wash. By referring to them you will easily find my position. The village of Falls Church is just in front of me & occupied by my outposts. My camp is at the forks of the Leesburg turnpike, & the road leading to Wash. by way of Ball's cross-roads.

I have now got my regiments together & shall probably have some new ones added to the command.

Last night was regarded as the night which should decide whether the enemy was likely to attack us here, or choose an entirely different approach. I was satisfied that they would not venture to approach us here, but everything was prepared for receiving them. I spent the first half of the night inspecting the position of the troops & arranging a plan of cooperation with the forces about me. I then threw off my coat & boots & lay down—got one hour's sleep & was awakened by Gen. [John] Hatch who wished to make some further arrangements. Slept another hour & was again aroused to receive reports of persons coming in from the front & who had been out to the battle-field looking after the wounded, & so on till morning, I got very little rest.

The morning came without any attack however & all reports confirm my opinion that the enemy has passed up the Potomac. I am not yet assigned to any Corps. Had I reached Pope I should probably have gone into Sigel's, but Pope's command is 'gone up,' & McClellan is chief now.

Camp North of Washington 6th Sept/62

Yesterday evening we were ordered to hold ourselves in readiness to march at a moment's warning, so I had the men cook three days rations ahead, & get all ready for a quick move. Shortly after midnight we got the order to report in Wash. to Gen. Burnside, & to march as soon as our pickets were relieved by McDowell's Corps. So, long before light, we drank a cup of coffee, struck our tents, & marched to Georgetown, thence through Wash. & out at the north eastern suburb, where we now are.

We expected to move forward at once to Leesboro, a little place some ten miles from the city, well situated to intercept an enemy moving from the Potomac toward Baltimore. But Gen. Burnside was delayed by the Cabinet for some consultation, & we shall not start before morning.

On the whole I am glad to be ordered to Burnside's Corps. I am not sure whether we shall remain here, but the prestige of his command is as little broken as any, & I have as much faith in him as in any of the Corps commanders, unless it be Sigel.

Gen. Sigel himself sent me word that he was very desirous that my command should join his Corps. I thanked him for the compliment, & said I should be glad to do so if the choice were left to me.

My command has a high reputation & we are gaining the very advantage I foresaw from comparison with other divisions. If we have half a chance now, I shall have strong hope of receiving a promotion.

Matters look blue, but I think that this is precisely the time when it is darkest just before day. The advance of the rebels will soon be rolled back & I do not believe they can muster a force to meet the half million new levies coming on. We must keep up good heart, & fight it out.

Goshen, Maryland, 10th Sept. 1862

Since leaving Wash. I have had the advance of Burnside's army & we are now here awaiting orders, & the arrival of the remainder of the Corps. We are about thirty five miles from Washington & perhaps ten from the Potomac, the movement being made to intercept a supposed advance of the rebels toward Baltimore.

Arriving in camp last evening just at dusk, hot and dusty from the march, I sat a little too long in the shade of the trees we were to pitch our tents near, & took some cold, which took the singular form of settling in one of my grinders, which is aching this morning, & preventing me from thinking of anything very consecutively.

It is entirely uncertain where we are to go, or what we are to do. The fact that we have had no battle yet, makes it doubtful whether the enemy proposes to give us one here, & we may have a wild goose chase, but nothing is certain, & as I am not now in a condition to know all that is known at Hd. qrs, it is hardly worth while to speculate.

Do not allow your fears to overcome you. Remember that the duty before me is a holy one, & that whatever risks I take are taken as a solemn obligation, & the result to me personally rests with God.

> On September 9, Lee, confident that McClellan would not be a threat for at least another week, disseminated Special Orders 191, dividing his forces. Most would focus on taking Harpers Ferry, Virginia, with only a small number stationed at South Mountain, near Frederick, to defend against any Union advance. McClellan was in fact nearby. However, because he erroneously estimated that Lee had over one-hundred thousand troops, he demanded reinforcements. Lincoln acceded to his request to send him Fitz-John Porter's V Corps, which McClellan would designate as his reserve force.[5] Porter, McClellan's closest friend in the army, had been court-martialed after Pope had accused him of disobeying orders at Second Manassas. Lincoln suspended action in the case in order to help McClellan's campaign.
>
> As the lead element of the IX Corps, Cox and the Kanawha Division played the key role in taking the city of Frederick on September 12. The

Jacob Cox's Portable Field Desk at Carter House, Franklin, Tennessee.
The Battle of Franklin Trust: On Loan from the Grafton Family Trust.

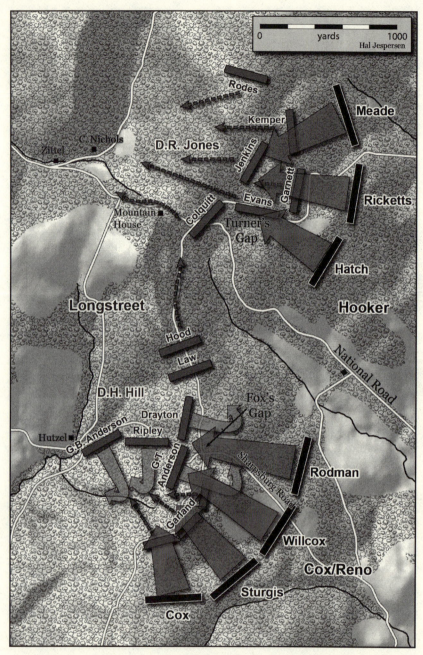

Map 2. Battle of South Mountain, September 14, 1862. Map by Hal Jespersen.

next day, Cox's division and others of the IX Corps crossed Catoctin Mountain and encamped in Middletown at the base of South Mountain. In his memoirs, Cox noted that, on that same day, McClellan had received a copy of Lee's "Lost Order," and knew the rebel forces were divided. However, McClellan did not inform his subordinates of this piece of intelligence, so Cox did not mention it in his letters. After the war, Cox would be very critical of McClellan's failure to seize the moment. He wrote, "If my men had been ordered to be at the top of South Mountain before dark, they could have been there . . . but the value of time was one thing McClellan never understood."[6]

On September 14, Cox's Kanawha Division broke through the Confederate lines on South Mountain. However, because of his uncertainty of how far he should go, given McClellan's erroneous estimates of the size of the rebel force, Cox did not pursue his advantage. Nevertheless, the Union won a solid victory there, the first in many months. Also, with the death of General Reno that day, Cox became acting commander of the IX Corps. After the battle, Lee moved to Sharpsburg and set up a defensive line to await McClellan's advance near Antietam Creek. That great battle would be fought on September 17.

Because of the events' rapidity, Cox only wrote one letter between the Battle of South Mountain and the Battle of Antietam, but it revealed his inner thoughts about the praise from McClellan and Burnside that he received for his victory and his hopes that this triumph at South Mountain would lead to the ultimate defeat of the rebellion.

Camp near Boonsboro, Md. 16th Sept 1862

On Sunday the 14th we had a battle & a victory—Burnside's army was the one engaged with the enemy, & my division had the advance. They say we are covered with glory—perhaps it is so, we had a warm time of it, & tried to do our duty.

Gen. McClellan & Gen. Burnside both specially congratulated me on the success. Gen. McC. came to me yesterday in the field, in the presence of a member of his staff & chief officers, such as [General Edwin] Sumner, [General Joseph] Hooker & etc. and said we had done more than our duty—we had done magnificently. Gen. Burnside said he was personally grateful to me for the credit I had given his command.

The work before us was carrying a low crest of the blue ridge which the rebels held with infantry & artillery. We charged over an open space to reach them while the musketry, & the grape & cannisters from the artillery were very galling. The ridge was carried by two bona fide charges with the bayonet

—no paper soldier charges, but the cold steel was in steady line as our men rushed forward, & the rebels broke when the bayonets were within three yds of them.

They made several strong efforts to retake the crest, but I was well supported by the divisions of the corps, and after an all day fight, lasting till ten o'clock at night, we were completely victorious, the enemy retiring hastily leaving us in possession of the field covered with their dead & wounded mixed however too plentifully with ours. This fighting was by the 9th Army Corps, on the left of the line.

At some time Gen. Hooker's [First] Corps were engaged on the right of the turnpike, & beat the enemy there. So both wings of the army were successful. Maj. Gen. Reno commandant of our corps was killed in the afternoon, & by order of Gen. Burnside I was placed temporarily in command of the whole, being the next-Senior officer.

I am still in command, & if more than one corps is left under Gen. B. shall probably retain it. The Corps consists of four divisions. [Orlando] Willcox, [Samuel] Sturgis, [Isaac] Rodman's, & the Kanawha, which stands now exceedingly high in repute. It is universally conceded to be one of the finest divisions in the whole army.

So you see all the tedious work in Western Va. has not been wholly lost. I have made some good soldiers. The div has done credit to itself, & given me some reputation, & all in a few weeks, almost a few days active work after taking position in the old army of the Potomac.

On the Fri. before the battle of the Blue Ridge [South Mountain] we had a lively little affair at entering the city of Frederick. Being in the advance, my division had a brisk artillery skirmish with the rear-guard of the enemy consisting of the well known [General J.E.B.] Stuart's cavalry, which is supported by flying artillery. There was a cavalry melee in the town, in which Col. [Augustus] Moor cmdg my 1st brig. was unhorsed & captured, he being rather rashly in lead of our cavalry. I pushed forward the infantry, who drove the rebs out, but they carried off the Col. who was paroled two days afterward, being thoroughly robbed however.

Part of the time I have been writing this, our batteries have been skirmishing just in front with the enemy & the cannon reports were more rapid than you could count. The rebels are retreating & we are following up. I have just received the order to put my whole command in motion.

> September 15 and 16 saw both armies maneuver into place. During this period, Cox was in the middle of one of the worst examples of the rivalries and maneuverings with the army, one which would ironically

place him in an unexpectedly powerful position. On the fifteenth, McClellan diminished Burnside's responsibilities by removing Hooker's I Corps from his wing. Some historians believe he had solid military reasons for this action. Others believe it was to accommodate his friend Fitz-John Porter, who was seeking revenge against Burnside, who had forwarded messages to Washington from Porter showing the latter's disdain for his commander, Pope, which in turn had led to his court-martial.

Burnside was upset by this decision and he decided that, as a wing commander, he could not only command his remaining Corps, the IX. As a result, he gave Cox field command of the Corps. As Cox would write later to Helen, "there is nobody but me that he is commanding, & through me, the corps." Getting that responsibility, with the IX Corps acting as the entire left flank of the Army of the Potomac at Antietam, would be the culmination of Cox's startling and rapid transformation from duty in the backwoods to a central role in the bloodiest one-day battle of the war.[7]

At Antietam, the role of Burnside and Cox on the left wing was to await orders to attack while the right and center wings of the army engaged in combat from dawn until 10 a.m. Even though Burnside had been told that his and Cox's troops were to be a diversion to keep Lee's right wing in place, they were not ordered to attack until after 9 a.m. After about 10 a.m., Cox's men attacked the "Burnside Bridge" again and again, while Isaac Rodman's Division was attempting to ford Antietam Creek downstream.

Both Cox and Rodman got across Antietam Creek by 1 p.m., but the resultant delay until 3 p.m. in renewing the attack to replenish ammunition and bring up reserves let victory slip from their grasp. When Cox's men were within sight of Sharpsburg at about 4 p.m. and were about to sweep Lee from the field, Confederate General A.P. Hill's men, coming north from Harpers Ferry, hit them from the left and stopped the advance. Having promised Burnside that he would provide reinforcements if needed, McClellan nevertheless rebuffed Burnside's request at this critical time for help, in part based on the advice of Fitz-John Porter. Most historians agree that reinforcing Cox at that moment could have destroyed Lee's army.[8]

Cox had no choice but to withdraw to a line above the bridge. The IX Corps stayed there all day on September 18 and, that night, Lee retreated over the Potomac, his first attempt to take the war to the North a failure. Burnside went to McClellan on the evening of the 17th to ask

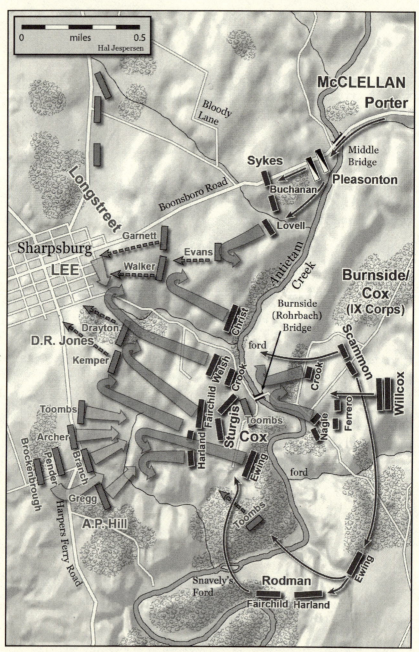

Map 3. Battle of Antietam, September 17, 1862. Map by Hal Jespersen.

for five thousand men to renew the attack on the 18th. Once again, he did not get his reinforcements.[9]

Early on September 19, after he was sure that Lee had retreated, McClellan telegraphed Halleck that "we may safely claim a complete victory." He wrote that Lee had abandoned the field and "[o]ur victory was complete. The enemy is driven back into Virginia. Maryland and Penna. [Pennsylvania] are now safe." There were a few subsequent minor altercations, including the Battle of Shepherdstown on the nineteenth between the retreating rebels and Porter's forces, but, by September 21, the Antietam/Maryland campaign was effectively over.

At Antietam, only two non-West Point Union generals had major responsibilities, Cox and Alpheus Williams. The latter, who took over the XII Corps when its commander, Joseph Mansfield, was killed early on September 17, played only a peripheral role. Cox, who was nominated by both McClellan and Burnside for promotion to Major General of Volunteers, performed as well as any professional soldier on the field. Cox now believed that he had proven himself worthy of further advancement and responsibility in important campaigns. However, it was not to be.

Cox's three letters to Helen about Antietam show his pride in his (and his men's) accomplishments and the promotion to Major General of Volunteers that he was promised. He also criticized his friend McClellan for the first time, presciently claiming that he and his men could have won the battle if they had been reinforced. In his last letter, Cox regretted that, in his absence, many of his gains in West Virginia had been lost, a fact which would soon mark a major turning point in his career.

Near Sharpsburg, Md. 19th Sept. 1862

The turmoil of war has never so completely separated us from our usual opportunities of communicating with home as for the week past. Instead of having our own line of messengers, & providing for our own mails, we are dependent upon chance for every opportunity of sending or receiving letters. I find myself unable to telegraph, for the present movement being a hasty one & probably brief, the usual system in that respect has not been followed.

Day before yesterday we were in another great battle. And whilst we drove the enemy from their ground & held the battle field, the success was not as decided as to force them to a precipitate retreat. It is reported that they evacuated last night, but it is not yet certain. They are now in possession of so small a foot-hold in Maryland that I see no object to be gained by them in remaining, & suppose they will try to hold Harper's Ferry, & put their army in Va. behind the Potomac.

My division has borne the brunt of two severe fights, & is much cut up. It has less than half its former efficient strength, & has lost many of its best officers. So we go, the old regiments cut down, & then instead of recruiting them, they are left mere handfuls, & the new regiments made of raw men, who of none of the esprit or confidence of the old ones.

My life has been preserved in a good deal of danger, & I have lost none of the staff, though Bascom is sick with overwork & exposure. I hope they will be ready for service again in a day or two. Dory [Cox's brother Theodore, who had joined his staff two weeks before] has been of great use to me as an extra aide, & in carrying orders & messages, has had two or three very narrow escapes. He behaves as coolly as an old soldier.

Write and tell Ma [Cox's mother] & Lottie [Redelia, Cox's sister] so. When I get home I shall have many incidents to relate that will interest you, but cannot write them now.

I believe the true policy of the Govt. when once the war is carried out of Maryland, will be to hold up a bit & organize the new lines. If this is done, we shall also organize our communications with home, & regulate our affairs better.

Hd. Qrs. 9th A.C., Mouth of Antietam Creek 22nd Sept./62

Last week was the heaviest campaigning we have had anything to do with. Sleeping most of the time on the ground without even a bush to cover us, & getting a cracker or piece of bread when or where we could with no regular meals or chance of getting them, it seems quite a luxury to get our wagons up, & have once more the shelter of tents, & the comforts of our mess chest. Providentially we have not suffered in health, & are rapidly getting over the physical & mental fatigue.

As I wrote last the Sharpsburg battle was not really decisive though we held the battle field. It was confidently expected that McClellan would renew the attack next-day, but he did not regard it wise to risk it with his exhausted troops, short of ammunition & provisions, & the enemy solved the problem by retreating across the Potomac in the night of the 18th.

The only criticism I feel like making on the conduct of the battle is that we were not supported on the left by part at least of Fitz John Porter's Corps which was near us & was not brought into the engagement. With its aid, after we had carried the stone bridge by desperate fighting, & driven the enemy from the hills above the Antietam, we could have made the victory decisive & cut the enemy's line in two. This would have driven his two wings back on the Potomac by different lines, & probably in a panic rout. Not to seize the moment to throw his fresh reserves into the scale seems to have been McClellan's error, & the result is that we shall have to follow up the enemy & fight him again, when it seemed possible to have crushed the Southern army so that it never could have reorganized.

Our corps was the extreme left of our line. Its advance was a powerful diversion in favor of the right, & though we were not able to hold quite all the ground we at first gained, it is universally admitted, that it gave the success of the day by forcing the enemy to concentrate his troops on us, & so enabling our right wing to push forward & occupy new ground, driving the rebels from their position. The enemy massed his troops on our left flank, completely out flanking us, but we held the stone bridge, & the heights above it, in spite of his assaults, & under cross-fire from a dozen batteries.

The artillery fire was entirely ahead of anything I ever conceived. It was one continuous & terrible roar, & the shells burst on every side & above us, with constant & deafening din. In order to conduct the movement I was necessarily exposed to the hottest of it all, & between the cannonade & the insidious sounds & as it were, malicious humming of the rifle balls around, I reckoned very little on my chances of coming out whole in life & limb.

The intense occupation of my mind necessarily withdrew my attention in part from the danger, yet no one could fail to be conscious of it.

Our experience has now taken us through every variety of soldiers' life & duty, this last being a pitched battle which for number of troops engaged & the sanguinary results will rank among the great battles of history. I shall never be in love with arms as a profession, but most earnestly long for the over throw of the rebellion, & the return of peaceful life & pursuits.

The taking of the stone bridge was the most difficult part of our work. It is a strong structure of three arches, with stone parapet on each side of the roadway. The valley of the Antietam is narrow, the hills rising close to the water & steep, though not very high. The enemy had the bridge commanded with cannon, & had infantry breastworks of wood & stone covering all the approaches to it, & the road from it on the other side. The stream was not fordable near the bridge, though we subsequently found a ford above & one below, within a mile. Several charges across the bridge were made, but our men could get no foothold on the other side to make a stand & hold on, until we succeeded in getting a battery in position to aid in sweeping the road at the head of the bridge, & with the aid of this the enemy were dislodged after several hours of hard fighting.

There is much jealousy of western troops in the army of the Potomac, among the subordinate commanders, & our men & officers are a good deal indignant that fuller credit is not given the Kanawha division for the South Mountain battle. It had not only the advance, but had practically won the battle, before the supports came up.

The enemy made two vigorous efforts to retake the position, & on these the other divisions gave me good help, but the brunt of the fight was in taking the mountain top in face of the batteries, & great masses of infantry the enemy had stationed there.

Mouth of Antietam, 27th Sept. 1862

My last letter has given you such knowledge of my position & etc. that you will be able to trace us in the newspapers, I hope.

Still my command is a somewhat anomalous one. The 1st corps which also belongs to Gen. Burnside, has been temporarily detached (Hooker's) & the 9th is the only one at present under his immediate command. By his order however I am in command of the 9th & he prefers that it should not be changed at present, therefore it is in fact, nobody but me that he is commanding, & through me, the corps. The result is, that in all the published reports, my position is ignored, as Gen B. is spoken of as the corps commander & Col. Scammon has the command of my division.

As I am always a modest man, it makes little difference to me, & I presume the present condition of things will not long endure.

I believe I told you in my last that in the great battle of the 17th I was the actual commandant, in the field & under fire, of the corps., & handled it so as to get the applause of both Burnside & McClellan. The latter is accordingly cordial, & puts me at once in the old familiar footing, urging me to come to his hd. qts. frequently & as an intimate friend without ceremony.

I am afraid I shall stir up the embers of worldly pride in you in what I am going to tell, & I am under great 'concern of mind' lest the thing should some way leak out in the papers before you get this, & yet hereby prepare with a stock of humility &e.&e.

I fear I have lost the knack of writing a good homily. Please consider a good one written on the text 'all is vanity.' & then I'll tell you that McClellan & Burnside both have recommended my promotion to the Major Generalship made vacant by Reno's death, & that there is a pretty fair chance of my getting it.

Gen. B. himself I have taken a great liking to. He is a noble, quick, manly man. He was offered the command of McClellan's army when it left the Peninsula, but refused to take it, & told the Prest. & Cabinet that McC. was a better man to have it. I fear not many of the M.Gs. would have had the modesty or generosity to say that. Yet I think it to be true so far as they have shown themselves, none has exhibited the military genius & power of mind necessary to handle so large an army successfully. We have good division and corps commanders, brave men and good soldiers, but great generals are rare.

Our hd. qrs. today are some three miles nearer Harper's Ferry than yesterday. It seems probably that we shall be delayed here some days. With his present army McC. will hardly cross the Potomac in face of an enemy, or put himself in the condition Lee was in, of having to fight with his back to the river. What he wants is that they should give him a hundred thousand of the new recruits, who are said to be already in Wash. to that number, & then with an army of some two hundred thousand men he wants to push on to Richmond.

I think it should be given him with a hearty God-speed, & every help the administration can furnish. We shall then be in R. & further before long I warrant.

The loss of the Kanawha valley I can't think necessary. The odds against our forces there was not nearly so great as against me in Aug. & Sept. of last-year, when I expected to be surrounded & prepared for a siege. The trifling loss shows that there was no stubborn resistance, & that the labor of the year past has been abandoned without a struggle.

4
Paper General

> In regard to all my late disappointments, I think I have got them pretty thoroughly under my control, & am quite cheerful about the whole matter. I don't think I am hurt at all, even in public estimation so far as I can judge. I meet troops of friends, & influential men of all classes have taken great pains to assure me of their great satisfaction with my career hitherto.
> —Dolson to Helen, April 17, 1863

In early October 1862, a pleased Cox looked forward to the remainder of the war as a corps commander and a Major General of Volunteers, with two senior generals, McClellan and Burnside, protecting his interests. However, during the next six months both McClellan and Burnside were fired and Cox's promotion was annulled. This would be the most dismal period of his career as he was both effectively demoted, as well as removed from active campaigning, and forced into a series of desk jobs.

McClellan did not actively pursue Lee after Antietam, in part because, he told Lincoln, he did not have sufficient forces. He specifically pointed to his dismay that, on October 4, Cox and his Kanawha Division were ordered to return to the Kanawha Valley, which had fallen in September to a resurgent Confederate force.[1] Cox hoped that regaining the lost ground would only take a few weeks and that he could return to his IX Corps command. That did not happen. Instead, Cox left on October 5 for Washington to get his orders, not knowing that it would be over a year before he returned to an active field of combat (other than West Virginia).

Cox's next letters cover the latter part of 1862 when he succeeded in repelling the Confederate advance and strengthening Union control in West Virginia. As he did so, he continued to look for orders to return to a major campaign. However, this was also the time when both McClellan and Burnside were fired as commanders of the Army of the Potomac. With no stronger advocates in Washington other than Chase (who was increasingly at odds with Lincoln) and Garfield, Cox was now out of sight, out of mind. He would use the next months effectively to solidify his political base and control civilian opposition to the war. While these were important for the advancement of his reputation, Cox nevertheless would frequently lament that he was fighting the war behind a desk instead of on the battlefield.

Helen visited him for several weeks in early 1863 and he also took some leave in the early spring, so there are no letters in the typescript between December 5 and March 21. Those were the only happy events of the first three months of 1863, a period which Cox would later call the worst of his military life.

Antietam, 5th Oct. 1862

I am realizing that in war more than in anything else, we never know what a day will bring forth. Last night I was taken all aback by an order to go back to Western Va. & try to retake the Kanawha valley which our men recently ran out of. If I could take my old division, I should feel pretty well over it, but to take command of beaten troops, or raw ones, does not suit me. I go immediately to Wash. & shall there make an effort to have the Kanawha div go along.

The order is reported to have been procured by the united & persistent efforts of Govs. [Francis] Pierpont & [David] Tod,[2] & the Western Va. influence generally. It is of course complimentary in itself, but to make it satisfactory, I must have the means of making a reasonably sure thing of the campaign. As soon as I have a consultation with Gen. Halleck & the Prest. I shall know what to expect.

I may write to you from Wash. or I may not. My haste while there will be the criterion. I doubt if any very decisive movements will be made on the Potomac soon, & if I get the force to do anything with, I may have livelier work on the Kanawha than they here.

The question of promotion may be acted upon before I leave Wash. in view of my going West, though we had not expected action for some weeks. Such things usually wait for receipt of full official reports & etc. when they come for military services.

Wheeling 9th Oct. 1862

If you received my telegram of the 7th you must have been astonished at my sudden departure from the Army of the Potomac, but I myself was astonished no less. Gens. McClellan & Burnside shared in the astonishment.

It was brought about by the urgent request of the Governors of Ohio, Indiana & Western Va. and although at first I felt disappointed, the thing has been done in so complimentary a way, & my command is so important that I have no reason to complain. I am put in command of the whole of Western VA, & my promotion was given me as a preliminary.

The honor of being the first Brig. promoted 'for gallantry & distinguished services in the battles of South Mountain & Antietam,' added to the assignment to so important a command, was of course flattering.

Besides this Sec. Stanton, Secy. Chase, Gen. Halleck & others were personally very complimentary. The Prest was at Cabinet meeting when I called, & I did not see him. I saw him however at Antietam, & he was very kind. He said he was very glad to see me & that Secy Chase had often said to him 'You ought to know my friend Gen. Cox.' Showing both that the Prest. felt cordially, & that Mr. Chase has been a warm friend.

I go tomorrow to Cin. to see Gen. [Horatio] Wright & complete my arrangements for the campaign & then back post haste to Gallipolis. If I am fortunate & successful in my campaign, as I expect to be, I may get a little rest when I get the rebels out of the Kanawha valley. I have had occasion to learn pretty thoroughly however, that not many calculations can be made on the future in time of war.

Much depends on the season. If the roads break up early, little can be done in the mountains, & I shall either be at leisure, or shall be ordered to a new field. If the former, I shall hope to be able to leave my subordinates to take care of the country after it is won, & establish my hd. qts. somewhere nearer civilization & home, where I may get a visit from you, or get leave to visit home myself. But these castles in Spain are very unsubstantial at present. Work is to be done & dangers faced before they can be realized.

When we parted McClellan said to me that if I got matters straightened in Western Va. he would be very glad to have me come & take command under him, even for the Winter campaign alone, whilst matters would necessarily be quiet here.

Burnside said he had calculated on my being permanently assigned to command the 9th Corps, & was seriously grieved at parting. The officers of my old division came & begged me not to leave them behind, but to take them wherever I went, & at Wash I succeeded in having them ordered out here, though they may not get to the Kanawha immediately.

All these tokens of respect & regard are pleasant after the rather trying period of probation I had, & I am thankful for them. God grant my present campaign may be a successful one! I sometimes am sad when I think of the increased expectations of me, & feel my own deficiencies keenly.

Gallipolis, 14th Oct. 1862

I went from Wheeling to Columbus, spent four hours there calling on Gov. Dennison & family, Gov. Tod, & a few others, & thence to Cin. where I arrived late Fri. night, was detained there till Mon. morning, there being no train on Sun. & came through yesterday, reaching here this morning.

Last night we reached Portland, & as we had no horses of our own, had to travel in a four horse hack. We had only got a mile on our way in pitch darkness, when by a blunder of the driver we were upset from the end of a sluice-bridge, into a mud-puddle of soft sand fully eighteen inches deep. Fortunately the horses were stopped at once, & as we climbed & crawled out, you would have died with laughing to have seen the figure we cut. Plastered from head to heels with mud, we were the sorriest looking Gen. & staff that ever was seen.

After partially cleaning, we waited for the moon & then drove on about ten miles & stopped for the night, finishing our journey this morning. I was most cordially rec'd every where on the route.

At Cincinnati I went to church & then home to dinner with Mr. [Aaron] Perry, a leading lawyer there, an intimate friend of Gov. Dennison & Mr. Bascom, who has been a very pleasant acquaintance of mine also for sometime. He has a beautiful little place on the hill above the city, & what with the pleasant drive, a nice dinner, & a very pleasant chat with himself & his agreeable family, I had a very good time of it. I met there a number of notables also.

It will take me a few days here to get my command together, clothed, & etc. & make ready for a start. I trust then to make short work of clearing the valley, God willing, & then who knows? Either a stay here, or a command in more active service. If the former, my present notion is to make my hd. qrs. at Marietta which [is] a refined, pleasant, old-fashioned Ohio town, where I could have you with me part of the winter at least.

The congratulations I receive on my promotion seem very hearty—indeed quite enthusiastic. The warmth of the greetings I receive, & the evident good-will of the people I meet, are good compensation for the labors of the year past—& prove that a sincere effort to do one's duty with patience & fortitude, will come out right in the long run.

My command takes in Western Va. & the border Ohio counties. This makes the arrangement I spoke of above a feasible one.

Gallipolis, 18th Oct. 1862

I have four Brigadiers in my command. Gen. G.W. Morgan who was at Cumberland Gap, Gen. [Robert] Milroy & Gen. [Benjamin] Kelly who were here with Rosecrans & Gen [George] Crook who was promoted in my Div.

I understand that Col Scammon has received his promotion. If so he is the fifth Brig.

It is not probable that we shall have the means of doing more than to reoccupy Western Va. this fall as the mountain country will be impracticable when the winter fairly sets in. I fear we shall see mud & chilly rains before we reach Gauley. The report now is that the rebels are retreating at the mere rumor of my preparations here & at Clarksburg to follow them, & that it is not probable that we shall get a fight. Part of the troops assigned to me are over at Portland on the Railway—twenty five miles from here, waiting for shoes & clothing, which ought to have been sent from Cin.

My movement has been delayed waiting for them, but on Mon. I shall start whether or no. That is to say the troops now here will move up the river some distance removing obstructions from navigation, clearing roads, & e[tc.].

Gallipolis 24th Oct. 1862

To my great surprise Charlie [Charles, Cox's younger brother] dropped in upon me yesterday P.M. & his appearance, together with press of business prevented my writing as I intended.

I shall start in the morning to go up the Kanawha to join the advance division which left some days ago. Our reinforcements have been coming in very slowly, and in no very encouraging condition. The whole of Gen. Morgan's div, since its retreat from Cumberland Gap has been sorely in want of everything in shape of clothes & supplies, & their destitution has caused great delay. Part of them are still delayed a day or so, but I hope to be able to push forward with what I now have.

The reports from the valley above are that the enemy have returned to Charleston in force & intend to give us battle. I do not however regard this as certain although acting on the presumption that it is true.

I find my command will be made in many respects unpleasant by the jealousies & envies of petty men, & a small clique have already commenced exercising their literary proclivities by newspaper correspondence questioning my loyalty!! or at least intimating that I have been in the habit of favoring rebels. So we go. The gnats must buzz & bite in their small way, & were it not for them we might lose our humility.

I hope to be able to do my duty decently & fairly, but would much rather be in my old position in the Potomac Army. I suppose many think my return here was at my own instance, & because I prefer an independent command. How mistaken they are!

A few days will now enable me to tell better what to expect in the Fall campaign—whether it is to be fight, or only march.

Point Pleasant 26th Oct. 1862

We are having today one of the most disagreeable storms, a mixture of rain & snow, & a most raw chilling atmosphere. I came yesterday from Gallipolis expecting to go on up the Kanawha, but pitched our tents here when the storm began. We were well housed at Gallipolis & feel the change more than we should otherwise. The storm may cause some temporary delay in our movements, but will undoubtedly be worse for the rebels than for us.

The accounts from the upper valley are not very definite, but the prevailing report is that the rebels continue in pretty strong force at or near Charleston. The probabilities of their remaining are not great, & they will be likely to pull back as we advance. Our delays have been innumerable. The force sent to strengthen me, being destitute of everything & being forced to wait for a new outfit before they could possibly move. If the storm continues long enough to raise the river, we shall profit by it when once it is over. Meanwhile we must bear it as we can.

Charleston 1st Nov, 1862

Again at Charleston, & in the old hd.qrs. The rebels made a show of standing a battle until we were within five miles of them, & then decamped pell-mell out of the valley. The supply of Brigadiers in my command renders it useless for me to go forward in person, as there is no chance of anything but a chase to Gauley, which we shall probably re-occupy tomorrow. I shall then reorganize affairs here & wait further orders.

Charleston, 4th Nov, 1862

Nothing of interest is going on here, & I am busied re-organizing the means of supplying & sustaining our troops in this valley. Gauley Bridge is again in our possession, & the rebels have gone back to their old positions beyond the mountains.

Catching the scamps is as hopeless as flea-catching, for when they begin to run no advancing army can keep near them. There has been some disposition at Dept. Hd.qrs to try to push over the mountains this fall, but with any means of doing it they are likely to be able to use here, there is little prospect of much being done, and I regard it as very doubtful whether it is at all practicable to attempt anything further than the reoccupation of the country this Winter.

The town is relieved of a number of the more violent secessionists, & they have had such experience with the rebel army as has made a good many sick of it, who formerly were quite inclined to sympathize with the rebellion.

Charleston 9th Nov. 1862

It is now decided at Dept. Hd. qrs. that nothing further than the reoccupation of the Gauley country will be practicable this season, & so after making arrangements for the organization of the force left here just Gen. Morgan's div. being here, I shall determine the question of Hd.qrs. for the Winter. I must first make a trip to Gauley to inspect the condition of things there.

It would not surprise me if I were to receive orders to join McClellan again about the time I am preparing to settle down for a month or two of quiet, so you must not calculate too largely upon the Winter. I fear Rosecrans has a heavier load than he will be able to carry, but I wish him success with all my heart.

We had a snow storm yesterday, but it is clear & bright today. I may go to Gauley within a day or two if the weather continues fine. Shall take Dory with me to let him see the country.

Charleston 15th Nov. 1862

We are just now having a report of Stonewall Jackson being at Winchester with forty thousand men threatening a raid into the northern part of my Dist. If we have him on our hands I shall be busy for awhile, but as soon as the prospects are more clearly defined I will know what to do.

I have written to Dept. Hd. Qrs. in regard to making my Winter Quarters at Marietta, & shall expect to have the thing determined within a week. When it is settled whether I go, I will immediately write to you, & if things are so arranged that you can leave the children safely, I would like to have you meet me there soon after my own arrival. Then whatever time we may have for a visit will at least be secure & we shall not run the risk of losing all.

Charleston 24th Nov. 1862

We have been kept in uncertainty by reason of a notion of Gen Halleck's that it might be needful to remove part of the force out of this valley to help guard the rail-road in the northern part of the Dist. As I felt sure this would result in a fresh raid into the Kanawha I have opposed further changes here, & it was only a day or two since that Gen. H acquiesced. It is not yet fully determined whether I go to Marietta. That will be in many business respects the most convenient position for me, & by the facility of reaching it by rail it will be a good place for you to visit.

As to public affairs I am in the position of patient watching. I scarcely venture to form any hope, & refuse to entertain fears. I am desirous of affairs being brought to a crisis & having it distinctly & speedily determined whether we have the ability to subdue the rebellion. My great anxiety in regard to results arises chiefly from the fact that the old policy of dividing the army into numerous columns is persistently adhered to.

Burnside runs the risk of finding his army too weak by just the numbers that will be used in some expedition to Texas or Florida, & Rosecrans will not have concentrated under his command more than half the force that is nominally operating in Ken., Tenn. & Miss.

Charleston 30th Nov. 1862

You will realize soon, I suspect, that uncertainty is the only certainty in war times. The question where I shall have hd.qrs. this Winter is not yet settled, & I should have urged you to come on at once, were it not for the fear that by the time you reached here, I should be en-route elsewhere.

The trouble is now that there is a strong expectation that Gen. Wright will take a command in the field, & in that event I may be ordered to Cin. to assume command of the Dept. I understand there is some talk of this, though I have as yet no official information on the subject except that Gen. Wright has desired my going to Marietta postponed for a short time. We are to have a Thanksgiving dinner today at our staff hd.qrs. having failed to learn in time of the day set at home.

Charleston 5th Dec. 1862

Last night I received a dispatch informing me that matters at Cin. will remain in status quo, & that there is no objection to my establishing hd.qrs. at Marietta. Accordingly I propose to go there on Mon.

Should you think best to come on to Marietta at once, the directions I gave you in my last will probably be sufficient.

> During his time in Marietta, Cox repeatedly applied for new duties, but to no avail. His lack of influence in Washington was the key reason, but his skills and success as an administrator may ironically have made him too valuable to send elsewhere. While he was unhappy about his idleness, Cox typically used the time to good effect. Most importantly for his future historical writing, he wrote to several correspondents about a variety of issues, including racial matters, war objectives, national politics, and military strategy, which had arisen during the war.
> In letters to his friend Aaron Perry and to Salmon Chase, he sup-

ported the idea of creating the "United States Colored Troops," noting "blacks would make good troops—they are easily disciplined and ruled and are susceptible of military education." As a believer in freedom but not in equality for blacks, he wrote that a postwar solution for the black community would be to create "a military colony on the southwestern frontier which can absorb the surplus black population and solve the emancipation problem with a system of colonization." Those views would be the seed of his concept of resolving the "negro problem" through domestic colonization on the southeast coast, which he would re-introduce during his gubernatorial campaign in 1865.[3]

As he brooded about his lack of active duty and his experience dealing with both West Point-trained and citizen generals, Cox seized upon an announcement that the army was seeking input for a reassessment of its organization. In response, Cox wrote lengthy letters providing his thoughts about military leadership and training. Showing his pride in the citizen-soldiers and his resentment that West Pointers were getting all the major leadership assignments, irrespective of their qualifications, he advocated creation of an open system in which all generals could compete for leadership positions. He wrote, "the army must be a unit, because if the regular army organization is so narrow it can't be expanded in time of emergency, what use is it? If a volunteer organization is fit to decide the *great* wars of the nation, is it not ridiculous to keep an expensive organization of regulars for the petty contests with Indians or for an ornamental appendage to the State in peace? The thing to be aimed at is to have a system flexible enough to provide for the increase of the army to any size required, without losing any of the advantage of character or efficiency which, in any respect, pertained to it as a regular army."[4] His sentiments, which would ultimately be reflected in army policy, were ignored in Washington and no action was taken.

Cox's resentment at the treatment he received, as well as the favorable dealings with even incompetent West Pointers, was exacerbated in early March. As he wrote in his *Military Reminiscences*, he suffered "the one severe disappointment of my military career" when he learned that his promotion to Major General of Volunteers had not passed through the Senate and that he would become a brigadier general again. His commission expired and his rank was decreased on March 4, 1863.

Cox attributed this decision to the fact that he had fewer political contacts than others; however, there was another reason about which he apparently never learned. One of his Colonels in the Kanawha Division, Hugh Ewing, had judged that Cox had been a poor leader at Antietam.

Ewing, who was General William T. Sherman's foster brother, had dropped out of West Point in his senior year, likely because of alcoholism. Angered at Cox because of Antietam, Ewing had asked his father, Thomas Ewing, an influential Ohio politician, to block Cox's promotion, which apparently worked.[5] Cox's complaints to Helen about his shabby treatment and his consideration of resignation would underline what a significant blow this was to his career and his ego.

In late March, Cox was assigned to Columbus to aid Ohio Governor Tod in organizing the troops called out under a new enrollment and conscription law.[6] On April 9, Cox unexpectedly met an old friend, Burnside, who also had been "condemned" to administrative duty as commander of the Department of Ohio after his disaster at Fredericksburg. But this was only to be temporary and Lincoln intended to have Burnside put together a force to re-gain control of east Tennessee. As part of that process, a new corps, the XXIII, was to be created out of a variety of forces, including new recruits. The XXIII would ultimately be Cox's home corps for the final years of the war.

Burnside made Cox commander of the District of Ohio and the two men soon were again working closely together in Cincinnati with overlapping responsibilities, as at Antietam. Burnside promised Cox that, when he finally was given an active command, he would bring Cox with him. In the meantime, Cox took advantage of the slow pace of life to visit Helen and the family in Warren.[7]

The next letters deal with the first part of this administrative interregnum and Cox's uniformly unhappy thoughts about his exile, including, as noted in one of his letters below, having to act as "a sort of chief of police" while the real war went on without him.

Marietta 21st March 1863

I reached here safely last evening, having been unable to leave Wheeling on Thurs. there being no boat bound down the river on that day. We reached Wellsville on the Ohio about 2 past 8 & remained till four in the morning when the Pittsburgh & Wheeling train came along, carrying us to Wheeling at about six. The little business I had to do there occupied but little time, & a call on the Gen. & some of the officers of the post, was the only sociality I had, the rest of the time being spent in reading.

We left W. at eleven yesterday A.M. on a boat chartered by the government to go to Parkersburg for troops bound from the Potomac army for Rosecrans, & had as pleasant a trip as the blustering snow-squally day would permit.

I find matters here very quiet. The transfer of Western Va. to Gen [Robert] Schenck's dept. has been made, but in such a way as not to transfer me with it, & I have accordingly reported my return to the Secy. of War & asked for orders. Till I hear from Washington therefore I shall regard myself as without a command, & have nothing to do but look after the odds and ends of business which need to be attended to before taking what I hope may be final leave of Va.

The staff is all here. They have been greatly exasperated by the management of promotions & at Wash. but are gradually recovering from it.

Marietta 25th March 1863

The parting day was a gloomy one for us all. I suppose the sense of disappointment & the uncertainty of my own future made it gloomier than it would otherwise have been to me. Still the visit was a great satisfaction to me, & I trust it was to you & Jute [Helen's sister Julia].

Nothing has been determined yet as to my command, & I am waiting orders here with nothing to do. I have written Gov. Dennison & Mr. Chase pretty fully on the subject, & am daily in expectation of some definite orders from the War Dept.

Yesterday I heard that Gen. Burnside was to be at Parkersburg on his way to Cin. & I went down to meet him, but it turned out that he had taken the Northern route, & I missed seeing him.

Marietta 29th March 1863

I am sitting this P.M. in the old room we occupied when you were here. The little round table with red cloth cover is moved up into the corner by the window with the hanging flower basket, my back is to the fire & the uncertain sunlight of this chill March day comes occasionally in upon my paper. The madeira vine in the other window has reached the top of the casing & is looping down upon the strings again. The little bedroom is locked. I don't use it now, having my bed in the corner of this room where the table used to stand. My camp candlesticks with star candles in them are on the mantle on each side of the little clock which keeps ticking away. My trunk stands before the door into the next room, my camp chair before the fire, my sword, pistol, field glass & overcoat hang from the hooks on the wall; half a dozen military books, an atlas, bible, prayer-book, Tennyson, Lucille by the younger Bulwer, & Sidney & other poems are on the table.

News I have none to tell. After finding the uncertain condition of my command, I wrote to Gen. Wright reporting my return to duty & informing him that I had written to the Adjt. Gen. for orders. He replied that it was his understanding that I was transferred to Gen. Schenck's command with my district. I then of course reported to Gen. S.

Baltimore, 5th April, 1863

Everything tends to make the surroundings unreal. Here in a southern city it ought to be spring, but I woke this morning to look out on five inches of snow, & sit hugging the fire as though we were in Quebec. I came here expecting orders assigning me a command in Gen. Schenck's dept. I find on the other hand no such orders, but am sent back to Ohio to fix my hd.qrs. at Columbus & aid Gov. Tod in organizing operations under the new enrollment & conscription law.

This change is one which gives me very mixed feelings. I am satisfied that if I were kept in Gen. Schenck's command he could or would give me no larger district than my old Kanawha country, & that I should therefore be practically reduced to the position heretofore held by my own subordinates. This would be most distasteful to me, more so than any other change.

The present order has these unpleasant features, that it sends me out of active field service, though I am told that will only be temporarily, it gives me no large command of troops, it puts me in what may become disagreeable relations to the state government.

It has on the other hand some advantages. It saves me from the unpleasantness of serving in a subordinate position where I have commanded in chief, it puts me in more direct & immediate contact & communication with the friends who will interest themselves in aiding me to get an important field command when the chance occurs, it separates me I hope finally from Western Va. associates me with Burnside, & leaves me uncompromised by the Spring campaign which I regard as the most doubtful in results of any we have undertaken.

Circumstances are making the western armies far more unhealthy than they have been, sickness prevailing alarmingly. The commanders Grant & Rosecrans are neither of them men in whom my confidence is large, & I should be at a loss if the choice were forced on me, in what active column I would fight. Whilst therefore the natural desire of active duty made me request that I should be sent to one of the large columns, I am determined not to grieve over the disappointment, but to look on the bright side, & console myself with the reflection that it might have been much worse.

I feel that I have been shabbily used, & am determined to find out fully & in what proportions I am indebted for it, but seeing that matters are decided in a way foreign to my expectations, & in spite of my entreaties, I strongly incline, as heretofore to believe that providentially the thing is determined better than I could determine it for myself.

Personally I receive abundant compliments on my standing as an officer & my reputation both with the army & with the people, but I am convinced that two adverse influences are at work. One the jealousy of some officers appointed like myself from civil life, & the other the determination of Halleck to put every active command into the hands of the regulars when it is possible to do so.

I shall leave for Marietta in the morning train, & from there go to Columbus as soon as I can provide for moving Hd.qrs. I do not know what will become of the staff, nor how many except my aide I shall keep with me.

Don't suffer yourself to be fretted or annoyed by the vexations of my position—it would only add to my discomfort. My friends at Columbus all agree that it will never do to think of resigning as the motives would not be understood or appreciated, & express themselves very confident that justice will soon be done. I am taking matters very quietly 'biding my time.' I say with Aeneas, 'Forsan et haec olim meminisse iuvabit.' [From *The Aeneid*: Cox provides his own translation:] Perhaps we shan't be sorry twenty years hence.

Columbus 9th April 1863

I have reached here, having traveled between eleven & 12 hundred miles by rail within the week past. It is the intention of Gov. Tod that the whole state should be put into a military district under my command, so that I should have the supervision of the organization of the enrollment & of the camps for recruits & etc. If this arrangement is perfected the command will be important & honorable, though I should have preferred an active one in the field.

I am glad it makes me report to Burnside, for whom I have the highest regard & respect, & as it promises to be only temporary I shall hope to be in the field before the close of the season under the General's immediate command.

Cincinnati 12th April 1863

I am getting to be a perfect Arab, wandering about & staying scarce two nights in the same place. I got orders to come down here today, & the probabilities now are that my hd.qrs. will be here. I say now are, because what may turn up tomorrow the Lord only knows.

I had a very pleasant visit with Gen. Burnside this evening & he has determined to assign me the command of this Dist, comprising the State, & perhaps the Kanawha district added to it. He thinks & I guess he is right, that Cin. is the proper place for Hd.Qrs.

I may go back to Col. tomorrow or next day, or I may stay here & send for my baggage. Tomorrow will determine. Don't let the uncertainty keep you from writing. I will keep you advised fully of all my movements &e., so that you will not be at a loss longer than necessary.

Columbus 17th April 1863

I have come up to get my baggage, horses, &e., & make the final move to Cin. today. I say final, but prospects have changed so often & so rapidly the two or three weeks past, that I hardly venture to form any expectations a week ahead.

In regard to all my late disappointments, I think I have got them pretty thoroughly under my control, & am quite cheerful about the whole matter. I don't think I am hurt at all, even in public estimation so far as I can judge. I meet troops of friends, & influential men of all classes have taken great pains to assure me of their great satisfaction with my career hitherto.

My reputation as an officer is I think so well established that I should be foolish to be troubled about it, or to fear that the failure to secure the confirmation of my rank will be an injury to me in the estimation of sensible people. So many of such classes have assured me that the reflection is rather upon the 'powers that be' than upon myself, that without arrogance or egotism I think I am justified in saying I have been treated as if the slight put upon me had called attention to & secured a more general recognition of my services, rather than injure me in the opinion of those worth considering.

If I had not been so hurried in writing for the week past I should have said more to you of the universal kindliness of feeling the people of Marietta showed you when I left. Some thirty or forty gentlemen called on me to tell me good-bye the evening before I left, & their hearty good will, & the messages of love & good will from their wives & daughters to you touched me deeply.

Hd.Qrs. Dist. of Ohio, Cin., 18th April 1863

We came down yesterday as we intended, reaching here a little before seven o'clock. In the evening some fifteen or twenty gentlemen, prominent businessmen, called upon me, & about half-past-nine, I was surrounded by a brass band, & called on for a speech. As. Gov. Tod was there however I said to him that as the civilian I should depute him to do the talking—& got off with about five minute's speech.

Cin. 21st April 1863

Much of the statement in regard to my being in command of the camp of paroled prisoners was true in form, though incorrect in substance. The Secy.

of War & Gen. Burnside did not thoroughly understand each other at the start & it took a few days to regulate the matter.

I have no fears that Gen. B. [Burnside] will not do for me anything which is reasonably within his power, & therefore I feel quite content with the present arrangement as a temporary one.

The position itself will be full of embarrassments. A field command has the simple duty of organization & fighting, here a thousand quasi-military & quasi-civil questions will be arising which will be full of knotty points, & on which different parties will demand action in different ways. I can hardly promise myself a great success in it in any event, & shall have reason to be satisfied if I do not exasperate strong partisans of either extreme of sentiment. I shall try to reach the aiders and abettors of the rebellion with a stern & consistent rule, & enforce the stringent order of Gen. B. against them as firmly, yet as justly as possible.

I retract one of the criticisms I made when at home upon the Prayer book version of the Psalms, compared with the authorized version. Or rather I retract a criticism of one phrase. When in Baltimore on Sun. the 5th I was not surrounded by very cheering circumstances, having just rec'd the order to go to Col. & not knowing that my command would extend beyond the parole camp. Reading the selection for the evening service of that day, the phrase in the Psalms 'O! tarry thou the lord's leisure' seemed in its homily pithiness to be more apt than the more dignified & compact form of the authorized version 'Wait on the Lord.' The latter would hardly convey to a casual reader all the meaning of the former, & the kind of patience inculcated & the associations of ideas from the phrases, would under such circumstances give peculiar meaning to the first.

Cin. 26th April 1863

I am not yet settled in my new office, but shall get possession tomorrow or next day. My most unpleasant duties will be in regard to the rebel sympathizers. Some of the women seem to be monomaniacs on this subject, & court martyrdom for their sentiments as women are apt to do. Several have been arrested & ordered to be sent beyond our lines.

In Indiana they are having trouble. Several collisions have occurred between the Union men & the copperheads, & several lives have already been lost on either side. Gen. B thinks the outbreak might have been prevented by a more judicious administration of military affairs there, & has relieved [General Henry] Carrington of the command. I doubt the policy of this, since whether Carrington was quite right or not, the Union men there have such confidence in him as to feel alarmed at his removal.

It is this disturbed condition of affairs that makes such duty as mine disagreeable. Any collision in our own state would be most painful & I would far rather be in the front where the fighting with the Confederates is hottest than to act as a sort of chief-of-police in a great state like Ohio. Still whatever is duty must be done & thoroughly.

For the next few months, Cox acted as Burnside's second-in-command, and he often had to do both his own paperwork and that which the notoriously unsystematic Burnside failed to do. Cox also helped pick up the pieces when Burnside impulsively issued his famous General Order No. 38 on April 13. That measure threatened punishment by death or banishment for persons who "commit acts for the benefit of the enemies."[8] When notorious Ohio Copperhead leader Clement Vallandigham tested the decree by giving a fiery speech, Burnside arrested him and he was convicted with Secretary of War Stanton's solid support. But when Lincoln criticized the decision, Stanton characteristically reversed himself, chastising Burnside.[9] In his memoirs, Cox defended Burnside's actions, but said he thought Burnside should have consulted with Washington first, as well as with Cox, whose legal and political background would have provided him with a broader perspective.[10]

During May and June, 1863, both Cox and Burnside were hopeful that orders would be forthcoming for the latter's return to active fighting in Tennessee in support of Rosecrans, then in command of the Army of the Cumberland. In the meantime, aside from administrative duties, their only military activity dealt with Confederate General John H. Morgan and his cavalry raiders. In June and July, Morgan and his three hundred horsemen made a sensational foray into Ohio, which had previously been spared of any fighting. While the populace was unnerved for a time, Cox and the militia caught Morgan quickly. Cox later mused that, while this raid caused much excitement, it had very little military importance.[11]

In early August, Burnside finally got orders to take command in Knoxville, Tennessee. As he departed, he again promised Cox that he would do his best to get him a command there. In the meantime, Cox now had to undertake both his and Burnside's jobs. The only political event of consequence during this period was when Vallandigham, having gained the Democratic nomination for Governor, said publicly in August that he was coming back to Ohio to campaign. Cox made known that he would be arrested if he tried to return. Vallandigham did not return and was soundly beaten by the Union Party candidate, John Brough, in October.

The only military event of consequence for Cox came November 9. Cox heard that there would be a Confederate attempt to attack from Canada on Lake Erie to free the Confederate officers at the military prison at Johnson's Island in Sandusky. Cox immediately ordered five hundred new recruits and a battery of cannon to Sandusky and he traveled there personally to supervise the defense. His quick action helped ensure that the raid never took place.[12]

As Cox learned of the victories at Gettysburg and Vicksburg that summer, his unhappiness and envy continued to grow as he believed the war was passing him by. He exhibited some *schadenfreude* at the news in June that one of his former subordinates, Robert Milroy, who he considered incompetent, had been defeated in Winchester, Virginia. Cox's description, by contrast, of his former commander William Rosecrans's defeat at Chickamauga was proverbially more in sorrow than in anger. Garfield, who was Rosecrans's chief of staff, visited with Cox during this period. Since Garfield was about to take up his position as a congressman, Cox appealed for Garfield to lobby for him so he could obtain an active position in the field. During this period, Cox notes in the letters that his Warren, Ohio friend Emerson Opdycke was serving nearby.

Helen's visit in July took his mind off his concerns, as it did for her. Afterward, she wrote to Lucy Garfield, "I enjoyed the visit completely, apart from the fact that I was with my husband which you know was enough in itself to insure complete happiness."[13] In November, while he was in Sandusky, he would tell Helen that he had gotten a note from Burnside about the promised command—but still nothing was certain.

Cin. 30th April 30, 1963

I took a horseback ride yesterday over the defensive line of works on the Kentucky side of the river. My aide accompanied me, beside the officer in command of the fortifications, & his aid. It was a very pleasant ride. The country over there is beautiful, & the nature of our errand took us long the best points for seeing it. We were some nine hours in the saddle, though we came back covered with mud, we enjoyed it greatly.

I suppose you have seen that Western Va. is in trouble again. The state officers at Wheeling have been calling for help in most piteous tones, the rebels having got entirely this side of Gen. Schenck's troops. Managing that country from Baltimore will prove a costly experiment.

In this case however, as usual, the force of the rebels & everything pertaining to them has been grossly exaggerated. We have had to send all the troops we could scrape from our corps with artillery, gun boats & etc. It seems impossible for me to sever my connection with that region.

Cin. 11th May 1863

It has been oppressively hot today, & I feel the exhausting effects of the heat tonight. I have been all day in the court-room of the U.S. Circuit Court listening to the argument of the application on behalf of Mr. Vallandigham for a writ of habeas corpus. The argument will be continued tomorrow. I do not think the court will interfere with us.

Gov. & Mrs. Dennison were in town from Fri. till today. Yesterday P.M. I went with them out to Mr. [Aaron] Perry's where we spent the evg. I had my saddle-horse brought out & rode back about 2 past nine, they remained all night. I had a very pleasant visit. The hills beyond Mr. Perry's are looking charmingly in the early green of Spring, & the air is redolent of the fragrance of blossoms.

We had a good deal of excitement in town on Sat. night from the report that our troops were in Richmond. It was not generally credited in army circles, & lacks confirmation today. I fear we have no such good fortune in store for the Eastern army at present. Hooker was manifestly out-maneuvered and whipped at Chancellorsville but there will be a desperate effort to support him.

Cin. 6th May 1863

We expect the decision of the Court on the Habeas Corpus in Vallandigham's case this A.M. & instead of going to my office, I shall go to the Court-Room & may be detained there most of the forenoon. We are quite confident the decision of the Court will be to refuse issuing the writ, & we shall start him on his way to his place of confinement immediately after the decision.

I expect to run up to Col. this evening to see the Asst. Provost Marshall Gen. & have some conferences in regard to his action in the state.

Cin. 7 June 1863

I hope your journey north was as safe & speedy as mine South. I reached here at four-o'clock Fri., & found to my astonishment the streets full of soldiers. On inquiring, I learned that the Ninth Corps was ordered down to Vicksburg to reinforce Grant, and Burnside's campaign into East Tenn. necessarily broken up in consequence.

Yesterday the Gen. himself & staff returned to the city. The young men who had signalized their departure so publicly were a good deal crest fallen at their ludicrously quick return. Gen. [John] Parke goes in command of the Corps. The removal of his troops together with the Pres's revocation of his policy as to newspapers & etc. disheartens Gen B. very much.

He requested to be allowed to go himself in command of the Corps & to turn over the dept to some one else, but this was refused. He was then strongly inclined to ask to be relieved of his command altogether, but concluded it would not be patriotic to do so.

I had a long talk with him this morning, in which he read me a letter from the Secy. of War to him, which practically revoked the whole of his famous 'order no. 38' & provides that he shall confer with the War Dept. before making arrests of civilians or suppressing newspapers. This is practically saying it shall not be done at all.

I should not object to this if it took the form of an announced policy of non-interference with speaking & printing under all circumstances, leaving the liberty of speech & of the press as broad as in time of peace: but any such declarative policy they will not make, & their conduct therefore takes the form of a tactical retreat before a theatrical popular storm.

There is some excitement about another raid through Western Va. & some anxiety at Col. about our own border. The carving process still goes in Western Va. I see by the papers that Western Penn. & part of W. Va. are to be created into a new dept. under command of Maj. Gen. [William] Brooks.

We expect on Thurs. of this week to move into our new quarters & boarding place. The staff are prophesying that as soon as we get comfortably settled in permanence we shall be ordered into the field. I have been hoping it might be so, but the strange lack of coherence & unity of purpose in our military movements gives me so little to hope of great successes that I find myself growing indifferent as to the part I may personally take in so aimless & scattered a campaign.

Columbus 17th June 1863

The news from the East & Gov. Tod's proclamation for more troops has brought me to Col. to make arrangements for their organization, & for the opening of camps. The union convention meets here tomorrow, & I have already seen a greater number of old friends & acquaintances than I have met in a long time.

There is said to be a speck of war in Holmes Co. & we are sending up a battalion to take care of it.

I have received a request from a meeting of officers & soldiers at Murfreesboro to represent the Ohio soldiers in convention & may, if I can find time, go in for that purpose. My only objection is that I may have to make a speech, which you know I am on principle opposed to.

There is a good deal of excitement over the Eastern news, & there may be hot work there very soon. I shall go back to Cin. on Thurs.

Cin. 24th June 1863

You will recollect that my greatest chagrin at the injustice done me last Spring was that [General Robert] Milroy, my subordinate, was promoted over my head, without merit, ability, or military character. The recent disaster at Winchester turns out to be chargeable wholly to him, with all the train of evil consequences. He made a most disgraceful flight as I predicted he would do. No one who had known him in the field would have expected anything else. His fall has been more rapid than I looked for, but I felt sure it must come, & that the country would pay sorely for his ill-judged advancement.

Cin. 2nd July 1863

The hurry of events at the East is fulfilling my expectations & prophecies faster than I had anticipated. The rapidity with which humbugs & falsely inflated reputations have been collapsing is the most encouraging thing connected with our present experiences.

I have little doubt that a few days must put McClellan again in command & am hopeful that will be the signal for my own recall to active service. With [Nathaniel] Banks as Secy. of War & McC. at the head of the Army of the Potomac, I shall feel that we are entering upon the healthiest phase of military administration we have yet had.

Cin. 12th Jul/63

We are having a little stir here with the raid of the rebel Gen. John Morgan into Indiana. He appears to have felt sure that Lee was to be successful in the East, & determined on making a bold dash on Indianapolis. The Gov. of that state has been in a great panic, but has succeeded in gathering militia to head him off—whilst Gen. B. has been collecting a force from Ken. to follow him up. Being thus beset before & behind it looks today as if he might break out on this side, & as we have sent away all our troops that were available for immediate use to West Va. & Louisville, we shall have to make a stir among the militia here tomorrow if he continues moving this way.

He is expected today about fifty miles from here, heading in this direction with some four or five thousand troops. Our gunboats are patrolling the river to prevent his recrossing, & we are trying to make this his last adventure of the kind.

Cin. 15th Aug. 1863

Gen B. is at camp Nelson Ken. on the river below Lexington, organizing his column for the advance into Tenn. I see no further prospect of my getting into the field at present, & must I suppose watch & wait a while longer.

[On August 27] Gen. Burnside is now near the Tenn. line, & a day or two must determine whether the rebels under [General Simon Bolivar] Buckner will dare give him battle. In his absence, I have a general supervision of his hd.qrs offices & business here.

Cin. 30th Aug. 1863

The necessity which keeps me so closely here, is one of possible rather than actual existence. I am put in general superintendence of the administrative part of the dept. business, but my habit of systematizing enables me to dispose of all that is to be done with very little burden of labor. It is still important however that Gen. B. may feel that some one is here in whom he will have confidence, whatever exigency arises.

I have been annoyed for a little while by the efforts of the Probate Judge to produce a collision between the sheriff & the military force. His writs of habeas corpus have not been obeyed, in consequence of the decision of the supreme court of the U.S. that we are only amenable on such writs to the U.S. courts. This Probate Judge has issued attachments for the officer in charge of the barracks here for contempt of court, & has ordered the sheriff to take the officer if he has to call out the whole population of the county for the purpose.

Though both are Vallandigham men, the sheriff sees that the personal execution of such an order will not be as easy as the issuing of it. He called on me to know what I would do, if he attempted it. I told him I would suppress his posse as I would any other mob by severe means & then hand him & the Judge over to the U.S. courts to be tried for their lives for treason. This was no attractive prospect, & he complained bitterly of the Judge who put him in the dilemma of making war on the U.S. or losing the favor of his party.

I have no idea that they will muster nerve enough to come to an open outbreak. It is probable that these Vallan. men will control most of the old Democratic party vote in this city & county, & will carry the election here, but this is not certain, though there is chance enough of it to make them very impudent.

If I am kept here I propose being quite a student this winter, hoping that the war will soon end, & that I shall get back to professional life in some measure prepared to take it up where I left it off. If however I am ordered to the field I shall rejoice in the opportunity of having one more rap at the rebellion & of being active in the closing scenes of the great conflict. Either way, I am determined not to fret.

Cin. 22nd Sept. 1863

The surrender of the man who shot the officer at Dayton was not to a mob, as you say, not until after the mob dispersed & everything was perfectly quiet. I then coolly investigated the matter, consulted with the U.S. Dist. Attorney & concluded that we could not lawfully try the villain by a military court, as he was neither in, nor in any way connected with the military service. It was necessary to try him before the Court of Common Pleas, & I therefore ordered him to be delivered up to the civil authorities.

A few days after one of the same set assaulted an officer there, & got shot down for his pains. This officer being under our jurisdiction I ordered not to be given up, but to be examined by a military court, which will doubtless acquit him. I refuse to let the civil authorities take the officer on the same principal that I refuse to keep from them the civilian.

The news from Rosecrans will I hope be better as we get more of it. All his engagements indicate the same fault: He is caught unprepared & with wholly inadequate preparation for battle. His men are scattered, & fight piecemeal. His first troops in action are overwhelmed & it is only after the battle is half lost that he succeeds in getting the rest where their hard fighting can in some measure retrieve the fortunes of the day. In every instance he has allowed the enemy the advantage of the initiative, & has been content if he was able simply to beat them off.

Cin. 25th Sept. 1863

I am very glad to hear that Col. [Emerson] Opdycke & the rest of the Warreners in the Army of the Cumberland [Rosecrans's army] are safe. Give Lucy [Opdycke, Emerson's wife] my most hearty congratulations. I see that Garfield [who was then serving as Rosecrans's Chief of Staff] had a horse shot under him, but was not injured personally.

The effect of the battle of Chickamauga we can hardly estimate as yet, for the movements pertaining to it seem hardly completed. I hope however that the rebels will not feel strong enough to push Rosecrans further, & that reinforcements will soon reach him which will enable him to resume the offensive. Every effort will be made, I do not doubt, to increase his army largely. I had rather lose almost any part of the country than East Tenn. & am anxious to see every effort made to keep it secure.

Cin. 13th Oct. 1863

Mr. Chase arrived yesterday, & we gave him a little reception, firing a salute at the station & escorting him with music on a small military procession to the Burnett House. In the morning he spoke at Mozart's Hall, & the union men had a magnificent torchlight procession.

Voting is being very quietly done today, & I hope everything will pass off without disturbance. We are prepared to put a quietus upon any mob, & the roughs know it. I think therefore they will use some discretion in their valor. The loyal men are very confident of the result of the election & I heartily pray they may not overestimate their strength. I can not endure to think of the possibility of defeat.

I voted at the soldier's polls this A.M. a full Trumbull Co. ticket which will be sent home in the usual course of events. We have allowed nearly three thousand soldiers, convalescents in hospitals, paroled prisoners &e. to go home to vote, & although there may be a few Vallandigham men among them, the great mass will vote the straight Union ticket.

Cin. 15th Oct. 1863

We are all jubilant at the result of the election. Never was there a more complete triumph, & no victory in the field has been of more importance to our cause either at home or abroad. The election went off with perfect quiet here, there being not even a common street fight near the polls.

Cin. 24th Oct. 1863

The past two or three days have been very busy ones, not in the way of ordinary business, but in matters extraneous to the usual business of the Dist. of Ohio. The day before yesterday we had the funeral of Gen. [William] Lytle, which was an imposing affair, being one of the largest civil & military processions ever seen here.

Garfield arrived the night before, & acted as one of the pall-bearers. He returned with me by way of Mt. Auburn where we stopped at Mr. [Alfonso] Taft, he having invited us to tea there. Gov. & Mrs. Dennison, Mr. and Mrs. Perry & some others were there.

This week has been a livelier one in the way of society than any I have spent since you left here. Garfield goes on to Wash. under orders to lay before the Prest. the condition of the army there. While there, he proposes in accordance with the wish of the circle of my best friends, to sound the Prest.

& Sec. of War in reference to their feelings toward me, & to report what can be done toward getting for me the command and the rank they have so often admitted I have earned.

Cin. 27th Oct. 1863

The return of my birthday makes me think of home & wonder how many more such anniversaries I must spend away from my family.

You must not be astonished if you hear of my being ordered into the field yet this Fall. I think it best that I should assert my claim to a field command, & have requested Garfield to push it, whether they give me my rank or no. A fortnight will prove whether it will be acknowledged, & as I am sure I can be more useful, I shall hope to spend the Winter in my tent.

I am under great obligations to Mr. Perry for the interest he has manifested in getting my friends to cooperate in their efforts to have justice done me. He has taken hold of it in earnest, & when Gov. D[ennison] & Gen G[rant] came here insisted that now was the time to see what could be done.

Cin. 31 Oct. 1863

Garfield is, I see in Wash., & I shall hope to hear in a few days what the prospects are for my getting more active service. I am confident that great efforts will be made to have an active campaign in front of Chattanooga this Winter, & for this reason I am desirous of going there, although the hardships will no doubt be great. So much more glory in enduring them you know.

I have done what I thought right in getting G. to bring the matter before the War Dept., & now I shall quietly abide the result & do my duty wherever it be. The changes being made have seemed to make this the fittest time for a change with me also, although it would be more uncomfortable physically than at another season.

Cin. 5th Nov. 1863

I am waiting with some anxiety to hear from Garfield the result of his effort to bring my claim for active service before the War Dept. I notice with pleasure that he has received promotion himself, being as flatteringly received as I was after Antietam. He will not however have his seat in Congress I imagine, & will no doubt resign as soon as it is time for the session to begin [Garfield did not in fact resign, and he remained in Congress until he was elected President in 1880].

I have very little expectation that the Sec. of War can be induced to do anything for me. Everything I hear of the mode of doing business at Wash. satisfies me that 'out of sight is out of mind' there, & that being once drifted aside, nothing but accident will move me into the current again. If the present move is unsuccessful, I shall make no further effort of any sort to secure their attention, & try to systematize my leisure, so that it may be made as profitable in an intellectual way as possible.

I should not feel quite right in resigning—the war may last sometime yet, & changes may occur which would give me employment more to my mind: so I think it best quietly to accept what Providence seems to order, & not to fret about it.

Sandusky 16th Nov. 1863

My plans are sorely interfered with by this little scare in regard to an invasion from Canada. I had proposed being at home tomorrow in order to attend the demonstration dinner, ball &e. at Cleveland in celebration of the opening of the Atlantic & S.W. RR.

On Thurs. morng. I rec'd orders from the Sec. of War to come at once to this place & make arrangements for the defense of Johnson's island against any attack of the rebels. I came at once stopping in Col. a couple of hours to make arrangements there, & reaching here about midnight. Since then my hands have been full providing for the regiments of militia called out, & getting them in condition to endure the weather which suddenly changed, becoming very stormy & rainy. My expectation is that I may be kept here several days yet, though everything is uncertain.

I had a dispatch from Gen. Burnside night before last saying there was a chance for me to take a command perhaps a corps in East Tenn. I sincerely hope that this may be so, for although it would be rather uncomfortable taking the field just as Winter sets in, if I get the command of the corps, it would probably lead to my permanent assignment to it by the Prest. with the additional grade.

The importance of this to me is such that I think it ought to outweigh all questions of comfort & even of a visit with you. The matter will probably be decided before I leave here, & it is possible that I may get a single day to run home & see you.

I had made an arrangement to meet Garfield in Col. about the 20th & hoped you might make one of the party, but for a day or two all must remain unsettled. Should any important change be made in my orders, I will telegraph.

While Cox was still in Sandusky, Burnside formally offered him command of the XXIII Corps in Tennessee. On December 3, an exultant Cox was ordered to report to the "general in command" at Knoxville. When Cox got to Cincinnati, he learned that General John B.

Foster had replaced Burnside. Cox hurriedly left Cincinnati with his staff on December 9 and reported for duty in Knoxville on December 18. The description of his travels on the way over muddy, rutted roads underlined the difficulties of travel at this stage of the war. When he arrived in Knoxville, he learned that Foster had assigned him to command the District of Kentucky. However, once Foster saw Cox's determination, as well as his unhappiness at being "condemned" once again to administrative duty, Foster assigned him to field command of the XXIII Corps.[14] Cox's long, unhappy duty in administration was finally over—or so it seemed.

The next letters involve Cox's pleasure at finally going back to the warfront and the difficult paths, both political and geographical, that he had to traverse to get where he was.

Sandusky 22nd Nov. 1865
I am still here chafing at the interruption of my plans by the long continuance of my delay.

Some siege guns are on the way here, & it is now probable that I shall be kept some days to receive them, & see that the arrangements are all completed for putting them in fortifications on the Island. I shall know definitely tomorrow.

Garfield writes me that he can meet me in Col. on Wed. night. If you can do so I would like to have you meet me at the Dennison's at that time, & I will run down even if I have to return at once. If you should get this too late to reach C. on Wed. do the best you can for Thurs. Nothing further has come from Gen. Burnside & I feel utterly unsettled in regard to the future.

Cin. 4th Dec. 1863
I reached here at 4 this morning. I report by telegraph to Gen. Burnside. The evidence increases that I am to have the corps, & shall probably go to Knoxville not stopping in Ken. The roads to Knoxville are reported horrible. It will take near a week of horseback riding to carry me there after I get started from Lexington, & the mud is said to equal West Va. in its muddiest.

Cin. 9th Dec. 1863
I leave on the noon train today, my baggage being packed, the horses &e already gone ahead in the freight train, & all ready for the move. We go to Lexington, KY. & thence to Richmond, Ky, Big Hill, London, Barbourville, Cumberland Gap, Tazewel &e. to Knoxville. I have heard nothing from Burnside or [John] Foster.

Foster told everyone that I was to have the 23rd Corps. & I do not question it, but am anxious to get forward lest there should be some slip. I have the order from the War Dept. to report in person & so am going. You must expect a great irregularity in getting letters from me. It is said to take the mails about two weeks to get to Knoxville. I shall write as frequently as possible.

After leaving Lexington we have more than a week of horseback travel to get through, & will have to pick up such accommodation on the road as we can. We take two large four horse wagons, & a two horse ambulance with us, with selected teams which we hope will not break down on the road, though we expect a repetition of West Va. mire after the first thirty miles. We expect to have a cavalry escort if necessary.

London, Ky. Dec. 13th 1863

Have just reached here after three days hard riding since we left Lexington. The last fifty miles of country has been very mountainous & rough, & the roads like those of West Va. Yesterday noon commenced a steady pouring rain, & we rode in it till night-fall. Then stopped at a log house, owned by a widow Jackson, where they gave us two beds, the rest of the party sleeping in their blankets on the floor. Twenty miles a day is about all we can make without running away from our wagons, which we do not wish to do.

We learn here that [General William T.] Sherman's and [General Gordon] Granger's Corps are both in East Tenn, & that Sherman is in command of the whole. These changes of command make me uncertain about my command of the Corps, but I shall at least get a good division, & shall be in active service so I shall not complain.

The soaking rain of yesterday did not penetrate my thick coat, & I rode perfectly dry, giving my rubber coat to Dory. The country is exceedingly wild here, & grows no better till we get quite near Knoxville, the journey taking us probably six days more. Some of the incidents of the road would be amusing if I had time to tell them.

One of the party was groaning this morning over his soreness & the lameness of his horse, saying the weakness of his horse was a punishment for riding on Sunday. Oh, said another, if your horse is so weak on Sunday, what will become of him on a week day!

Knoxville Tenn. Dec 19th 1863

I arrived here last night, yesterday being the eighth day in the saddle since leaving Lex. The roads are horrible, & the crossing of the Pine & Cumberland mountains were about as hard bits of travel as I have ever experienced.

As we were keeping with our wagons (the country not being reliable for supplies) we made only five miles the day we crossed Pine mountain and fourteen the day we crossed Cumberland mountains. On other days we made about twenty miles each, sometimes a little over.

Yesterday morning met with a member of Gen. Foster's staff (Col. Strong). I left the wagons behind, & rode from Jacksboro to this place, making forty miles for one day's ride. As we approached the place we heard all sorts of rumors as to the whereabouts of the enemy, & many of the people seemed to think Foster would be besieged here as Burnside was, but like most rumors, there was very little foundation for this one.

A brisk cavalry skirmish between the rear-guard of the rebels & our advance guard being all the apparent material out of which the story was made. It however served to stimulate us a little by the spice of danger it gave us, since our escort was a mere handful of less than twenty men, half of whom we left behind with the wagons, & a strong troop of rebel horsemen might have gobbled us up.

I found Gen. Foster absent at the front—but expected back tonight—when I hope to have my fate decided. On reaching here I learn that Gen. F., notwithstanding his declaration at Cin. that he proposed giving me the 23rd Corps, as Gen Burnside had determined to do, has put Gen. [Orlando] Willcox in command of it, & assigned me to the Dist. of Ky. Against this I propose protesting with all my power, as I do not mean to be deprived of field service if I can help it.

The officers of the 9th Corps all served with Gen. F. in North Carolina under Burnside, & they seem to have used their influence of old acquaintance to get Willcox appointed to the 23rd, so as to get him out of their way in the 9th.

As you may imagine I do not feel very pleasantly over this state of the case, & in the uncertainty whether Gen. F. will on my statement of claim revoke the arrangement, am in a very vexatious suspense. To ride back to Lex. to take command of Ken. is not a satisfactory addendum to my recent muddy trip across that state.

On our route we met Gen. B[urnside] & staff returning to Cin. I was wakened about four o'clock in the morning at a farm house near the Cumberland river where we were spending the night, by the voice of one of the Gen's staff, Capt. French, in the room below saying that Gen. B. was a few miles back, & wished fires made, &e., so that the party might stay there. I immediately dressed and went below stairs, when presently the Gen. came.

His staff were all with him, & all covered with mud & nearly frozen. They had reached a little place on the other side of the Cumberland the evening before, having broken down their wagons & ambulances, & were obliged to pack what they could carry upon mules & abandon the rest, except an old-fashioned stage coach which they had picked up somewhere, & which still hung together, a team of mules drawing it. About midnight they had been awakened by the report that the Cumberland river was rising & that they would not be able to ford it unless they started at once. Accordingly they started at once & in the darkness were thoroughly soaked & in no little danger in crossing the river. They warmed themselves & rested a little and then pushed on, & a more jaded, dirty, & unkempt set of beings you never saw.

The news of the rapid rise of the river was not cheering to us of course, but I had long before learned that little was gained on a wild bad road by starting before light, so I had everything ready at day break, & went along smartly, found the river still fordable, & got everything over without worrying my teams or my party. We had a careful wagon-master & an experienced quartermaster also, & although the road was strewn with wrecks, & in the single space of a day's march a hundred & fifty dead mules & horses were counted along the wayside, we came thru without accident or serious delay.

P.S. I have just seen Gen. F[oster]. He received me very kindly, & said the order assigning me to the Dist. Ken. was made on the supposition that I would prefer that arrangement. As soon as I said I would prefer the Corps, he at once directed the order to be countermanded, & assigned me to the command I wished.

5

East Tennessee and the Struggle for Position

About this time last year, I went through the experience of learning that intrigue, pretense, & self puffing are surer roads to promotion than modest performance of duty. It was not a pleasant thing to learn, & the time marked more distinctly than is common perhaps, the transition from the buoyant confidence of early manhood to the soberer (though I think not cynical) view of human ambitions & so-called successes, which belongs to the maturer years & steady middle age of man. I saw how success in mere position is obtained. I saw more clearly than ever before how mere a sham it is, & how entirely unworthy the seeking. I believe I long ago adopted in all honesty the faith that being & not seeming to be is the only true ambition, but it needed some such lesson to make the faith quicker & more lively.

—Dolson to Helen, February 26, 1864

During the next few months, Knoxville was the scene of a variety of feints and threats from Confederate commander James Longstreet. The miserable conditions and the strong position the Union held in the city made any substantive military activity unlikely. Cox, using his experience training his men in West Virginia in terrible weather, immediately set to work organizing his corps to enhance discipline and to keep them busy. The poor conditions that his troops had to bear were, he wrote, worse than what he had experienced in West Virginia. Many men had to suffer with having no shoes or blankets and with wearing tattered uniforms. Additionally, their morale needed constant bolstering.[1] Cox and his staff fared better, though, and Cox was able to invite his friend from Warren, Ohio, Emerson Opdycke of the IV Corps, over for a sumptuous Christmas dinner.[2]

Cox's letters explain in detail—because there was so little fighting—the unpredictability of his campaign to obtain field duty, including the miserable conditions which he and his men had to endure. He also took the time to describe almost poetically the countryside and how the men were adapting to their conditions. Finally, noting that he believed Helen was more disappointed than he about his situation, Cox examined his personal philosophy about warfare and his fate.

Hd. Qrs. 23rd A.C. Blain's Cross Roads, Dec. 23 1863

Once more under canvass, though it is a rather inclement season to begin camp life again. Our camp is about seventeen miles from Knoxville on the road to Rutledge where the enemy are supposed to be. I am busy trying to get hold of the condition of the Corps & put matters in train to supply its wants which are legion. The almost impassable roads are the cause, in part, of the destitution & the investment & siege of Knox. by shutting off all possibility of supply for a time increased the difficulty. Abundance of everything is at Cin, & on the way, if it could only reach us.

Our present position was taken upon a movement of Longstreet being made which seemed to indicate a purpose of immediate attack on his part. The nature of the country is such that neither party inclines to take the offensive & how long this condition of affairs will continue we do not clearly see. I found my predecessor, Gen. [Mahlon] Manson, occupying an old log house too small for himself & staff. He had a bed, but the rest slept on the floor. I stayed there one night, slept with Gen. M. & my staff officers wrapped themselves in their blankets & slept on the shed-porch at the back of the house. We have succeeded in getting four old tents without flies, & are in them, which however is very preferable to the log house arrangement.

We have had clear freezing weather for about a week. It is now raw & cloudy, threatening snow. The soldiers make such shelter as they can with rails & branches of trees, & so get along not comfortably, but endurably.

I learned on arriving here that Opdycke was encamped near me, his regt. being in Gen. Granger's command. I took the opportunity the same evening of going over to see him, found him in the woods, his tent made of canvass thrown over some crotched sticks as to make a lean-to resting on the ground on one side, & open on the other. Before the opening he had a camp fire of huge logs which threw the heat into the shed, & made it quite comfortable. He was just opening a batch of letters, the first received since he left Chattanooga. As I rode up through the trees he did not see me till I was quite near, when I astonished him with 'If your name's not Opdycke, what is it?' He had heard that I was expected & had been looking for me sometime. You will not need to be told that we had a warm greeting & a pleasant chat of home & friends.

Granger's command is as destitute of supplies as mine, but they are managing to live on the country somehow. Opdycke says they get enough to eat, but sadly lack clothing, &c. I have met also Lt. Col. Stratton & Capt. Miller of the Warren boys. They are all well & in fine spirits. It is uncertain how long any of them will remain with us probably until we either have a fight with Longstreet, or he retreats out of Tenn.

We seem very far removed from the civilized world here. I have seen no newspapers later than the one I brought with me. Everything therefore that has happened since the tenth is new to us.

Blain's X roads, 26th Dec. 1863

The disorganization consequent to the siege of Knox. has left the mails in so uncertain a condition, that the encouragement to write letters is greatly reduced by the absence of all assurance that they will reach their destination. I have not yet rec'd a letter from Ohio since leaving Cin., & am quite skeptical as to the future.

The mountain roads would be called entirely impassable if the necessity for using them were not as imperative as anything connected with the existence of the Army can be. I do not believe you can conceive the condition of the roads over which we passed in getting into East Tenn. At London in Ky. we left the road to Cumberland Gap & turned South to Williamsburg, which as the man who gave us the route said 'isn't much of a burg neither when you git thar.' This route was reported to us as decidedly better than the others, & as giving some chance of finding feed for our animals on the route, which was out of the question on the Cumberland Gap road.

Knowing that the Army was on less than half rations, we endeavored to purchase our meals and lodging on the road, so as to save the supplies as much as we could, to eke out necessaries for our mess after getting here. Some of the experiences we thus encountered would be well worth drawing if I had time, & you would greatly relish I'm sure, some of the pictures I could give of life in the mountains of East Tenn.

Fourteen miles north of Jacksboro we reached Pine mountain, the most precipitous of the range over which this road passes. We had four stout horses to each wagon, & the loads light, but still had to double the teams & the eight animals had all they could do to crawl up the hill with all the stimulus the drivers, one to each pair, could give with whip & voice, all shouting in chorus & yelling to their teams like mad. Every little distance they had to halt & breathe the reeking horses, then to it again. When half had thus reached the first summit, after a little rest, the teams were sent back for the remaining wagons, & so we went on, making but five miles that day & that with the most strenuous exertions of man & beast.

The strata of rock often forms staircases in the road with several steps, in succession from one to even four feet in height, the edges being only a little rounded by the wear of wagon tires, & up these, scrambling, slipping, falling, & striking fire from the rocks, the horses have to haul their loads. An immense outlay of labor & money must be made before even a tolerable road for military purposes can be made into East Tenn. from Ky.

The condition of the Army here is a sad one. Many of the men are barefooted, all need much clothing, but a part have army blankets or overcoats. Tents are scarce, & the troops shelter themselves as they can with such huts of rails & boughs of trees as they can hastily construct.

The enemy were when I arrived, at Rutledge, interrupting our communication with Cumberland Gap, & stopping the supply trains which had reached that point. Since then they have been made uneasy by our demonstrations upon their left, & have fallen back to Russellville & Morristown about 25 miles from here, near Bull's Gap & upon the east side of the Holston river.

The supply of the army seems to be the first duty, & I think Gen. Foster will not incline to move till he gets the most pressing wants of the men in some degree satisfied.

I find many things 'at loose ends' & it will take some time to bring all to proper order, but the spirit of the troops is magnificent. It would hardly be believed, but yet it is true, that these brave fellows lying here on the frozen ground, without shoes, clad in tattered rags, & fed on half rations are re-enlisting for a new term of three years by whole regiments, & for three days the camp has resounded with the cheers with which the completion of the enlistment of the separate companies is greeted. In one regt. all re-enlisted but some fifteen, fifty-five going in out of a company of fifty-six, & still others going in solid. Is not this magnificent considering the circumstances surrounding them? All they ask is the thirty days furlough at home which is promised them on entering the veteran corps.

I have had a chimney built at the back of my tent with brick from a ruined house near by, & have a comfortable open fire place before which Col. Sterling, Dory, & I all sit writing. This is a great improvement on the arrangement we had before.

Yesterday being Christmas we had Col. Opdycke & two or three other officers to dine with the mess, & our recent arrival from Cin. gave us the opportunity of putting on the table some stores which are not commonly seen here now, whilst a foraging party twenty miles into the country had added a turkey, a pair of fowls, & some good mutton to our larder.

Strawberry Plains, Tenn. 30th Dec 1863

 We had just begun to feel comfortable in our quarters at Blain's X roads, with brick chimneys to our tents when on Sun. morng. 27th we were ordered to march to this place, which is about the same distance from Knox. but directly on the railroad, where it crosses the Holston River. Our march was made through rain and mud, & we came to our camping ground just before night fall, the spot we selected being the only one in the vicinity which had not already been cut into mud holes, & defiled by the cavalry which had been here several days before. Our camp is on a rounded hill, which was densely covered with a forest of oak & pine when we came, but which has been a good deal thinned by the cutting of trees for fuel & for huts & shelter by the troops.

 My own hd. qrs. are on the summit where in our little quadrangle of tents we are as romantically situated as one could desire. When we arrived however the rain was pouring in torrents, the dead leaves, wet & deep, soaked our boots, & made it slow work to get a fire, & as we stood about in our overcoats heavy with water, we were not specially impressed with the romance of the scene. But after the heavy smoke of the damp leaves changed to a bright blaze, as we succeeded in finding a few old pine knots to start the fire with, & the tents were pitched, a cup of hot coffee made, & we sat around the fire watching its flashing light on the deep green of the pines & the beautiful russet of the oak leaves & the white of the tents, making the few square yards about us as beautiful as a fairy scene, shut in by the impenetrate gloom beyond, the old witchery of camp life came over us, & we forgot rain and cold, singing & chatting as merrily as if care were dead, & finally rolling in our blankets under our tents, went to sleep as soundly & sweetly as children.

 Today is a calm bright day, & I am sitting in the open air before the camp fire of great logs writing upon my atlas on my knee, this mode being more comfortable than attempting to write in the chilly shade of the tent.

 I wish you could have seen our camp last night. We were sitting & lolling upon the logs of wood drawn up for the fire, & on our camp chairs, in as picturesque a group as you can imagine—the smoke from the camp fires of the troops about us made the whole air hazy, over the tents, through a vista of pine trees the moon was rising red through the smoke and haze, overhead the stars were shining & the wonderful perspective the fire-light makes in the trees, here bringing out & deepening the mass of color of the evergreens, then making the bare trunks & limbs of a leafless oak stand like a chalk drawing against the black back-ground, & again giving a rich warmth to the brown of the dead leaves which hang thickly on some trees, while the a gloom beyond, & the snug enclosure of our little rectangle of tents about the fire, shut us in with a sense of shelter, made a picture Rembrandt would have died of envy at.

Our continuous exposure as usual hardens us quickly, & we sit about the fire till past ten o'clock without discomfort, though the nights have been generally cold enough to freeze pretty sharply, & we often wake as we did this morning to find the leaves which make our carpet, crisp and stiff with frost. Still, the climate is a milder one than yours, or we should find it impossible to live so completely under canvass in mid-winter.

We expect some light snows, but they seldom lie longer than two or three days here, & the inhabitants say that ice never forms more than couple of inches thick on the ponds. The supplies for our troops come in very slowly—beef is plenty, but bread stuffs are very scarce & vegetables not to be got at all. Our men get their bread by seizing the mills of the vicinity & foraging through the country for corn to grind at them. Still we should not feel like complaining if they were only clothed, but it is hard to see them ragged & tattered as the sorriest beggars.

We are hoping the route by rail to Chattanooga & thence by river to Knox. will soon be used to an extent which will relieve us of the destitution the troops are now suffering.

There is no change in the military condition of affairs. Maj. Gen. [John] Parke commands the forces in the field, consisting of the 4th Corps, the 9th, & my own. Gen. Foster has his hd. qrs. at Knox. & I have little opportunity of learning anything of prospects or plans for the future. I am hoping to hear something from Garfield as to the prospect of my affairs at Wash. My strong desire is to get the grade & be permanently assigned to this Corps, so that I may work away feeling that there is some lasting effect to be produced.

Strawberry Plains, 5th Jan. 1864

Still nothing from home since leaving Cin! When I wrote last I was showing how attractive a camp might seem even in cold weather.

On New Year's eve we had a change. It had been raining nearly all day on the 31st, but about ten o'clock P.M. it began to blow a hurricane, and we had all we wanted to do to hold our tents down & keep them from blowing away. The front of one of our huge mess tents blew in, the whole roof & sides were bellying out & flapping like the sails of a ship half clewed up. I caught them & held the door flaps down to the poles, shouting to the black boys to turn out before the whole should fly away. Then we had a lively time for an hour, going round to drive the tent pins tighter & secure everything.

We just had got things snug as we thought & began to listen to the roaring of the wind with something like defiance, when a stick & clay chimney which Sterling & Dory had at the back of their tent, took fire & had liked to have set the whole encampment on fire with it. Then there was another rush & shout, till the chimney was torn away from the canvass & the fire extinguished. The gale was so great that the sparks from the camp fires rolled along the ground instead of rising & we should have burned up had not the rain kept the tents pretty well soaked. It soon began to grow cold, & we woke aching with numbness in the morning, the wind still blowing a gale, though the thermometer had sunk to zero!

The men in the camp slept little, being obliged to keep awake & near the fires to keep from freezing to death. The ground was frozen solid, & no one who has not spent nights & days in tents in such weather can tell what it is to suffer from cold. The gale blew the fires so that on the windward side you could get no good of them, the wind blowing the fire away from that side of the logs while on the leeward side the smoke & sparks suffocated you.

Luckily in two of the tents little stone stoves had been put up, & by making use of these as places of shelter for the poor men, many of them without blankets, or overcoats or tents, & whose rations were reduced to less than three ounces of corn meal for several days, the meat ration alone being near full weight. No sugar or coffee had been issued for weeks, in whole brigades they have had no soap for two months. Matters are improving a little now, but the clothing does not come yet. Men turned out on last inspection without pantaloons, simply a blanket like a petticoat about their legs covering their nakedness. Fully one third of the command is suffering from more or less destitution in these respects.

Great efforts are being made to open the Chattanooga route, & Gen. Grant, who has been here for a few days, promises that the clothing &e. shall be along in about ten days. The siege of Knoxville by the destruction of supplies & interruption of trains was the proximate cause of these troubles which only time will cure.

The men bear the suffering heroically & we hear no complaining. I stopped at a camp fire where a little knot of men wrapped in their blankets were shivering & trying to warm themselves, 'Well my lads,' said I, 'how did you stand it last night?' They smiled cheerfully & one answered, 'We didn't quite freeze, but its pretty rough sir.' Under these circumstances nearly everyone of the old regts. are re-enlisting as veterans for another term of three years!

My command is now moving again, some fifteen miles up the railroad to Mosey creek, where we shall build huts & prepare to stay till the clothing

& supplies arrive to put us in better campaigning order, Gens. Grant & Foster agreeing that it is ruining our own troops to attempt active campaigning till they are better clothed & fed. Forage has been so exhausted in this vicinity that battery horses have died of starvation at the picket ropes & all the remaining wagons of the command are kept constantly out, going fifteen & twenty five miles to collect corn & hay fodder. There is no more to be got west of the Holston river, & I fear we shall not find much on the East bank, our superabundant cavalry force eating up the country like Egyptian locusts.

Strawberry Plains, 10th Jan 1864

When I wrote last I expected to be up fifteen or twenty miles further at the front before this, but the severity of the weather, & the insufficient & dangerous means of crossing the Holston have delayed us.

I never saw an army so utterly destitute of tools to work with, as well as of everything needed for comfort or subsistence. Everything moves slowly because we have nothing to make motion with. Axes, saws, hatchets, shovels, spades, picks, are almost worth their weight in gold, so scarce are they.

I am tired of saying no letters yet but have to continue the same tale. The weather has been quite cold since New Year's, but still changeable—Sometimes bleak, & windy, then a flurry of snow & a sharp solid frost.

By a little carelessness, I came very near being made sick a few days ago. I took a severe cold which I felt in all my bones, as well as in my lungs, where I had some symptoms of congestion, but by taking it in time, fasting, & using simple means to get up a sweat, I got rid of the worst of it, though I have some cough remaining.

The condition of our Army as to supplies is very little if any better than it was a week ago. Meat is the only thing of which we have a tolerably regular supply, though of poor quality. Corn meal & coarse wheat flour are our reliance for bread, & of these the men get some times half rations, sometimes much less, & sometimes none at all.

We are constantly living in the hope however that the Chattanooga route will soon be open & our condition ameliorated. There is no discouragement or grumbling. Hardships are acknowledged to be such, but are met without flinching. I am without the staff I need, the old officers having gone off with Gen. [George] Hartsuff & nothing can be less satisfactory than the attempt to get along in this unorganized condition, especially when food & clothing & everything else are lacking. I am gradually working matters into shape & am hoping before Spring to have the corps in satisfactory condition, if Gen. Grant's promises in regard to supplies hold good.

Strawberry Plains, 14th Jan. 1864

We move tomorrow to Dandridge, if the order is not again changed before we leave, as it has been four times already. Opdycke will be near us there again as his encampment is also ordered over. A good many things in the condition of affairs are vexatious, as they are likely to be everywhere. Our men are receiving their clothing, & we are full of expectation that in our new location we shall find the means of subsistence more plentiful. The weather has moderated gradually for several days, but the light fall of snow of a week ago has only today been sensibly disappearing. My cough improves.

Hd.Qrs. 23rd A.C., 20th Jan 1864

When I wrote last we were just about making our move to Dandridge. Since then we have marched four days, & that about as rough a bit of Winter campaigning as soldiers often see, though we have had no very severe fighting.

Our movement was partly to threaten Longstreet by moving toward his left flank, & partly to get into a country where forage & grain was less scarce than in this vicinity. It now appears that L. had been reinforced & was making a move across to our right flank at the same time, & the heads of our columns came together at Dandridge. We had pretty sharp skirmishing both days we were there, when Gen. Parke (who commands the three corps in the field) learning the situation determined first to cross the French Broad river so that stream might not be at our backs & we might, if it seemed advisable, still move up to the North East as first intended.

A temporary bridge was ordered to be built, & Gen. [Phillip] Sheridan took charge of construction. When it was reported ready some troops were moved across, when lo! it appeared that it only reached an island in the river! I understand the brigade in which Opdycke is, was the one moved over, & which found itself in this dilemma. Gen. Parke then determined to move the troops back here at once, & we had a retreat & a night movement very similar to that I made in Rosecrans command from Sewell mountain in '61.

Willich's (Wood's) div. of the 4th Corps had the rear & we were next him, the trains being ahead of us on one road & the rest of the troops moving unencumbered on other parallel roads. My command was moved into the road between 8 & 9 in the evening, but the horrible roads, blocked up the trains as usual, & when day broke at about six o'clock next morning we had made less than two miles, & Willich's div. had only got out of the town & past the first wooded ridge where a rear-guard could make a good defense.

The enemy did not trouble us until we had made some six miles, when their cavalry came up & gave us a pretty lively skirmish, but we did not halt the column, the rear guard brushed them off, & we moved slowly but steadily on. No one who has not seen an army train moving in bad roads in Winter can conceive what our half-starved animals had to do. The hills were high & hard, & the roads deep rutted, & the mud tenacious as putty. We had to take up the artillery one gun at a time, using the teams of several pieces to move one, & in some instances more than twenty animals were thus hitched to a single piece or caisson, besides having men on foot at the wheels as thick as they could cluster, pushing & lifting, the drivers beating the animals & shouting & cursing till all was blue. Add to this a cold rain turning at evening into snow, & you can form some idea of the beauties of Winter campaigning.

We halted at dark having made only sixteen miles in nearly twenty-four hours unresting & almost superhuman exertion. We found a deserted log cabin partly furnished where I made hd. qrs. for the night. It had a stick & mud chimney, but the floor was only half laid, & the chinking was out of the logs, so that the roof & the fire were the only advantages it gave us. Our wagons were far ahead, but some teamsters of one of our forage trains which we had overtaken shared their supper with us, & we got a hold of some corn stalks out of which we made a bed, & wrapped in our wet overcoats & saddle blankets we lay with our feet close to the fire & passed a tolerable night notwithstanding the snow blew through the open logs all over us.

The soldiers made shelter of pine & cedar boughs & by the aid of their shelter tents got along better than we expected, though having less than quarter rations of everything but poor beef. I slept less than anyone else, having to be up every hour or so to answer dispatches from hd. qrs. & issue orders for the troops, writing on my knee by the firelight—in a pocket dispatch book or manifold writer, like my letter book which you remember. We got the single meal which the teamsters gave us in twenty four hours, & were glad enough to get that, taking a piece of pork in our fingers & dipping some coffee out of an iron camp kettle with battered tin cups, munching a piece of corn pone meanwhile. Yet in the wet, cold & fatigue, this really seemed like luxury, especially as we had expected to get nothing till next day.

Yesterday morning we marched back to this place 3 miles from our camp at Strawberry Plains, crossing the Holston river again & are now some sixteen miles above Knox. though we expect the development of events to put us on the move again by tomorrow. In the midst of this exposure & exertion my health has been improving. Only half my command are with me in this late movement, the rest being scattered in detachments at different points.

Knoxville 24th Jan. 1864

The determination has at length been reached to put the troops in Winter quarters, our late march having fully satisfied everybody that it costs more in men & money to march armies in such weather over such roads than to fight the enemy in an ordinary season. My command is at different points of the circle about this place & my hd. qrs. are established here for a time.

It will not do to calculate upon the future in war, but our present expectation is that we shall be here for two or three months. We have not secured permanent quarters as yet, though we hope to make our arrangements tomorrow. I have a parlor & bedroom in a neat square cottage, & the staff tents are pitched in the grounds of a private residence just across the street. We hope to get rooms & board (by crowding) in a house close by & if we succeed, I shall give up those I now have, for the sake of being with the staff, as it is almost impossible to conduct business unless I can have some of them within call.

In our movement down here, we were followed by a heavy force of the enemy's cavalry & were skirmishing with them most of the way. About five miles from town the rebs pressed our forces pretty closely. I had been ordered into town to make arrangements for the disposition of my troops, when the report came that there was expectation of a battle which the Gens. on the ground with the forces seemed a little nervous about.

Gen. Foster immediately ordered me out to assume command of the 9th Corps as well as my own. I reached the field just before dark. The enemy were drawn up in line & were in perfectly full view. A glance satisfied me there was nothing but cavalry & mounted infantry, though the force was large. I stopped the retrograde movement of my troops, ordered some hills between us & the enemy to be occupied, & as it was then dark, put our men in bivouac in line of battle, ready to move on the rebs at daylight. I then in accordance with orders rode back to town to report the condition of things, & rode back to the front again before midnight through the mud.

Dory rode with me. We took each a blanket on our horses, & wrapped in these & our overcoats slept on the board floor of a log house till daylight. I then ordered the line to advance, but the enemy had taken the hint from the movement the night before & decamped. I pushed our troops back in detachments some eight miles, & finding the rebs had got quite out of reach resumed the original movement & brought the troops to the allotted positions without molestation. This however necessitated my staying out another night from our hd. qrs. tents which had been sent forward into town, & we lay on a floor again & got a bite to eat as we could catch it by accident or luck.

Take it all in all we have had a rough week of it—no regular shelter, food or sleep, and all the time in cold, wet, & mud. We now need some rest as well as our troops.

I have been getting stout & hearty all the time however, getting rid of my cold & feeling that my whole system is getting in better condition than before.

This town must have been a pleasant one in peaceful & prosperous times: the situation is beautiful, there were many comfortable & some rather fine residences, & a good deal of thrift & business. Now all is desolate enough, except that portion which escaped the effects of the siege, & in which my hd. qrs. now are. The grounds in which our tents are run down a hill to the Holston, which curves gracefully among wooded hills, out of sight either way.

The view is a very beautiful one, the range of the Great Smokey mountains forming the background toward the South East; as picturesque a distant range as one often sees. Here as elsewhere the more wealthy & influential people seem to have been rebels, though the division was perhaps less disproportionate than in most parts of the South.

If our expectation of remaining here a short time is realized I shall be able to report more of the people in another letter. I hear nothing of the news in the outer world, much as I am interested in knowing what is going on especially in Wash.

Knoxville 28th Jan. 1864

We can hardly call ourselves settled as yet, though in army life we shall probably never be more so. I have Dory with me in the house I mentioned in my last. He sleeps on my camp cot opposite my bed in the same room ready to be called on an emergency, as Christie did at Charleston. My room is a very pretty room, high ceiling, large windows opening on a verandah fronting the river, rosewood furniture, brussels carpet &e. with warm air register heating the room. I have beside the use of a parlor opening from the same hall, & regard myself nicely fixed for the present.

Dory & I have taken board with the family, a young gentleman & wife, with one child, & everything promises to be very comfortable considering the difficulty of getting the supply of marketing, & etc. which the presence of armies has created. The name of the family is Corwin. The hd. qrs. tents are in the grounds immediately across the st. in front of us, & the tents of the infantry company forming the hd. qrs. guard are just at the left on the terrace above the river, the sloping bank here being sixty or seventy feet high from the water to the plateau on which the town is built.

There is no evidence that the rebels have moved their infantry nearer us, though their cavalry keep about, dashing in on our pickets every day or two. Our cavalry near Sevierville gave them a handsome thrashing yesterday, killing some fifty, capturing over a hundred, & taking two pieces of cannon.

Early in February 1864, Cox began to hear rumors that General John Schofield was going to replace Foster, who told Cox of his resignation because of ill health. Cox was unhappy because he had developed a good relationship with Foster and he knew the new commander would want to name his own deputies, which Schofield did soon after arriving.[3]

Cox was now again without a formal position and he forced himself not to be bitter about his fate. Having learned from his earlier experience, he worked hard to make a positive impression on his new commander, Schofield. They soon became fast friends, in part because they were both scholarly—Schofield had been on the faculty at West Point soon after his graduation from that institution—and had similar interests, as well as, in part, because Schofield, who had had little field experience, was open to Cox's ideas and suggestions. Schofield was so sufficiently impressed that he offered Cox the position as his chief of staff. Not having heard from Grant, to whom he had applied for a transfer to the Army of the Cumberland, Cox accepted the staff position, while telling Schofield he really wanted a field command.

For some time, Cox would once again be disappointed; but he finally got a field position after Schofield was named commander of the Army of the Ohio. This group, which consisted primarily of the XXIII Corps and some cavalry, was one of the three elements of Sherman's combined army that was going to launch the "Atlanta Campaign" from Chattanooga in May. Schofield gave Cox command of the 3rd Division of the XXIII Corps. Because of his seniority, Cox would be in charge whenever Schofield was away. When Schofield went to Knoxville on business in early April, Cox took command as he and his troops prepared for Sherman's campaign.[4]

Schofield would be Cox's commanding officer for the rest of the war. The next letters include frequent references to the evolution of their excellent working relationship, as well as such mundane matters as Cox's having his brother supervise the burying of dozens of dead horses and mules. Cox's comment that, though Schofield was unpopular (in part because of his Democratic Party membership), he would follow his orders meticulously underlined Cox's reputation as a quintessential subordinate.

Knoxville 2nd Feb. 1864

We had marching orders yesterday, & expected to be off at daylight this morning, but the information received last night found the movement unnecessary & it was countermanded. Most of the horses have been ordered to the rear to reduce the quantity of forage required, & my own three horses will be the only ones at our hd. qrs. for a time.

The rumors now are that Gen. [John] Schofield is coming out here to assume command, relieving Gen. Foster, who goes East to have an operation performed upon his leg, which is disabled from the effect of an old wound, aggravated by a recent fall from his horse. As Gen. Schofield has not been confirmed, & the last reports indicate that it was very doubtful whether he would be we do not credit the report. Gen. Foster will perhaps be relieved, but we are entirely in the fog as to his successor.

I hear nothing from Garfield since his letter of 16th Dec. in which he told me of the Prest. recommending my promotion to the Scy of War & Gen. Halleck, which did not to my apprehension promise well. My mind is accordingly made up that I need look for no recognition from the powers that be, & that I must do my duty irrespective of such hopes or stimulus.

Knoxville 7th Feb. 1864

We have been in a state of uncertainty here as to the command, amid various reports of names of different officers who were to relieve Gen. Foster, who himself has asked to be relieved on account of his increasing difficulty in his knee & leg. It now seems to be settled that Schofield is to come, & we look for him every day. There is also a report that Maj. Gen. George Stoneman has been assigned to this Corps as permanent commander, which if true would show that Garfield has failed in his efforts to do anything for me at Wash.

Gen. Foster took occasion upon receiving the report of Stoneman's coming to say to me that he sincerely hoped it was not true, & that were he to remain here he would wish no other commander for the Corps. I determined if relieved, to make some move to obtain a div. in the Army of the Cumberland, & at Gen. Foster's suggestion wrote him a note expressing my unwillingness to take a division from my subordinates & he forwarded it to Gen. Grant, with some remarks of his own which are quite as complimentary as I have a right to expect on so short an acquaintance.

If I could have a strong division in the Army of the Cumb, I would on many accounts prefer it to this weak corps, especially as it would have the grand line of operations to act on, whilst we may play a very subordinate role here at best.

I continue to occupy the rooms I described in a former letter though the family find themselves unable to board us, partly from the scarcity of provisions, & partly on account of Mrs. Corwin's health, which she finds unequal to the increased care. As a specimen of the unsettled condition of all slave-holding here, Mr. Corwin said to me the other day that their cook is a slave woman whom he hires from her mistress, but he has to pay the cook herself beside in order to keep her, & has moreover to keep their secret from the mistress. So he is paying double wages.

Anyone with half an eye must see how hopelessly slavery is destroyed here, when such a state of things exists, & that this must necessarily be a transition state to systematic & exclusive free-labor.

We have had the most charming weather for two weeks past, & should enjoy it extremely, were it not for the apprehension that we must pay for it by a back Spring, when we shall be impatient to be moving.

Knoxville 11th Feb. 1864

Maj. Gen. Stoneman has arrived & today relieved me of the command of the Corps. Gen. Schofield has also arrived & relieved Gen. Foster of the Department.

Gen. Stoneman was originally ordered to report to Gen. Grant with expectation of being his chief of cavalry, but it not being convenient to have him that, or an infantry Corps suiting his taste better, after consultation with Grant he was assigned to my Corps, which I suppose they thought a Brigadier should not keep, much less a volunteer when regulars were plenty.

Gen. Schofield treats me very well, desiring me to wait a few days till we hear from Gen. Grant in regard to the papers sent him by Gen. F[oster]., till which time I shall be off duty, awaiting orders. Gen. S. offers me the Dist. of Keny. but though I should be personally well situated, with hd. qrs. at Lexington I have declined accepting it as long as there is a chance of my getting a good division in the field. I want to have active field service in what promises to be the last great campaign of the war.

Gen. Stoneman has offered on my recommendation to endorse the applications I have made to give Bascom the position of Adjt. Gen. & Commissary of the corps with rank of Lieut. Col., & I advise him to stay, though he is willing to follow my fortune. The only ones I keep with me now are Dory & Capt. Saunders.

Knoxville 16th Feb. 1864

I am still unsettled, the delays of mails having prevented an answer being received from Gen. Grant as to my transfer to the Army of the Cumberland. I think it more probable that I shall remain with this command however, & that in all large movements the two armies will be united.

I shall have no objection to serving under Stoneman more than any other Corps commander. He seems very gentlemanly & pleasant in his manners and is quite as clear & apparently accurate in his military perceptions as the Corps commanders of my acquaintance. He is about forty two or three years old, tall as myself, or taller. He has treated me with great consideration & politeness as has also Gen. Schofield.

Did I mention in my last that Gen. Schofield had tried to persuade me to act as his Inspector Gen. The position is one requiring such confidence on the part of the comdg officer in the strictly military qualities of the Inspector that I regard it as personally complimentary, but the command of a div. I prefer to any staff position.

People have been a good deal excited about here for some days with rumors of Longstreet's approach, & of a new siege to be had here. The whole is based upon a movement of part of Lee's command down to Strawberry Plains, 17 miles from here, but in my judgement it will turn out that it is rather with a view to destroying the railroad so that we can't use it in the Spring than with any intention of attacking us. The arrangements now made are such that he would be pretty sure to 'catch a Tartar.[5]

Knoxville 21st Feb. 1864

Gen. Grant has not yet finally decided whether he will give me a command in the Cumberland Army. Gen Schofield is now pressing me to take the position of chief of staff with him, & unless we hear favorably from Grant in a day or two, I shall probably be obliged to do so or forego any connection with the movements at the front & take a territorial command.

If I was sure of the proper support from the Government, I should not have been so averse to the Ky. command, although my preference as you know has been for active field operations. In Ky. however I should be forced to a collision with politicians on the slave question, with a reasonable probability of falling between two stools like Fremont & Schofield in Missouri. There is no decided policy determined on by the Government for settling the question in Ky. & so long as events seem to be so rapidly drifting toward the desirable end, I am not sure but it is best to keep hands off & let them drift.

There has been a good deal of discussion among our officers for a few days on the question whether Longstreet means to attack us. His forces are in some strength at Strawberry Plains where he is said to be bridging the river with pontoons, but I cannot believe he will be foolish enough to undertake another siege. The odds are or will be every way in our favor, & therefore I think the only rational conclusion is that he is making a demonstration for some ulterior purpose.

Several things have occurred to me as possible solutions: 1. That he is attracting our attention in front, while he slips by a part of his force to rejoin Bragg's old army. 2. That he is trying to draw part of [George] Thomas' army up here to support us by way of making a diversion in this way in favor of [Joseph] Johnston's army or to prevent us from following up the movement being made by Sherman in Miss. 3. That he is covering a movement by another column in his rear upon Cumberland Gap & Ky. If we could learn of his being heavily reinforced, I should regard the latter as the most probable supposition, but as we cannot, I regard it least probable.

One thing I shall be sure of, even if he attacks us, & that is that he does not & cannot seriously expect to take Knox. with his present force.

Knoxville 26th Feb. 1864

No permanent assignment has been made yet of myself, but I have consented to go with Gen. Schofield as chief of staff in the field, on a movement we are about to make following up the retreating rebels. I shall leave tonight or tomorrow morning for Strawberry Plains, & if the weather proves favorable we shall probably be gone some ten days or two weeks.

Longstreet appears to have received sudden orders withdrawing his command, & we suspect is en route for Georgia. At any rate after demonstrations as if about to make an immediate attack upon us, he has suddenly pulled up stakes & started for Va.

As Gen. Foster had sent off most of our animals before he left the dept., we are in no condition to make a rapid pursuit, but shall follow up as well as circumstances will permit.

Gen. Schofield has urged me to take the position of chief of staff permanently, but I have been unwilling to make such an arrangement at present, & have agreed with him to postpone all final determination till we see more clearly what the plans for the coming campaign are to be.

I see that the bitterness of disappointment at my being relieved of the command of the corps has been chiefly on your side. I have been a little impatient at being so completely uncertain what I should do, but have otherwise been tranquil. About this time last year, I went through the experience of learning that intrigue, pretense, & self puffing are surer roads to promotion than modest performance of duty. It was not a pleasant thing to learn, & the time marked more distinctly than is common perhaps, the transition from the buoyant confidence of early manhood to the soberer (though I think not cynical) view of human ambitions & so-called successes, which belongs to the maturer years & steady middle age of man. I saw how success in mere position is obtained. I saw more clearly than ever before how mere a sham it is, & how entirely unworthy the seeking. I believe I long ago adopted in all honesty the faith that being & not seeming to be is the only true ambition, but it needed some such lesson to make the faith quicker & more lively.

I would rather have died than not to have had a hand in this war for human progress, & have therefore been glad to do what I could in the fight. Rank, as giving greater power to act, has been welcome, but I have not been fool enough to think our armies would be beaten unless I commanded them.

Hd. Qrs. Army of the Ohio. New Market, Tenn. 4th March '64

Until today I have had no opportunity to write since leaving Knox. on Sat. last. We have made a short movement to discover the extent of Longstreet's retreat, but were stopped by heavy rains at Morristown, 42 miles from Knox., the roads becoming very bad, & the rise of the streams carrying away our bridges. We consequently fell back eighteen miles with our hd. qrs. to this place, leaving the troops in camps four miles above here. We should however have remained at Morristown notwithstanding the rains had not Gen. Grant stopped further advance by directions indicating other work for the troops, or part of them, & this in connection with the storm made the retrograde to this point necessary.

We found no enemy near us at Morristown, & all the evidence points to the evacuation of Tenn. by the rebels, as fast as they can get away with their stores & supplies. The coming on of a storm just as we marched was true army luck & we had to ride in a drenching rain. The morning after reaching Morristown we expected an attack if any of the rebel force should be near us, our information showing that they were some thirteen miles in advance, & it being probable that unless they were determined to continue their retreat they would turn upon us, & we should hear of them at about daybreak. This was the more probable as the storm had prevented part of our force from coming up, & he knew that we were very inferior in numbers to Longstreet's army if it was at all concentrated.

Accordingly I was called an hour before day & went the 'Grand Rounds' visiting the outposts & pickets & putting them on the alert. I don't know that I have ever described such a trip & as this was a good specimen of the kind, I will tell you something of it. When my horse came to the door of the house where we made our hd. qrs. (it was an empty one left by a rebel, & we slept in our blankets on the floor) it was dark & raining heavily. I took an orderly with me, buttoned my cape together over my overcoat, pulled down the brim of my felt hat, & started off, trusting to the horse to keep the road till I should be able to see better in the darkness.

As usual where armies have been, the fences as soon as we got out of the village were gone, the wagons had cut tracks right & left of the old road, & it was impossible to follow it. We therefore struck out guiding ourselves by the campfires, & when we passed those, by the smaller fires of the outposts & picket reserves.

Beyond all these, we felt our way along in the dark, till presently we heard the expected challenge of the solitary sentinel, 'Halt, who goes there.' We could see no one, but reining in our horses, & turning in the direction of the voice I answered, 'Friends with the countersign'. I sent my orderly to give the pass-word, & learning this was the outer line of infantry pickets, I pushed still further out to find the cavalry outposts, from which I wished to send forward a small reconnoitering party before daylight. Presently we saw some glimmering lights in a wood & upon nearing them found the cavalry in an old rebel encampment of log huts.

The first hut we reached contained an Irish dragoon, & him we turned out to conduct us to the Capt's quarters, for the camp fires were burning low & only served to make the darkness visible. The Irishman told us to follow him closely, & 'look out' says he 'for thar's pits every little way, where them ribils dug foundations for their chimneys.' He started on & I kept my horses nose close to his shoulders, when suddenly he disappeared, & as I jerked my horse back on his haunches, the Paddy sung out, 'Och, I've found one sir!' Sure enough he'd gone in head over heels into one of the 'pits.' He scrabbled out, & I cautiously went around the hole, but had hardly gone a rod before Pat went out again with, 'Be jabbers, I've found another.' But he took his mud baths good humoredly & led us without further accident to the Capt.

From him I got the reports from the cavalry at the front, & after ordering the reconnaissance, turned back to inspect the infantry line of sentinels. This was simply a succession of hails & challenges such as I first described, & we went splashing through the mud, across fields, over ditches & fences, the pouring rain soaking my cape till it seemed to weigh fifty pounds, but not penetrating my coat.

We came full upon one sentry asleep in a fence corner, where the poor wretch had tried to make some shelter from the storm. When the horses halted beside him he sprang up bewildered, & stood bolt upright, trying to look at us, evidently uncertain whether we were rebels, but too confused to utter a single word. I asked him if that was the way he guarded the camp, & he began to stammer denials of his being asleep with a strong German accent & broken English in which his stupidity seemed more stupid. I reported him to the Capt. of his guard as we came in, but could not find it in my heart to order a courts-martial, which would perhaps condemn him to death, & so only ordered some lighter summary punishment by the immediate commander.

After examining the more important part of the front, I splashed back to the quarters, getting in just as the gray of dawn was broadening into day, got a fire built in our cheerless room, hung my coat beside it to dry & crossed my mud cased legs before the fire-place to have half an hour of rest & recovery, listening for any carbine shots which might show that my scouting party had found an enemy, whilst the staff lay snoring in their blankets in the corners of the room, oblivious to wars alarms, making the most of the night to be ready for the day. No attack came, & the day went as usual.

New Market 8th Mar. 1864

By the date you will see that I am still at New Market. Gen. Schofield has been several days at Knoxville, leaving the care of the Army up here with me, & I have been quietly enjoying myself, Dory & Capt. Saunders being the only staff with me.

We are stopping at the house of a good Union woman, whose husband died in a rebel prison charged with no crime but patriotism, & whose two sons are in our Army. We live quite comfortably, & are as well contented as we should be at Knoxville.

We are expecting some troops from the North to increase the 23rd Corps & relieve the 4th Corps. When they come if I like the quality of them I shall probably take a division which will supply the place of the 1st division of the 23rd, which has been broken up.

Opdycke is mistaken in his estimate of the troops of the 23rd. They have never had the advantage of being long together in the field & acquiring the esprit which perhaps the 4th has, but I doubt if any troops will fight better, & if they could have a brief period of drill & discipline together, they would be as good as any others. Such an arrangement as he speaks of, giving me a div. in his corps would please me very much but there is no chance of it.

Sherman's expedition has failed, it seems. The cavalry part of it was entrusted to the most easily 'stampeded' man I have known in the army, & if it was expected that he should take care of Sherman's flank & rear, it was morally certain a priori that there would be a failure. I am very sorry it should have turned out so, for it spoils the beginning of the campaign badly, & will necessitate new combinations throughout, giving the rebels the chance to seize the initiative.

I never liked the movement thinking it too hazardous, & false in principle, but being started, I earnestly hoped it would go through successfully, &

result either in the capture of Mobile or a lodgment of our troops in central Alabama within communicating distance of the rest of Grant's army.

New Market 11th March 1864

We now expect to start tomorrow for a forward movement, though the frequent rains we are now having may make the roads impassable. We are hoping a short campaign here may put affairs in position to secure the safety of East Tenn. & leave us free to act elsewhere if necessary. Till we get through with this movement I shall continue my present duty, but expect that a permanent arrangement will not be delayed longer than our return. The condition of affairs in our front is doubtful, & we shall probably get no satisfactory information till we advance. My own belief is that the force in front has been a good deal reduced & that we shall find no stubborn resistance this side Watauga river.

Morristown, Tenn 16th March 1864

This army seems fated to be a sort of shuttlecock. When we came up here before, we had no sooner arrived than Grant ordered us to suspend our movement, expecting to take away the 4th Corps. This took us back to New Market. Now no sooner are we here again, than he takes away the 9th Corps & this again suspends our advance.

I find Gen. Schofield a pleasant man to be with, & that my influence upon affairs is undoubtedly much greater than it would be as a division commander, indeed more weight is given to my opinion than I could ask. I am sure no position in the army is a more influential one, & if the command were larger & a more prominent part in the campaign assigned us, I believe there is no other position in which I could do so much good. My personal preferences are known to have a division, & the promise of new troops to supply the place of those removed, will we expect bring about the desired result.

The fact that Gen. S. is unpopular has no influence with me. He is the military commander here, & I, like the rest of his subordinates, am bound to give him the best assistance in my power. By the course I have taken I am sure I have secured the hearty good-will of the Generals in the army here, & if I take a line command again, it will be with more influence & consideration than if I had not consented to serve in the staff for a time.

Gen. S. is an honest, loyal man and a good soldier. He has the confidence of the Prest. & of Gen. Grant, & I can learn no good reason for his being opposed by the radicals. He is opposed to slavery, believes in emancipation, & in fighting the rebellion earnestly & thoroughly till it is conquered.

I have not enquired into the particular quarrels involved in Missouri politics, & cannot judge of the merits, nor do I care to do so.

Our hd. qrs. here are in a large house wholly bare of furniture. I sleep in my blankets on the floor. Dory is with me. My mess is separate from Gen. S. We have our cooking &e. at a neighboring house. Gen. S. with his aids & Adjt. Gen. messing here.

Strawberry Plains 19th March 1864

We returned here today, Gen. Schofield being persuaded that no good could come of remaining longer at Morristown. The rebels under Longstreet held Bull's Gap some thirteen miles in front of Morristown, & though undoubtedly stronger than we, would not venture out to meet us in open country whilst we were not strong enough to attack their position in the mountains, or to detour to turn their flank.

The withdrawal of the 9th Corps from the command made our advanced position hazardous, & other points were threatened which we could better look to from here, & hence the wisdom of withdrawing. I hope it will not be long before the arrival of the troops from which my div. is to be made, & which will give me the independent command I desire.

Strawberry Plains, 24th March 1864

Gen. Schofield has been kept at Knoxville since we came back from Morristown, & I have been here by myself managing the affairs & routine of the army. We are in the only house on this side of the river near this point. I use a large room on the first floor with open fireplace for office during the day & three of us sleep in it at night—I on my camp cot, & the other two, Dory & Capt. S. on the floor in their blankets, Treat & the qtr. Master & engineer in the room directly over us & the remaining room upstairs is the telegraph office. The stairs go up out of my room.

The family, consisting of an old man, his paralytic wife, two grown up daughters, unmarried, one married with her husband & three small children occupy the other room below & the kitchen wing. Our servants cook in another wing at the end of the house, & our office is our eating room. So you see we are quite comfortable, with our guard camped about the house, the horses of the cavalry escort picketed in front, & our own horses in the only stables.

The man who lives here owns some two thousand acres of land in this beautiful valley, & is reported to have had nearly a hundred thousand dollars in cash when the war broke out, but you cannot conceive the utter slatternliness of the whole family. You wouldn't believe to look at the women that they ever saw a quarter of a dollar. Dirty, unwashed, their hair hanging every way about them, in homespun woolen dresses of which the original color can't be told for the dirt. Any servant in Warren would lose her place who couldn't look neater on washing day than these do at all times & hours.

In peace times a winding country road came by the house & ended at the ferry a few rods in front of it, called after the owner of the place McBee's ferry. The village of Strawberry Plains is perched on a mass of broken rock & hills across the river, the bend of which leaves a strip of bottom land on this side. Now there is not a fence in sight, the last rail having disappeared long since, & instead of one seldom used country road, the whole region is one vast road, cut up & cross cut in every direction, with tracks leading to the railway station a few rods above, where our great wagon trains for the supply of the army are parked at night & where the mules with their whistling bray, keep us in music night & day.

The house stands in a wilderness, with a singular appearance of bareness about, which can only be realized when one has seen how clear of trees, bush, & shrub an army can clear a tract of country where it is long encamped. Yet the land is fertile & the hills most picturesque.

When we arrived, the whole region was thickly dotted with dead mules & horses which had died during our encampment here last Winter. I immediately ordered a burying party of fifty men, & Dory set them to work. They worked hard two days, & I think I can find another day's work for them yet before all the odorous carcasses will be under ground. There are none now within smelling distance of my quarters, which is more than could be said three days ago.

> The next letters describe General William T. Sherman's consultations with Schofield and Cox about their role in the upcoming Atlanta campaign. This was the first time that Cox met Sherman, and Cox quickly recognized that Sherman was the kind of leader that he and the army needed at that point. As Cox wrote in his reminiscences, "Of all the men I had met, he was the one to whose leadership in war I would commit my own life and the lives of my men with most complete confidence."[6] For his part, Sherman would ultimately recognize Cox to be a dependable and trustworthy general, eventually offering Cox a brigadier-generalship in the regular army after the war.
>
> In these next letters, Cox described an additional horror of the war for Helen, the ongoing guerrilla war in Tennessee. He recounted almost nonchalantly how pro-Union guerrillas "disposed" of their pro-Confederate enemies in a "take no prisoners" approach.

Knoxville 28th March 1864

Gen. Sherman is expected here this week, when the work we are to do in the coming campaign will be more distinctly marked out. There is a faint chance of my getting the command of Sheridan's div. in which Opdycke is. Sheridan is ordered to Washington & will probably be assigned command there in some capacity, & this leaves his div. open. Gen. Schofield will assign me to it if it is left to him, & on Gen. Sherman's coming we shall know more positively about it. I make no calculations with confidence in regard to it only refer to it as possible.

Knoxville 31st March 1864

Gen. Sherman was here yesterday, arriving the evening before & left this morning. He has had a pretty full understanding with Gen. Schofield & we feel that we know pretty well what will be the arrangement for the coming campaign. I shall have a division, one of the 23 Corps enlarged, & it is probable that changes will be made which will make the command every way agreeable, & which will give us an important part in the general campaign for the Summer. So far as my own command is concerned it is settled definitely by my understanding with Gen. S. since Gen. Sherman left. We shall probably leave Strawberry Plains for another move up the country in two or three days, but do not anticipate being gone much longer than on our former trip.

Bulls Gap, East Tenn. 6th April 1864

Here I am once more at the front, & in command of the 23rd Corps, though only temporarily. Gen. Stoneman has been assigned to a cavalry command, & his connection with the corps will probably not be resumed, & I have been assigned to a division, which makes me as ranking officer present commandant of the Corps.

Our expectation is that Gen. Schofield as commander of the department will also be assigned to the permanent command of the corps as it includes all the troops which regularly belong to the dept. As he is at Knoxville & will doubtless be kept there by his duties for some time, it leaves me in command in the field.

We are some thirteen miles further up the country than we were at Morristown, the 'Gap' being a deep cleft in Boys mountains, through which the rail & country roads run. The rebels left Tenn. destroying rail road bridges & putting obstructions in the way of our following them. We may follow them fifty or sixty miles further up, but it is doubtful whether this will accord with Gen. Sherman's plans for concentrating everything for a campaign in Georgia. I think it will not be long before we shall be on our way to Chattanooga.

I am very glad to be once more settled in a field command. I have as Brigadiers under me Gens. Manson & Hascall, the same who commanded divisions when I took the Corps in Dec. & as my div. will be increased till it will be nearly as strong as both have been, you see there will be little difference except in name between my permanent command & the old corps. A large number of Maj. Gens. are being ordered out to Sherman's command, & in the crowding which is taking place, I consider myself very well off to get a good division, especially when it is under circumstances which show that Schofield will regard it as the most reliable portion of his command.

I had my choice of divisions & took the 3rd, which contains the oldest & best troops of the Corps, & the most Ohioans. Sterling's regiment is in it, & I shall expect to have him with me as Inspector Gen. My hd. qrs. are a sort of shingle palace which was a railway hotel, in which the rooms are separated from each other by partitions of unpainted boards, & the whole building being without lathing or plaster, every noise is echoed from end to end of it. Still it gives me shelter, & that is about all we need of it.

I came up day before yesterday in a hard rain which continued till last night, & threatens to begin again. The streams are unfordable, the roads muddy & deep, & we could not move far if we wished to.

Bulls Gap 16th April 1864

My health seems quite as good as usual again, though the vile diet we had for sometime makes it almost impossible to be free from bowel complaints. Yesterday we were gladdened by the arrival of an agent of the Sanitary Commission who brought us some onions, potatoes, & sour kraut—& never were vegetables more wanted or better appreciated. A good deal of scurvy has been manifested in the incipient stages among our men, & all of us were feeling the need of some change of diet. For sometime we have had nothing but bacon & flour with occasionally a little rice or white beans. And as we cannot get flour made into anything but heavy biscuit which I abominate, you may be sure I have not had much luxury in victuals at any rate.

Last night however, we had a regular feast, good boiled potatoes, sliced onions raw, & smoking sour kraut made our stomachs glad.

I don't know whether I mentioned in my last that the Corps has been merged in the Dept. & Gen. Schofield regularly assigned to command. This is as I had expected & we are now reporting from our div. hd. qrs. directly to Dept. hd. qrs. My div. is to consist of eleven regts. of infantry, two of cavalry, & two batteries of artillery.

The continuance of cold backward weather will I fear, delay the opening of the Spring campaign. We had a little flurry of snow this morning, not enough to show on the ground, but filling the air & accompanied by raw chilly winds which are anything but pleasant.

We have a little partisan warfare at the front, but there is no prospect of any considerable engagement in this part of the state. The loyal people here are terribly exasperated & our Tenn. troops when they meet bushwhacking bands of rebels neither give nor take quarter. A party of a little over a hundred which I sent out, composed mostly of Indiana cavalry but accompanied by some thirty Tennesseans came back this A.M. bringing fifteen prisoners & having killed ten men, the remainder of the party. The prisoners all surrendered to the Indianans, & the Tennesseans were quite inclined to complain of the cavalry for giving them quarter, & would have killed them in cold blood, if the Indiana men had not kept strong guard over them.

It is true the rebel party were peculiarly hateful, having committed most horrible outrages, & having been regularly engaged in hunting up the men fit to bear arms & forcing them into the rebel army, but the exasperation & disposition to slaughter seems as great as ever it was among the Spanish guerrillas in the Peninsular War.

One of our old Tenn. scouts & guides reported to me this morning on their return. 'Will Reynolds,' said I, 'what luck this time?' 'Oh,' said he in a sort of dejected nasal tone, 'some pretty good luck, & some bad luck.' 'What bad luck,' said I, thinking some of our men had got hurt. 'Oh them Indiana cavalry fellers let the Capt. of the gang & fourteen of his men surrender to em.' 'What became of the rest,' I asked. 'We had to deal with them, & they didn't surrender,' he answered significantly. Even this will give you no idea of the horrors of a real civil war, when it comes to a deadly feud between old neighbors & acquaintances.

I am very anxious to get away from it, & into a field where armies will meet with something like the chivalry of fair field warfare.[7]

Bulls Gap 24th April 1864

I am going up to the front to try my hand at destroying railroads for a day, & we shall then move toward the South & begin our campaign in earnest.

26th April

I had a busy day of it yesterday, destroying railroads, & trying to put matters in such shape as to make it impossible for the rebels to come in here with large force while we are absent on our Southern campaign. My orders now are to hasten matters. Part of my command is forty miles up the country, & as soon as it can march back we shall be in motion.

We are all glad at the prospect of having a part in a campaign on a large scale. Soldiers always are – the danger is no greater & the apparent accomplishment, or at any rate the éclat much more.

The weather has been delicious for three days, & we are hopeful that the reputation of the Tenn. Spring may at last be realized. As we march we shall at different points pick up the new regiments assigned to my division, or part of them, for I suspect it will be a month before one or two that are on return furlough will join us.

One of the advantages of being with a large army will be that the news agents &e. find it pay to take their depts. along in portable shape, & bring us the newspapers & magazines. Since I have been up here I have been supplied gratis with the Cin. Com. Gazette, Louisville Journal, two Nashville papers, a Chattanooga paper, Knoxville Whig, N.Y. Herald, & had beside the associate press dispatches telegraphed to me every night. So I have not lacked for news. The march will interfere with these convenient arrangements at first.

Charleston Tenn. 1st May 1864

We are encamped in one of the loveliest spots I have ever seen. The place is a small hamlet of perhaps a dozen houses, situated on the railroad where it crosses the Hiwassee river, the village being on the South side of the river which as you follow it upstream makes a long detour describing in fact two thirds of a circle & coming back to within a quarter of a mile of the railroad again at a point not over a mile from the bridge.

Just here at the narrow neck above the bend, I am encamped, my left resting on a ridge sloping down to the river & my right on the railroad as we face South. The rest of the Corps are behind me, nearer the railroad bridge. We are about a hundred and forty miles from Bull's Gap, & by the partial assistance of the railroad have made the transit quickly, the command having marched half the way & then carried the other half.

The weather has made one leap from Winter to Summer. On Monday last only here & there could I see a little green or an early tree on the hills, but today a fresh green color covers everything and the noon sun makes the shade of my clean new tent comfortable. The country is hilly, not mountainous, though we see far off at our left the smokey mountains piling their deep blue masses up against the horizon, while at our feet winds as beautiful a river as ever bore a musical Indian name. The hills just at the river bank on my left are about one hundred feet high. I should rather say, the bases of the hills are about a hundred feet above the water, for the undulating surface of my camp is about so high above the stream, the steep bank of which is wood covered, with zigzag paths leading down to a spring pouring out a steady swift stream two yds wide, six inches deep, which supplies our troops with fine sweet water. I know of no lovelier country than these valleys of East Tenn. & especially the more Southern ones. They are not so romantic as those of Western Va. because more quiet & rural.

The whole country is arable, & is susceptible of much richer agricultural wealth, while the surface is still broken enough for beauty & the mountain peaks are always in view to complete the landscape.

It will take two or three days to get our wagons & artillery together here, & then we shall be ready any day for a move still further South.

6

The Atlanta Campaign

> The orders had at first assigned that my command should assist in the assault [Battle of Kennesaw Mountain] nearer the center, but Gen. Sherman finally concluded that I could do more good by the flank movement & changed the order accordingly, for which I was not sorry, as I knew the result of the assaults must be very doubtful, & whether successful or not would have cost the lives of a large portion of my command, whilst the movement I did make was with little loss, & Gen. Sherman himself said accomplished the only valuable result of the whole day's fighting. The positions we took will be most important in the movements of the next few days.
>
> —Dolson to Helen, June 29, 1864

In May of 1864, the Civil War in the West was focused primarily on two armies commanded by Sherman and Joseph Johnston. Sherman would move out of Chattanooga with over one-hundred thousand men, aiming at Joseph Johnston's Confederate army of seventy thousand, then based at Dalton, Georgia. Grant's order to Sherman for the campaign stated, "You, I propose to move against Johnston's army, to break it up, and to get into the interior of the enemy's country as far as you can, inflicting all the damage you can against their war resources.... I leave you free to execute in your own way."[1]

Sherman's forces consisted of three "armies," of which Schofield's was by far the smallest, about thirteen thousand and five hundred men and a few calvary in the XXIII Corps. General James McPherson commanded the Army of Tennessee, which numbered approximately twenty-five thousand. General George Thomas commanded the Army of the Cumberland, by far the largest, numbering over sixty thousand. Since Schofield's army was the smallest and thus most mobile, it would be used primarily for flanking movements.

Unlike the parallel Overland campaign in the East between Grant and Lee, both sides in this campaign focused on flanking maneuvers and the defensive, resulting in far fewer casualties than in the East. The strategy Sherman chose was what the eminent military analyst Basil Liddell-Hart would later call the "indirect approach."[2] Cox summarized in his book about this campaign as follows: "Sherman's calculation . . . was that the Army of the Cumberland in his centre was always strong enough to hold Johnston at bay until one of the wings could attack his flank or rear. This simple plan controlled the whole campaign."[3]

For his part, Johnston was ordered by Jefferson Davis to stop Sherman's advance by attacking the Union army as much as possible. Johnston, who was on extremely bad terms with Davis, paid lip service to his orders while taking a defensive-oriented, Fabian-strategic approach. As Cox wrote later, "the days for brilliant detached campaigns . . . were over. Johnston settled down to patient defensive operations behind carefully constructed earthworks, watching for a slip in the strategy of the Federal commanders which might give hope of success to aggressive return blows by their smaller forces." Johnston also hoped to cut Sherman's tenuous railroad-based supply line and thereby force him to retreat.[4]

For Cox, the campaign began on May 5 when Schofield's army crossed the Georgia line. On May 9, Cox's 3rd Division was on the extreme left near Dalton. Making a demonstration toward the Confederates, Cox forced the enemy's advance troops to move back to the main trenches, retreating slowly. Then, on May 14 and 15, the first major battle of the campaign was fought at Resaca, where each side engaged in flanking maneuvers, with Cox's division making the only direct, frontal attack. Johnston retreated to Cassville during the evening of the 15th.[5]

Cox's first three letters of this campaign discussed the trials and tribulations of a new command, his role in the Battle of Resaca, his concern about his friend Opdycke, and the praise he received from Schofield. As usual, he also took the time to describe the flora and fauna.

Camp near Red Clay, Ga 5th May 1864

The past two days we have been within the state of Ga. & only far enough to say so, for we are less than two miles South of the state line, on the road from Cleveland to Dalton. I was boasting before leaving Bulls Gap of the abundance of newspapers I had, but the change has spoiled all that. I have seen a paper only once or twice since that time.

On reaching Cleveland I learned that the 4th Corps were here, but were only awaiting our arrival to move out. We however had got the start of them, reaching the town about 9 o'clock having already marched twelve miles, so we passed on through & went into camp four miles south of the place. There I sat in front of my head-quarters, watching for Opdyke as the Corps filed by. After watching perhaps an hour, my patience was rewarded by seeing him. He halted & sat down by me for a chat while the column moved by. It was very pleasant to see some one from home once more.

Their Corps are about 8 miles to our right, we forming the extreme left of the line of which the right is at Ringgold. We expect to move forward in a day or two, & the enemy must then give us battle or retreat. When we move we shall probably draw close together & form a connected line, sharing each other's work, & I trust each other's glory.

Yesterday & today are the only warm days we have had. The day we left Charleston the frost was thick on the ground at daybreak, & my feet were almost benumbed during our first hours ride. After the sun rose, however, it got warm. Today has been almost sultry. The whole surface of the country is wooded, & in the valley a dense undergrowth, mostly of young pines, makes it impossible to see or to move. It is the most unpleasant campground I have occupied this season. The season has been rapidly advancing during the warm days, and if I see any peculiarity in the climate it is in the sudden transition from March to June.

There seems to be no interval. The wild flowers are in the main those I have been accustomed to see at the North. The Spring beauties, dwarf-pinks, phlox, anemones, & violets, look very familiar and natural. The great abundance of wild azalea looks a little more foreign to us, & now & then we see brilliant clusters of to us unknown flowers which still more strongly remind us that we are getting South. Still the general features of the landscape & flora have nothing strange about them. We are however among the mountains & cannot expect a real southern climate or landscape till we get down to more level regions south of the Chattahoochee.

We have had some domestic trouble in our beginning of this campaign. In the hurry of moving from Bull's Gap my own mess chest was the only one brought with us by rail, the others being left in the wagon train which reached us only today, so we had about twenty persons living at our mess, with furniture for six only. This was bad enough, but we have a drunk sort of fellow for cook, being unable to find a better, & he knows almost nothing of his business, so that we can get our poor rations only poorly cooked.

The climax was that by some awkwardness, four of our six cups were tilted from the table & broken day before yesterday, & we can't supply their places for love or money. We cannot even get tin ones, & are ludicrously fixed having to borrow tin cups from our neighbors & postpone our meals till theirs are over, so that the borrowing may become feasible. But we laugh & grow fat. Rude health & a life of excitement make bad fare & few dishes seem of little account.

Camp near Tunnel Hill Ga. 11th May

The past few days we have been in motion without baggage. We have been almost constantly skirmishing, but have had no pitched battle, our movements being rather maneuvers for position than fighting. My division is on the extreme left, & has been in the most exposed position, but we have done the part assigned us without being seriously engaged, the casualties in my command not exceeding thirty.

The fourth Corps attempted to push along a very sharp crest to Buzzard's Roost, the principal position of the rebels, but the crest was so narrow that scarce a dozen men could stand abreast, & they were foiled. I hear that two field officers were killed & five wounded in [Charles] Harker's brigade to which Opdyke belongs, but I do not learn that he was injured, yet my news is so uncertain that I am almost afraid to speak positively. I have sent Col. Treat to learn definitely & hope to be able to say positively that O. is safe before sealing this.

We have had rougher times these four days than I ever before experienced in a summer campaign. My overcoat is the only bedding I have, & one night I passed on the rocky hill side without even it, having left it in an ambulance which could not get up to us. Our crockery & cooking utensils consist of one tin plate, one knife & fork, four tin cups without handles, three round tin oyster cans which do duty as cups, & two tin sardine boxes which answer for extra dishes. One coffee pot makes our coffee, & we are as independent as Kings of the Cannibal Islands.

Our tents, mess chests, & etc. are all left with the train, & we are in fighting trim, & there is no telling how long before we shall again have the luxury of our hd. qrs. tents. My baggage consists of one extra under shirt, handkerchief, a pair of socks, hair & tooth brushes, comb, piece of soap, four paper collars & a pair of candlesticks all carried in my saddle valise. The candlesticks you will remember are the round army pattern which screw together like a big watch.

We are merry as you please, & never had less grumbling about hd. qrs. Night before last I was awake all night, being just upon the enemy (within rifle shot) & having much work to do while my men slept. Since we began the move we are up at reveille at 3 o'clock, have our coffee & hard tack before four, & are on the move before five. We move again in the morning. God bless you all. P.S. Opdyke is safe—not a scratch.

Coosawattee River 17th May 1864

We have just completed a three days pitched battle at Resaca, over a very rough & difficult country, & have been victorious, gaining position after position from the enemy & finally taking the key of his last stronghold just as night closed on the 15th. Next morning he had evacuated Resaca retreating Southward, & we are in pursuit.

My division had the honor of the advance on the 14th the hardest day & we are proud of the honors awarded us for our work. We carried a line of rifle-pits & entrenchments under a very heavy fire, advancing in line over three successive ranges of hills, & once an open valley swept by a terrible artillery fire. The losses of my division are six hundred, but both myself & staff had our usual good fortune & came out unhurt.

After fighting till about 4 o'clock P.M. on the 14th & exhausting all our ammunition, some of the 4th Corps were ordered to relieve us that my men might rest & replenish their cartridge boxes. Harker's brigade was ordered to relieve my 2nd brigade, & you may judge my feelings when I saw Opdyke leading his command up to my position. They had to cross the same valley over which we had come, & the troops at our right had not succeeded in silencing the rebel batteries there, so that they suffered some as they came through that fire. Opdyke had scarcely got his men into position, & mine had not yet moved when he was led back pale and bleeding with a wound in his arm. Two men were holding him on his horse, & the loss of blood was making him both faint & sick at the stomach. He was taken a little to the rear & his wound dressed, but he could not be kept away from the field & as soon as his strength rallied a little from the shock he was back again.

They in their turn found the place a hot one, & were relieved before my first brigade had yet been, & I saw them file away with thinner numbers while I was waiting for the troops which were to take the place of the rest of my command. Three sets of troops were thus put in during the day to hold the ground I had gained. I cannot stop to give you even a sketch of this great battle.

When I reported to Gen. Schofield in the evening, he grasped my hand warmly, & said with evident feeling 'You have done nobly today, General, & I am glad to see you safe.' Gen. S. is so proverbially reticent & uncommunicative that I regard this as of much meaning from him. We all had our narrow escapes, & have good reason to thank God that we were spared in so great perils. We do not expect another battle till we get near the Allatoona mountains.

In the first days of the campaign, Cox's two fellow division commanders came under heavy criticism from Schofield, which underlined the importance of the dependable Cox. 1st Division Commander Alvin Hovey and 2nd Division Commander Henry Judah both were relieved from duty, Hovey because Schofield thought he literally might be suffering from mental illness and Judah because he made an unwarranted frontal attack which was bloodily defeated. Schofield then divided Hovey's and Judah's troops between Cox and General Milo Hascall for the rest of the campaign.[6]

Johnston, under pressure from Davis to go on the attack, determined to do so at Cassville on May 19. Johnston sent General John Bell Hood forward to initiate the attack, but Cox's and other batteries opened fire on the rebel line. Hood counseled retreat, which Johnston heeded, though he blamed Hood for inaction at a critical moment. This incident inflamed the already-volatile relationship between the two. Afterward, Hood wrote to Jefferson Davis, criticizing Johnston for not obeying orders to aggressively attack Sherman, while implicitly lobbying to replace him.[7]

The next major clash of the campaign was on June 15 near New Hope Church. Cox wrote later that the defensive strategy of both sides took the forefront. As each army attacked, "every advanced line on both sides intrenched itself as soon as a position was assumed." Sherman had been hoping that he would have a decisive battle with Johnston at some point, but instead the defensive tactics were leading to a stalemate. Both sides were learning the power of the defensive and, though obviously Cox did not know it, he was seeing a preview of World War I's trench warfare.[8]

On June 22, the battle of Kolb's Farm led to another extension of the trench lines, further exacerbating Sherman's frustration. That was worsened when, by the 24th, Johnston put his troops into what Cox told Helen was "nearly a horseshoe form . . . at Kennesaw Mountain, a high, isolated, double knob which stands out very prominently on the landscape." From there, the rebels were "unassailable by direct assault . . . and able to look down on and view every movement of ours . . . an advantage in itself worth half an army."[9]

Nevertheless, a frustrated Sherman decided to try a frontal attack.[10] Not unexpectedly, the Battle of Kennesaw Mountain on June 27 was a Union failure, resulting in massive casualties. Cox's division, originally ordered to be in the middle of the attack, instead flanked the rebel army and discovered an unguarded ridge which threatened the rebel position. Partly because of Cox's action, Johnston was forced to retreat south on July 2. On July 5, Johnston formed a new defensive line less than ten miles north of Atlanta, with his back to the Chattahoochee River.[11]

Cox's next letters include his pride at playing a key role in forcing Johnston's retreat; his happiness that he and his men had not been involved in the fateful infantry charge; his sorrow at the death of a staff member; his thoughts on his potential promotion; his fatalism as he ate dinner amidst an artillery barrage; and his annoyance at an infestation of "jiggers."

Cartersville, Ga. 21st May 1864

I wrote you a brief pencil note after the battle of Resaca, but have had no other opportunities of writing or sending a letter. We are having a day of rest here, & getting our clothes washed & preparing for another twenty days without baggage, & I take the opportunity of being once more near pen and ink to write to you.

We advanced to this point from Cassville yesterday, my division being in front & skirmishing all the way (8 miles). The rebels finally retreated over the Etowah river into the Allatoona mountains, burning the bridges behind them. Since we reached Tunnel Hill on the 8th not a day has passed without fighting more or less.

We are very hopeful that we shall force the rebel army to meet us in fair field before long, & then as we believe, the power of the Confederacy in the Gulf States will be broken.

Yesterday was one of the most wearisome days I have experienced. We rose at three, & were in the saddle at four, & got no rest till we got into camp & got our supper at ten in the eve. The day was a boiling hot one, & unfortunately we were accompanied by a brigade of cavalry which impeded while pretending to assist us. The roads were deep in finely pulverized dust, & often for minutes together when the cavalry were moving, you could not see even the outline of a man ten feet from you. The 'dust & the smother' were never so perfectly developed. It was terribly distressing on the men who were marching with knapsacks, though as we marched in line most of them were far enough removed from the road to be partly free from the dust nuisance.

A wash & a change of clothes were never so welcome especially as we had not got near our baggage or changed a shirt for nearly three weeks. The greatest of our annoyances however, was the absence of all mess-chests. To make a plate of a hard cracker, cut your bacon with a pocket knife, & drink your coffee out of an old oyster can, is rather more primitive a style of life than I should ordinarily choose. I think we shall manage to crowd our mess chest into the forage wagon on the next trip, & I shall have a change of under clothing in my saddle valise, & shall be very comfortable.

As for the sleeping on the ground in a blanket without undressing, it has become second nature to us, & we do not pine for the luxury of a camp cot even. At Rocky Face ridge it was a little uncomfortable, for the whole hill was a mass of quartz rock, so hard that the elements had not softened or rounded the edges of the fragments, & one slept on sharp stones, or rather tried to, for what with the discomfort of our bed, & the close presence of the enemy, my nap did not exceed an hour's length.

I used to wonder at the stories of Napoleon's making three or four hour's sleep suffice during an active campaign, but I have learned that in the presence of large armies, a commander even of a division, who does his duty, may think himself well off in getting even so much. Such work is of course wearing, & when we get an extra day of rest, like this, we try to sleep enough to make up in part for lost time.

Camp near Dallas 29th May 1864

Sunday happens to be a comparative day of rest, & I take advantage of the chance to write. Coming as we did from East Tenn. after a Winter which nearly starved our animals, we are much worse off for transportation than any other Corps here, & mail arrangements & everything else depending upon wagons & mules, or horses, are much worse with us than the rest. Consequently we get news from home seldom, & our chances for sending letters away are also rare.

We continue in light marching order, as I have described it to you in my former letters, except that for a week past we have had our mess chest with us, & have lived, so far as food & cooking is concerned, in a less heathenish style than before. Since the 5th of this month, no day has passed without fighting. The enemy gradually retreating through a difficult country to attack in, making occasional stands as at Dalton, Resaca & here, where we attack, usually by outflanking their strong positions & forcing them to fight at disadvantage. When after an engagement more or less severe they again retreat.

We are hopeful that we shall thus push them back on Atlanta where they must make their final & desperate struggle. Each army throws up breastworks & artillery parapets as it moves, & the process is a slow one, especially as most of the country is covered with forest so densely filled with undergrowth as to make it impossible to see your enemy, & on this line as on Grant's thousands of lives are lost on either side while we scarcely see a dozen of the enemy at a time.

No newspaper accounts of the Battle of Resaca have come back to us except one from the Cin. Commercial, written by a correspondent who has a long-standing quarrel with Gen. Schofield, & who tells lies without stint. This writer says my div. was lost in the woods & did not get into the action until an hour after its commencement. Such a thing might well happen in such country without fault, but it was simply untrue.

As I wrote you in another letter my Div. had the advance, Judah's Div. of our Corps following the movement on our right, & the 4th Corps coming in later on our left. We were in line full half an hour before the order to advance was given, waiting for the 4th Corps to come within supporting distance. This correspondent says Judah's Div. was badly cut-up before we got into line, whereas in fact, I sent back two staff officers at different times after our advance to notify Gen. S. that our right flank was exposed because Judah's Div. had not come up, & on account of Gen. S's dissatisfaction with the way that Div. was handled, & the complaints within the command itself, Judah was relieved after the battle & the Div. assigned to Gen. Hascall.

A continuous desultory engagement has been going on here for three days & while I write sharp skirmishing is rattling all along my front, with cannonade along the centre & right. We are habitually on the extreme left of the army, though temporary movements sometimes put other commands for a short period on our left.

The past three days Gen. S. has been too ill to be in the field, & I was in command of the Corps. Yesterday he came out in an ambulance & is again able to be in the saddle, using me however as a general assistant for the Corps to save his strength. We continue on the most pleasant terms & my respect for him increases.

In our present operations we find some new features, & gay. Our supper night before last was the liveliest I ever experienced (I can hardly say enjoyed) though we made very merry over it. The fighting had closed with the day, & in a little valley just in rear of my lines our servants had pitched a tent & cooked our supper, setting the mess chest table just in front of the tent in the open air. The air was so calm that the candles burned without flickering & we were enjoying a good meal after a hard days work, when the rebels took a fancy to open with their batteries all along our front, sending shells in showers above us. We could trace the flight of the shell by the burning fuse till the explosion with a flash & a din almost deafening. They dropped on every side of us.

Our servants would fall flat on the ground as they heard the rush of the shell, & then up again to wait on us, as if the whole party were struck with momentary epilepsy every other minute. Our div. surgeon came in from the hospital to see us, but though hungry would not sit down, & kept dancing like one with St. Vitus' dance, dodging now behind a stump, & again behind a tree, or imitating the servants in falling on the ground, keeping up a half hysterical laugh as if he were trying to think it very funny, but finally he broke & fairly ran off admitting it was too hot for him. There was a general stampede among the teamsters & ambulance drivers in the vicinity, the valley being regarded as an inferno from which they were anxious to escape as soon as possible.

As the enemy were firing in the dark & at random I knew it was of no use to move unless we went further to the rear than duty or inclination would permit, so I insisted upon quietly finishing our supper which we did, making all manner of fun at the 'grand & lofty tumbling' going on all around us. After about fifteen minutes very rapid firing the rebs became quiet & we slept through the night without disturbance. Providentially no one was hurt, though the escapes are always a marvel to me, when the shell fall all around & the air seems filled with the fragments after the explosion.

Nothing seems so formidable & ordinarily does so little damage as shelling. There is much less danger amid their clatter than when you hear the sharp ping of a bullet by your ear, which tells you a rebel sharp shooter is trying to pick you off as you reconnoiter their lines.

We continue in perfect health, the weather is pleasant, the days being often very hot, but the nights cool enough to make a blanket comfortable.

Camp between Dallas & Allatoona, 3rd June 1864

I don't know when I shall be able to write with pen & ink, & so will try to send a pencil line written on my knee in the field under shelter of a little slope near which the bullets of the rebel skirmishers are constantly singing.

This has thus far been the most wearisome campaign I have known. The enemy has adopted the policy of digging most industriously, & in country naturally difficult, they entrench each position with rifle pits & field fortifications so as to make the steps of our progress slow and siege like. It is now almost a month that we have been in constant presence of the enemy, & even the night has been made hideous by the din of war, one party or the other attacking some part of the lines, & getting up an alarm which runs like thunder along the whole front.

Yesterday was a black day in our calendar. We were advancing our Corps into a new position further to the left of the Army, & as we were going with the head of my division through a dense tangled wood our skirmishers got partially separated so that we came without warning upon the rebel pickets, who opened fire upon us. Capt. Saunders, my Adjt. Gen. was mortally wounded by a ball through his left lung. He died in the evening. To correct the line, push back the rebels & advance again was short work, but poor Saunders was gone, & some of the rest of us had narrow escapes. This is the first casualty among the members of my staff since the war began, & it made a gloomy day for us.

Add to this that a violent thunder storm came up deluging us with rain that soaked & drove through all covering & continued till near night, leaving us at the end of our advance, chilled, with chins chattering almost with cold, while we kept up a lively fight with the enemy, & you may imagine that darkness found us by no means a happy company.

When we got our lines in shape & hasty breastworks erected for night defense, I had a little space cleared in the rear with axes, & a fire made & before ten o'clock we were comparatively dry, our boys brought up a pot of coffee & some hard bread, & we rolled ourselves in our overcoats, with our feet to the fire, & finally slept well.

You must make strong effort to believe that all will go well with me, & that I shall be protected as I have been hitherto. I will endeavor to telegraph after every general engagement, but as I have said, the campaign is so anomalous that we can hardly tell when one battle ends & another begins.

I feared last night that I should be sick after my ducking & exposure, but find myself none the worse today. A few days more will, I think accomplish the present purpose of our movement, at least of another stage of it, & then I hope for a few days to rest & recruit our strength.

Allatoona Creek 5th June 1864

Our operations have resulted in again flanking the enemy's strong position & they have again retreated. We are by no means sorry, as it would have cost us terrible slaughter to have stormed their works, & we now hope to force them to fight on more even ground.

We shall move over to the railroad, re-open our communications by that means, & prepare to follow them up again. The preparations may delay us a few days, & we shall not regret the opportunity to rest a little, as we are greatly exhausted. I have never before seen so continuous & protracted a struggle, & although the loss of life has not been enormous, we have been in a constant skirmishing fight which has ceased neither night nor day for twenty days.

A new brigade was added to my Div. yesterday, making three brigades now in the command.

The weather has been very rainy for several days, making the roads very muddy & the fields too soft to move artillery upon them. The sun is shining again this P.M. however & will soon make an improvement.

Gen. Schofield told me this A.M. in a very flattering manner that Gen. Sherman & he agreed to recommend my re-promotion to a Major Generalship, & was only in doubt whether to do so immediately or to wait till a more conclusive time in the campaign should give the recommendation more authoritative force.

Camp near Lost Mountain 8th June 1864

Our left wing is now on the railroad again & I hope our communication with 'God's country' will be more regular for awhile, though when we move again we may have to adopt the old policy of turning Johnston's flank to force him from Lost & Kennesaw mountains.

We have been in this camp since I wrote last, the army moving around us, so that from being the extreme left flank, we are now on the extreme right & a couple of miles separated from the remainder of the line. This was so arranged to cover the movement of trains and hospitals, which have been gradually shifted over to the right, under cover of our presence here.

The rebs have evacuated a long line of tremendously strong works, and we feel quite content to have maneuvered them out, rather than assaulted them.

My camp is high and airy, well watered, & as healthy & comfortable as any camp can well be. We suppose this day will be our last here, new movements being planned for immediate execution. The rest we have had has however been good for us all, & we shall go to work again with renewed vigor. We can expect no decided pause till we have either taken Atlanta or been foiled in a determined effort to take it. First we have to drive the enemy across the Chattahoochee River & cross ourselves, & when we get to Atlanta, we have every reason to expect to find it fortified as thoroughly as Richmond. But we are strong & resolute, & shall not stop for trifles.

Camp near Lost Mountain 11th June 1864

We moved yesterday about four miles to close up on the rebel lines, but had no fighting except a little skirmishing & long cannonading.

The weather has played pranks with us for a week past which we have not liked. We have had very frequent pouring or driving rains, with terrific thunder and lightning. The latter accompaniments have not annoyed us, only keeping us doubtful whether it were not artillery firing when distant, & our batteries till they were quite out of countenance by the superior din when near. But the rain has come in sheets & torrents, miring the spongy ground and spoiling the roads & fords. If it continues so a day or two longer, or even as it is, I fear our movements for some days must be suspended. Between the storms the sun comes out boiling hot, & everything steams with the heat.

I had to laugh the other day at hearing of an article said to be in an Atlanta paper which said that some day the northern women would be made to blush with shame when it was proven to the world that the pictures on their walls, & the diamonds on their persons, were stolen from North Ga. We have not seen as yet, more than two or three houses with pictures on the walls, & none that would be worth removing. As to the diamonds, I suspect that it would be discouraging searching for them, for I have heard of no one who has seen any, or who has heard of anyone who has seen any.

For the past twenty days I have seen but one house other than common log shanties. That house was a very plain one story house, without any attic, having only two common size rooms, & three little closet bedrooms, sided with boards, & every way as plain a house as a day laborer at home would build & own. We occasionally have seen in a village or on a large plantation a respectable house, & one in some instances showily furnished, but they are so rare exceptions to the rule as to be sources of wonder, such farm houses as you may find any where upon our country roads at home, would here appear very stylish residences by contrast with the common houses we see.

Camp on Moses Creek, 5 mi. S.W. of Marietta, 20th June

There have been two little raids on the R.R. behind us since we left the Etowah river, & I fear some letters may have gone the wrong way in consequence. We have been gradually but steadily pushing forward for several days, our corps being now on the extreme right of the army, & it being our luck to turn the flank of the rebel positions and so force them to abandon their works. This we have done now three times in succession, & we are now some eight miles advanced from where we were when I wrote last.

Their works have been of very formidable character, being thick breastworks of heavy logs covered on the outside with several feet thickness of earth, with batteries placed at intervals along the line in commanding positions covered by still better fortifications. It has not been our policy to assault these lines in front, & by flanking them we have gradually forced them to give up one line after another. I doubt if any other country is so furrowed by field fortifications as this.

Our greatest discouragement, however has been the rain. There has been scarce any cessation for two weeks, & the soil is such that quicksands form everywhere, making it dangerous to cross the smallest rivulet. The country is full of little sandy bottoms which are here called lagunes, being a sort of quicksand marsh in which horse & rider are in danger of being swallowed up, & wagons or artillery become inextricably mired almost instantly.

Our command has kept ahead of the work assigned it, & has more than met the expectations of Gens. Sherman & Schofield. On our advance day before yesterday we turned the rebels' flank which rested on a rocky ridge covered by a low muddy creek in front. We pushed in past them, gained a ridge & knoll not quite as high as theirs, threatening their rear. They quickly moved back their flank, doubling it round & we opened on each other with artillery almost simultaneously, we being a few seconds ahead. The rebel battery was covered by woods, our[s] was on open ground just behind the crest of the knoll. It made one of the finest artillery duels I have seen, more interesting however, when seen a little on one side than it was from horseback just in rear of our battery as I rode from one part of the line to another at the moment they opened fire from both sides.

Two staff officers & an orderly were with me, & our progress as we trotted across the range of fire with shells exploding & solid shot plowing the ground around, was watched by a large & interested line of spectators. The infantry was covered from fire by the contour of the ground, & the artillery had it all to themselves. It was magnificent. We are confident the rebs must go back of the Chattahoochee as fast as they can get there, & the villainous weather is hindering us from hurrying them as we could wish.

The campaign has been a remarkable one for continuous hard work. We have been fighting nearly every day almost two months, yet have had no general & sanguinary engagement except at Resaca. The policy I have mentioned has kept us crowding on the enemy's lines, forcing him to leave one position after another, without severe fighting, yet always skirmishing.

It involves also daily personal reconnaissance from the skirmish lines & consequently I have been more frequently under fire & in range of the rebel bullets than in all my experience before. Usually we have a battle & then one side or the other is withdrawn, so that days or weeks intervene before we come to close quarters again, but here it has been ding dong day in & day out—& even night & day.

Near Marietta Ga 24th June 1864

This is the third fair day since the rain ceased. We keep moving little by little, & every day brings its battle large or small, though we get no general engagement. We are crowding in on Johnston gradually & expect to force him to abandon all his positions north of the Chattahoochee river. Line upon line of fortifications is constructed only to be abandoned, & so we go forward entrenching & fortifying step by step.

The rebels are now nearly in horse shoe form, the apex of the angle or sharp corner being at Kennesaw mountain, a high, isolated, double knob which stands out very prominently in the landscape. Some ten days ago their line was nearly East & West from the Mountain, but we have swung in on them both right and left, till the line is the form I have mentioned, whilst they still hold tenaciously to the mountain. They have a double reason for this, for the crest is not only unassailable by direct assault but affords them the most perfect opportunity of looking down upon & viewing every movement of ours, & the position of our camps, an advantage in itself worth half an army. Our operations aim to force them to abandon the mountain without attacking it directly.

It is rumored that an important step toward it was taken last evening by part of the troops of the center, but I have no particulars as yet.

I did not tell you that I was stunned by the explosion of a shell at Resaca, because it was not true. A shell exploded amongst three of us, Gen Manson of my div., Gen. Harker & myself. Harker was slightly wounded in the leg. Manson was knocked down, & has been off duty ever since, on account of the concussion of the brain, & I was simply deafened for a few seconds. It was a providential escape, for neither of us had the skin broken upon us whereas the bystanders thought we were all killed, & it was for a time so reported.

If I told you all the narrow escapes you would be kept uneasy all the time, & it is much better that you should only reflect upon the fact that so far I am unhurt, & the escapes will do to talk about at home, when the war is over, & I can fight my battles over again by the fireside.

Cheney's near Marietta 29th June 1864

Today is a day of comparative quiet after two busy days. I wrote you on Sun. of the movements I was then making, & on Mon. I followed them up by an advance of two other brigades of my command, driving the rebs from a strong entrenched hill in my front & gaining some two miles of ground on this road, called the 'Sandtown road'.

I am on the extreme right (south) flank of the enemy, & meet only their cavalry & detached bodies of troops, without running into their continuous & heavy lines of fortifications.

While I was making the movement, two attacks & attempts to carry the enemy's line by assault were made, in front of Thomas' & McPherson's Corps, both of which failed to break the line, which is a very strong one.

The orders had at first assigned that my command should assist in the assault nearer the center, but Gen. Sherman finally concluded that I could do more good by the flank movement & changed the order accordingly, for which I was not sorry, as I knew the result of the assaults must be very doubtful, & whether successful or not would have cost the lives of a large portion of my command, whilst the movement I did make was with little loss, & Gen.

Sherman himself said accomplished the only valuable result of the whole day's fighting. The positions we took will be most important in the movements of the next few days.

This morning I rode around my lines with Maj. Gens. Thomas, Schofield, & [O.O.] Howard, Brig. Gens. [William] Whipple & [John] Brannan with a cortege of staff & other officers & escort, making quite a formidable cavalcade which came to inspect my new position with reference to proposed plans, of which I will say nothing till they are in operation, lest my letter miscarry. In the assault by Thomas' Corps, Harker's brigade had the lead, & poor Harker was mortally wounded. A more gallant little officer the Army does not contain.

Opdyke had the command of the skirmish line (so Gen. Howard told me this morning) & was therefore in the fore-front, yet came out unhurt, for which I am personally thankful, & send Lucy my most hearty congratulations. I am glad he was there, since he came out safe, for he has added to the distinction he has already gained. If he were senior Col. of the brigade I should be sure he would be made Brigadier in Harker's place. I hope he will be anyhow.

The weather here has been very hot for some days past, the men occasionally dropping in the ranks from the heat. My hd. qrs. since Tuesday have been in an open grove in front of a house of a better class than we have commonly met, & we are very pleasantly situated (we shall probably move tomorrow) but before that we were in the woods, where I was attacked by the chizoes (commonly called jiggers) a species of wood tick which bite & burrow in the skin, causing the most fearful burning & itching, & even festering of the bite. I counted last night over fifty such bites in a space four inches wide around one ankle, & both my legs are almost covered with them to the knees. They form small purplish blotches from an eighth to a quarter of an inch in diameter, & even larger, & in spite of the application of brine, aqua ammonia & etc. burn & sting for days, & if scratched (as who can help scratching) fester & become sores that linger. My legs look as though I had the small pox.

I shall keep out of the woods in future if I can find an open spot to camp in, even if the sun is at 130 degrees. Scorpions with tail in air, occasionally march through our tents, or over our blankets, but I have heard of no one being hurt by them, & doubt if they are very venomous in so high a latitude.

Beautiful little lizards are very abundant, & though the soldiers say they are poisonous, I believe them harmless. They certainly are very timid, & get out of our way if they can.

The private soldiers find great difficulty in getting proper change of clothing, & keeping clean, & many naturally become careless, so that it is no strange thing to see men sitting around a camp naked, with their shirts in their hands, busily hunting the gray-backs as the common body-lice are called, 'gray-back' being also, as you have perhaps noticed, a soldiers name for rebels, which makes a grim kind of joke of it.

The cutting down of transportation & marching light, always lops off the little extras of the ration first, & so soap becomes scarce & cleanliness almost impossible. Of course there is the same difference among soldiers in the field as among people at home. Some will be clean and free from vermin, & others become pests to all about them by their filthiness, & the circumstances prevent the application of proper discipline, because we cannot furnish the means of cleanliness. The Jiggers have led me off on a theme I think I have never before written you about, but it is a very common feature of soldier life in a rough campaign, & is therefore part of the history.

Near Marietta, 3rd July 1864
We have been gradually pushing our right wing forward, & this morning find the rebels have been forced to evacuate Kennesaw Mountain, which has been their stronghold during the month past.

This is the third time our Corps has by its movements dislodged the enemy from their important positions. This however has occurred naturally from the fact that we have been kept on the flank & consequently it became our particular province to extend our lines past & around those of the rebels.

At every move we have been confident they would go South of the Chattahoochee, but having been disappointed several times, we now make no farther calculations, only as we can see. The weather is intensely hot, & the men often fall from sun-stroke on the march.

If we now succeed in occupying the line of the Chattahoochee, I think it not unlikely the paymasters will be ordered on at once, & the money question disposed of.

> Cox's next letter discussed his dismay at the horrors of war, not only for the soldiers, but also for civilians:

Camp near Chattahoochee River, 7th July 1864
We have passed during the last three days from the extreme right to the extreme left of the Army. We had turned the enemy's flank there, & so compelled his abandonment of Kennesaw Heights & Marietta, & the Army of the Tenn., McPherson's, passed to our front, leaving us for a day in reserve, then we moved across to the rail-road & are now, as I said on the left again, that being our original position when we joined the army in May.

The rebels are all South of the Chattahoochee except a small force holding the head of the R.R. bridge on this side, & even this may have crossed since yesterday P.M. We shall probably be delayed a day or two making preparations for further movements, & then will attempt the crossing of the river, & if we succeed in getting over, shall be only some eight or nine miles from Atlanta.

The weather has been intensely hot, & for some ten days has been dry, so that the streams are falling, & we are beginning to find some difficulty in getting camping grounds with sufficient supply of water for our troops. Even such a command as mine requires a great deal of water, & the common wells of the country are only as a drop in the bucket. Indeed, we make no account at all of them in our calculations.

My attention has been forcibly drawn of late, to some of the horrors of war which have been brought out in stronger relief in this campaign than I have ever seen them before. Most of the people fly from their homes on the approach of our army, & it would be well if all did, for the habits of pillage & destruction are so inveterate, especially with the troops which came up from the Mississippi, that nothing is safe & nobody respected. Soldiers enter houses & carry off the last quart of meal or bushel of corn, drive off the cows, slaughter the hogs, sack the house & go on, leaving a family utterly stripped & desolate—their food gone, their growing grain trampled down & destroyed when not used for forage, their gardens stripped of the last vestige of a vegetable, & so the people sit in black despair, with no hope of escape from starvation.

A case came to my notice day before yesterday which is only a specimen of what is occurring. Some soldiers went to a house & after robbing it of everything else they wanted, they drove away the only milk cow the woman had. She pled that she had an infant which she was obliged to bring up on the bottle, & that it could not live if it could not have milk. They had no ears for such appeals, & the cow was driven off. The natural result was, that in two days the child died, of starvation chiefly, though it went off quickened by disease induced by its mother trying to keep it alive on food it could not digest. I heard of this case when the child was dead, & two or three of the neighbors were getting stealthily together to dig its grave.

A woman came to me the same morning & said the cavalry had taken the last mouthful from her, telling her they were marching & hadn't time to draw their rations, but she would be fed by applying to us. The scoundrels knew that we are forbidden to issue rations to citizens, & so robbed her & her children of their bread. They sacked the house of an old man who has seven daughters, by a second wife, all young things, & he came to me in utter distress, not a mouthful in that house for twenty four hours—their garden & farm utterly ruined, the country in the same condition, & no means of traveling or carrying anything even if he tried to move away!

Of course in such extreme cases, I try to find some way of keeping people from death, & usually send them to the rear, in our empty wagon trains, but their helpless condition is very little bettered by going.

These things are done chiefly by stragglers & skulkers, against whom Gen. Sherman has issued very stringent orders, but orders don't reach them. The people cannot tell who has done them the mischief, & the rascals are gone before the case comes before anyone who will interest himself in it.

The evil is the legitimate outgrowth of the hue & cry raised by our Christian people of the North against protecting rebel property &e. Officers were deterred from enforcing discipline in this respect by public opinion at home, & now the evil is past remedy. You know the history of the matter, & how from the first I have insisted that the war was prolonged, the army disintegrated & weakened & the cause itself jeopardized, because discipline was construed as friendliness to the rebels.

I get heart-sick sometimes at seeing such things, & feel as though we mocked heaven in asking a blessing on such scenes of rapine & wickedness. War is bad enough however at best.

> From July 5 to 8, Sherman spent time trying to find a way across the Chattahoochee River in order to force Johnston to retreat into Atlanta. Cox and his men accomplished the task. On July 8, his division caught the rebels napping by moving stealthily to and over the river east of Atlanta, exposing Johnston's right flank. By the morning of the twentieth, Schofield and McPherson were just a few miles east of Atlanta.[12]
>
> Cox wrote several lengthy letters about his movements during this period, including the happy news that his position was so strong that he could take a long swim in the river. He also wrote with disgust that General Hovey, who had abandoned the army, had gotten a promotion despite his incompetence.

Isham's Ford, Chattahoochee Riv. 10th July 1864

We were expecting when I wrote from Smyrna Camp ground that we should remain several days quietly in camp, but the same night we received orders to take the advance & attempt the crossing of the Chattahoochee, which we have now safely accomplished!

As this crossing a river in presence of an enemy is one of the most delicate operations in war, I will try to give you some idea of it by describing more minutely than I commonly do, the steps we took to accomplish it. In getting Johnston out of Marietta & off the Kennesaw heights we had extended our right so as to turn his left flank & threaten his line of communications with Atlanta, & the great bulk of our army had thus been concentrated west of the rail-road. The enemy were thus made to suppose that we would attempt to cross somewhere in that direction, but instead of this we were suddenly moved from the right across to the extreme left, North East of the railroad, & at ten o'clock in the evening of the 7th I was notified that we would probably be moved to the Chattahoochee next morning.

I sent an aide to notify my brigades to be ready for movement at day break, & lay down with candle & matches close beside me. I dozed until half past twelve when an orderly brought a dispatch containing my orders to move the div. to the mouth of Soap creek on the Chattahoochee a distance of about five miles, starting at four A.M. To make necessary arrangements occupied half an hour, & I lay down again & slept a little, waking two or three times, & then rose at three, routed out the staff & servants, got a cup of coffee & was in the saddle at four, just as it was getting fairly light.

We marched quietly along in the cool early light, making only one halt for a few minutes to rest the men. The other div. of the Corps followed a mile or so at the rear, & behind it came the pontoon train. In about two hours we reached the creek, where we found the remains of a bridge smoking, the rebels having burned it the night before. The creek was at the bottom of a rocky gorge, with a dam a few score rods up the creek. The sides of the gorge were nearly perpendicular & some fifteen or twenty feet high at the bridge, while a little distance from it they rose to a height of fifty & sixty feet. Along the river ran a ridge some two hundred feet high, through which the creek broke, roaring over its rocky bed more like a romantic mountain stream than any I have seen lately.

I caused a few men to clamber down into the gorge & up the other side, where they deployed as skirmishers & advanced some distance to cover the crossing of a brigade, part of which followed the example of the advance guard, in clambering down & up the bank, & part picked their way along the slippery footing of the dam. Either was a slow process, but ordering Col. Cameron to get his brigade over & extend a line of skirmishers & pickets along the crest of the ridge bordering the river, half a mile above the creek, I directed the rest of the div. to turn into a by-road half a mile back & proceed down toward the mouth of the creek on the side nearest us.

All were ordered to proceed without noise, & if they met no enemy to allow none of our men to show themselves where they could possibly be seen from the other bank of the river. All fires were forbidden, & every precaution taken to keep the enemy ignorant of our approach. My brigades & the artillery were then massed in silence behind the wooded ridge bordering the river, & I took a few orderlies & the staff with a guide I had picked up, & climbed the ridge to reconnoiter the other side of the Chattahoochee.

On the summit was a large open field. As we approached this I ordered all to halt but Maj. Wells & the guide, & dismounting continued the ascent with these. The guide was so fearful of being seen that he led us a round about way, down ravines & through thick bushes, till we finally came out on the river side of the ridge & into the open at its lower edge. Here hidden behind bushes we used our field glasses & could make out a brass cannon bearing on the ferry, where we expected to lay our pontoon bridges, & could see some Confederate soldiers about, apparently on picket duty at the ferry. They seemed scarce a stone's throw from us.

We learned from the citizen that the rebs had occasionally fired their cannon at our cavalry scouts who had visited the river bank, but nothing indicated that any large force was on the other side, or that they had any warning of our movement. To complete our preparations in secrecy & then do our work rapidly was therefore our plan.

We learned of an old fish-dam formed of loosely laid stones a half mile up the river, & that upon this the water was probably shallow enough for our men to ford. The brigade which I had crossed over Soap creek was destined to cross the river by this dam at the concerted time when the canvas pontoon boats should be ready to launch, & as soon as they got a foothold on the opposite bank, a regiment was to dash across in the boats, the two parties would meet as soon as possible, drive away the rebel force & hold the opposite heights while the pontoon bridges were speedily constructed & the whole division thus crossed & put into position.

Hascall's div. was to remain half a mile back on the road ready to support us or cover our retreat as occasion might require. Our batteries were to be put in position along our ridge, out of sight from the other side, but where they could quickly open & silence the rebel artillery when the movement began. After examining the ground, I came down the hill, soaked with the heavy dew, which had not yet dried off the grass, not omitting to stop to gather a few handfuls of blackberries which were growing so lusciously in the open field that I could not resist their temptation. Surely none others were so sweet, picked cool & dripping with the morning dew, dead ripe (for the rebel rifles had kept all black berrying parties out of that field) they made an excellent lunch after my early breakfast, and none the less piquant because we had to dodge behind the bushes as we picked & keep them carefully between us & the rebel marksmen as a screen.

By this time Gen. Schofield had come up & I reported to him the results of my reconnaissance, & he went with me again to some of the principal points. The pontooners moved their trains as near as practicable, & went to work setting up their boats, which are simply a canvas cover stretched over a light scow-shaped frame of wood. On these light beams are laid, & across the beams a flooring of plank, the bridge being begun at one bank of a river, & boats & flooring successively added and anchored till the bridge reaches the opposite bank. Cameron's brigade found their ground very difficult & rocky, & the undergrowth so dense as to make it very slow work finding their way to the fish dam.

About noon, I sent Major Wells to see what progress they were making & to examine as closely as the ground would permit, the nature of the ford. He came back about two o'clock almost exhausted from heat & fatigue, & reported that the ford could probably be used, & that Cameron could reach it by three o'clock from the ridge. The day had become intensely hot, the sun poured down so scorchingly that though the pontoons were nearly ready it was thought best not to attempt the crossing till a little later.

An occasional straggler had been seen by the enemy & they had fired two or three cannon shot & shell at our side of the river, but they did not seem aware of any considerable force near them. I ordered Cameron to form an advanced guard of fifty strong & reliable men to try the ford first. If these got over, he was to push over all his brigade but one regt. which was to be kept in reserve. The whole movement to be covered by strong lines of skirmishers deployed on our side of the river, to keep down any fire from the enemy. This part of the movement was to begin at half past 3.

At four, two regts from the balance of the div. were to deploy as skirmishers under cover of the woods where I was, below the creek. These at a signal were to rush down across the open bottom lands & gain a line of trees and bushes on the river margin & engage any enemy which might appear on the opposite bank. Our hope was to surprise the enemy before they could accumulate any considerable force against us, & we were completely successful.

At the time fixed I stood at the edge of the open bottom land, concealed by a clump of trees, listening anxiously for any firing above on the river which would indicate that Cameron was meeting opposition. The half hour passed & no shots heard. 'Col. Byrd, you may advance your skirmishers.' At the command out rushed our men from cover & with a hurrah had reached the river edge before the astounded rebs were fairly aware that they had not seen an apparition. Had the men risen from the water they could not have been more astonished. Bang! goes their cannon, & bang! its shell as it explodes wide of our line, but quick as the puff of smoke showed the mark to aim at, one of our batteries opens on the spot, & our shell burst around the rebel cannoneers. Our riflemen however do the best work.

They quickly drove the rebel skirmishers from the river, & when the cannon which had been drawn back under cover to load, was pushed forward to fire, they poured in such a hail of bullets that the men left the gun unable to sight or discharge it. At the instant out float the twenty five white pontoon boats from the mouth of the creek, & each loaded with twenty men of the 12th Kentucky, & they pull with might and main for the opposite shore. They land, form a line & rush up the ridge on the run, cheering as they go. The rebs fire a few more shots & scamper leaving behind the cannon with the load in it which the artillerists had not dared to fire. Our men push on up the ridge & near the Summit, meet Cameron's men coming down from the ford above.

The only danger is that the enemy may be warned by the flying cavalry pickets & be down on us before we are ready. Every man works with a will. The boats continue to ferry over fresh troops, while the pontooners strain their muscle to lay a bridge with another set. Pioneer parties with picks, shovels & axes are set at work as soon as we have the rest of the hill to entrench. Three brigades are over before dark, & in an hour or two more the first bridge is done, & my fourth brigade & artillery are over, the division has a good breast work thrown up, we are ready for Johnny reb, & congratulate each other on being the first div. over the Chattahoochee.

Gen. Schofield comes down & joins the congratulations. He has watched the movement from a hill on the north side & is delighted with it. The signal corps telegraph the news to the rest of the Army that the dreaded obstacle of the Chattahoochee has been overcome by a successful surprise & we have a firm lodgment on Johnston's flank. The rebels saw that they were too late, & have made no effort to drive us back.

The rest of the army are to cross under protection of our fortifications, & I have spent the past two days in extending and strengthening my lines. I am as yet the only General officer on this side, though part of Hascall's div. has been sent over to me.

Johnston will not be foolish enough however to make an attack now as we have two good pontoon bridges behind me & the rest of the army can come whenever Sherman is ready. Therefore I feel secure though I stand here alone. I did not lose a man in crossing. The rebs were scared out of their senses, & were at best a mere outpost of cavalry with the one piece of artillery which we captured.

The risk we ran was that by some hitch in our plan, or delay in carrying it out, the enemy would get wind of our movement and quietly arrange a heavy force to oppose us, so that our advance would be cut to pieces or driven back before we could get a footing. As it was everything went like clockwork, & we are now the objects of a generous envy for our success.

Gen. Schofield said the movement was the prettiest thing he ever saw done, & one of his staff officers said the Gen. fairly clapped his hands with excitement when he saw the boats pull steadily across the river, & the line then form & advance up the hill with a rush.

The steepness of the ascent & the broken nature of the country has surprised some. My lines are nearly a mile from the bridge with steep ascent all the way, & the ridge is broken everywhere with deep & dangerous ravines. My hd. qrs. are in a grove beside a log cabin some 300 yards in rear of our breastworks.

Last evening we all went down from hd. qrs. & had a swim in the Chattahoochee by moonlight. The first swim I have had in three years!

Isham's Ford, Ga. 13th July 1864

We have had several days quiet in the pleasantest camp with one exception, which I have occupied since entering Ga. My hd. qrs. are in a pleasant grove near a log house which affords us a good well & a clear spot for our little encampment where we are free from scorpions, chizoes [jiggers or chiggers], & spiders, no small item in selecting locations for our camp.

My line of defense along a ridge in front is so strong that I feel as safe as if in Ohio, & until we move we are determined to enjoy the rest, our only labor being that of making up official reports of our campaign thus far.

We saw in the papers day before yesterday the notice of Dory's confirmation as Capt. This gratifies me as it relieves him of all doubt as to his remaining in the service, his regt. having completed its term of enlistment & being mustered out, & it also gives him a grade of deserved promotion in permanent staff duty.

As an offset to this the dispatches of yesterday are said to contain the news that Brig. Gen. Hovey has been made a Maj. Gen. If true, this is a wanton insult to the whole army in the field. This officer was the junior div commander in our Corps, through favoritism of Gov. Morton of Indiana having been assigned to a div. of new Ind. troops, whilst two senior brigadiers from the same state were commanding brigades in the Corps.

About a month ago he tendered his resignation in the presence of the enemy, an offense for which officers of lower grade are cashiered, the very last papers bringing an order of the War Dept. dishonorably dismissing a list of Capts. & Lieuts. for this very thing.

Gen. Sherman himself told me that he had endorsed Gen. Hovey's resignation strongly condemning his conduct & recommending that the resignation be promptly accepted. Gen. H. did not hesitate to say he resigned because he was not content with the relative importance of his command in the Corps & had not been promoted.

Only a short time before he resigned Gen. Schofield had asked to be relieved of him on the ground of incompetency to command a div. He left and his division was divided between me & Hascall. We have remained on duty in the field. Manson, his senior, is disabled by injuries received in the battle of Resaca where Hovey was in reserve & had no part in the fight, yet we hear that this skulker is made a Major Gen. & no recognition is given to the other general officers in the Corps.

The plain reason is the fear of Gov. Morton & the administration of his political opposition in Indiana, where he has had some prominence in the Democratic party! These are plain facts every one of which is susceptible of demonstration.

How the world is governed! Had we no higher motive for continuing this struggle than the expectation of honor & promotion for faithful service, who would stay in it a day? Among the discouragements against which men of honest determination to serve the country have continued this fight, I reckon the galling mismanagement of the army by the administration as by no means the least.

How long our delay here may be prolonged we do not know. Yesterday Gen. Schofield thought it not improbable we should advance today, but no orders have yet come, & we live on in the normal condition of soldiers, i.e. utter uncertainty what the day may bring forth. It is regarded doubtful whether the enemy can stand a siege in Atlanta, & the better opinion is that whenever in danger of being invested in the town they will retreat further South.

Three miles from Atlanta 21st July 1864

Yours of the 10th inst. came last evening, & was very welcome, meeting me as it did when I came to my hd.qrs. camp after a hot & wearisome day in which I had been pushing along the Atlanta road, gaining foot by foot all day in face of the enemy who obstinately contested our advance & kept up a hot skirmish incessantly.

We are in the centre. Gen. Thomas' army being on the right & McPherson on the left. We began the movement from the Chattahoochee on Sunday, pushing forward by converging lines which have now brought us very near the fortifications around Atlanta & into close connection with each other, so that the game begins to assume the general character of the fight about Kennesaw.

In the saddle at dawn & no rest till night, has been the rule since we started, & this must excuse the delay I have made in writing. We keep pushing along till night, then send back for our wagons, & when they get up, which is sometimes as late as nine o'clock, we have our boys cook a hasty meal, & to bed expecting to be roused by orders or despatches through the night, & up & off again at daylight.

We are now so close upon the rebel lines that the program this morning is a little changed, & I am seizing the minutes between six & seven to begin a letter, whether I shall be able to finish it or not. As I write I hear the whistle of the locomotive at the station in Atlanta & they are hearing the booming of our guns all along the North & East of their city. Last night there was not an hour of quiet, the pop-popping of the skirmish line being kept up without pause, & an occasional cannon sending a shell gave warning that they were awake in the batteries.

The advance along a road contested by the enemy is perhaps a little different from the idea of it you at home would have. Take yesterday as a sample of the whole. My camp of the night before was formed of three brigades in two lines across the principal road, another brigade in reserve, the artillery in the intervals all in position of battle, a strong skirmish line of pickets covering the front & flanks some three hundred yards in advance. In the morning we drew in the flanks of the skirmish line, reducing it to about the length of one brigade across the road, & it was ordered to advance.

The men go forward keeping the line at right angles to the road, stopping for neither creek nor thicket, down ravines, over hills, the skirmishers trotting from a big tree to a large stone, taking advantage of everything which will cover them & keeping the general form of the line & their distance from each other tolerably correct. The main body of troops file into the road & march four abreast, a battery near the leading brigadier. Presently a shot is heard off on the right, then two or three more in quick succession, & a bullet or two comes singing over the head of the column. 'They've the Johnnies,' say the boys in the ranks & on we move, the skirmish line still pushing right along. This proves to be only a rebel picket which has fired a gun to apprize their commanders that the 'Yanks' are coming.

We move forward a few hundred paces, & bang, bang, bang, & a rattle of rifles too fast to count. The column is halted & we ride up to the skirmish line to see what is up. A pretty strong body of rebs about some old log houses with a good skirmish line on either side, where our men must approach over two or three hundred yards of open field. A regt. is moved up to the nearest cover on either side of the road, a section of artillery catches up to the front, the guns are unlimbered & a couple of shells go careening into the improvised fort, exploding and scattering logs & shingles right and left.

Out rush the rebs in confusion, forward with a rush & a hurrah go our men over the open, getting a volley from the other side, then into the woods they go. The rebs run, two or 3 are caught, perhaps, as prisoners, & two or three of ours are carried to the rear on stretchers, wounded or killed, & on we go again for a little distance. This is what we call light skirmishing. Sometimes we find extemporized breastworks of rails & etc., requiring the use of more force to dislodge the enemy, & then finally we push up to well constructed lines of defense where we halt for slower & heavier operations.

A day or two will determine how protracted a contest we must have before Atlanta.

A few days before Cox wrote his next letter, John Bell Hood had replaced Johnston as the Confederate commander because of Jefferson Davis's unhappiness with the latter's defensive-oriented strategy. Hood promised he would be aggressive and, on July 21, he launched the Battle of Atlanta. Hood tried to swing around and destroy McPherson's army. While Hood was thwarted, McPherson was killed and was replaced temporarily by his deputy, General "Black Jack" Logan, a political general from Illinois.[13]

Sherman told Grant on the 25th that, since Atlanta was well fortified, he would try to force Hood to abandon it by cutting his supply line, the Macon Railroad to the south. To do so he engaged in yet another zig-zag movement, moving the Army of the Tennessee from the extreme left to the extreme right. This left Cox, as he put it, "on the extreme left flank again, necessitating a change of all my lines, a ticklish thing to do in the presence of an enterprising and desperate enemy."

In his memoirs, Hood admitted that "the holding of Atlanta depended upon our ability to hold intact the road to Macon." On July 28, he tried to stop Sherman's efforts to break the supply line at the battle of Ezra Church.[14] On July 25, Hood had issued a fateful general field order that said, in part, "SOLDIERS: Experience has proved to you that safety in time of battle consists in getting into close quarters with your enemy."[15] Ignoring the lessons his men had learned about the power of the defensive, Hood was issuing a trumpet call to return to Napoleonic-style frontal charges. His final such charge would be at the Battle of Franklin on November 30, 1864.

The battle at Ezra Church proved Hood's approach to be misguided. There, Hood's men were losing their stomach for assaulting intrenchments; Cox wrote later, "the implied conditions of his appointment to the command fettered him, and he could not adopt within a week the policy of his predecessor.... At one point, some rebels stolidly refused to continue the assaults and despite officers waving swords to encourage them, they remained motionless and silent, refusing to budge."[16]

Soon afterward, Hood moved into Atlanta and Sherman began a siege of the city. Cox hoped the city would fall quickly and he thought that his command, with responsibilities to cut the supply line, might get the credit. However, he was thwarted, at first, because of another political-military war. On August 3, Sherman ordered that "Major General Schofield with his own command and General (John) Palmer's corps [the XIV] will move directly on the [Macon Railroad] and not stop until he has absolute control of that railroad."[17] Palmer claimed he outranked Schofield and would not take orders from him. The offensive was delayed for two days while Sherman sorted out the matter of command and the opportunity to break the supply line was lost.[18]

Cox's next letters discussed these developments and his unhappiness about the lost opportunity and the pettiness of Palmer.

Before Atlanta 23rd July 1864

We found that our movements of the 20th past put our column considerably in advance of the others, so for a day or two had nothing to do but strengthen our lines & slightly advance some portion of them. I spent the morning after writing last in reconnoitering & carefully examining our position, giving such orders as were necessary & finishing other business for the day.

Yesterday we closed in on the city of Atlanta, the rebels taking to their interior line of fortifications. Hood, who has superseded Johnston made desperate efforts to drive back our flanks, but has been repulsed with loss each time. Yesterday we had a hard fight on our left, & for a time things looked squally there, McPherson being killed at the beginning of the engagement & the brunt of the action coming on his troops. I went over to their support, but was not under the necessity of going into the fight, being used only to cover their flank. I think we shall have Atlanta soon, & then perhaps a little rest.

Before Atlanta 27th July 1864

The past three days have been spent in the old way, closing in, fighting, fortifying, & pushing in again. The rebels have made some desperate efforts to break our lines but have been repulsed with terrible punishment.

Their losses in their attack on Friday last were not less than 12,000 & it is said the Atlanta paper admits even 20,000 loss. Either way they can ill afford it, as our losses were not over 3,500 all told.

The Army of the Tenn. has gone across to the right flank. They made the move between midnight & daybreak, leaving us on the extreme left flank again, & necessitating a change of all my lines, a ticklish thing to do in the presence of an enterprising & desperate enemy. We got through with it without confusion & in perfect silence, so that it was all complete before the rebs had any knowledge of what was going on.

We are full of hope that a very few days must see us in possession of Atlanta. Indeed I shall not be surprised if the rebs evacuate this very night. Our movements of today may well induce them to do so.

There is a point some eight miles beyond Atlanta, where if they make a stand it may be necessary for us to dislodge them. Further South than that it can hardly be that we shall go for a month or two, & if we are speedily successful here, we may look for a little repose.

Before Atlanta 31st July 1864

We are expecting to move over to the extreme right of the army again, being now [on] the extreme left. The rebels have made several desperate attacks before our lines, but have been uniformly repulsed with great loss. These assaults have not happened to come upon our div. front, though we were actively engaged in assisting in repelling the most desperate one made, our artillery especially doing them great damage.

We are gradually closing around Atlanta & are confident that we shall soon force the rebels to evacuate, by cutting off their only remaining railroad connection with the South. They seem inclined to hold on to the last, & have been using up their army rapidly in their attacks since we crossed the Chattahoochee. The most moderate estimates put their total losses within the past two weeks at thirty thousand, while we have not lost one third that number.

The season here has not been as hot as I expected, & we have not suffered from the drought which has scorched the country north of the Ohio. Showers have been frequent enough to keep everything fresh & green, & though we have had sultry days, we have as yet had no weather more severe than the ordinary summers of Northern Ohio.

Before Atlanta 3rd Aug. 1864

I have a few moments to write before the Postboy comes & scribble a line to assure you of my safety after the movement of yesterday which completed the change from our former position on the left to the extreme right of the army. Last night I was too fatigued to write after getting into camp.

From noon the day before yesterday I had had but one meal & two hours sleep, & was therefore prepared to do justice to the sleep, though not to the eating, for when I lose a night's rest, I must get some sleep before eating much, my appetite for food being gone till that time. We shall continue the flanking process till we get the rebs out of Atlanta.

Before Atlanta Ga. 7th Aug. 1864

I telegraphed you last evening that I was safe & well, thinking the papers might have some news of our fighting yesterday, which would cause you uneasiness.

The past three days have disgusted me exceedingly. It was intended to make a decisive effort to turn the enemy's left, & the 14th Corps was ordered to report to Gen. Schofield, so that he might push in with two Corps. [Aug 8th] I had just begun writing when I was called off & we began a movement which advanced the right wing of my lines about a mile, crowding in close to the rebels principal line of works, occupying those which we assaulted day before yesterday & a ridge considerably in advance of them.

I was about to talk of the unsatisfactory operation of the 4th & 5th inst. We had crossed Utoy creek, swinging round toward the railroad south west of A. & the 14th Corps were to act with us, under Gen. Schofield's orders. It became evident immediately that Gen. Palmer commanding that corps, would not act under Gen. S. if he could help himself, as he claimed to be the Senior officer.

My men were under arms & began their movement which was to support an advance by one div. of Palmer's when the commandant of that div. told me he had no orders to move. This was the beginning of cross-purposes, misunderstandings, half obediences, protests, &e. lasting through two days. No real effort was made to do what it was manifest must be done in occupying ground on the enemy's flank, & finally our corps had to exchange places with them, putting us on the extreme right again, in order that we might swing in with some vigor.

Palmer then was relieved of his command & sent home, but the enemy meanwhile had fortified the ground we might have taken almost without a shot.

Sherman was still anxious to gain the position, & we had to assault, not withstanding the experience of both parties in this campaign has shown how little chance of success there is in assailing entrenched positions. The work fell to my lot, & I ordered an assault by one brigade in column supported by two other brigades deployed in line in rear. We had a fierce fight, our men struggling nobly to get over the works but in vain. The undergrowth & saplings had been half cut off, bent down & interlaced for a hundred yds in front of the breast works, making an entanglement thru which it is all but impossible to make one's way if unopposed & in which an advance in order under fire is out of the question. The breastworks had what we call a 'head-log' protecting the heads of the troops within, & leaving simply a couple or three inches spare between it & the earth parapet, through which they fire. You can imagine the difficulties of struggling up a hill, tripping, falling, getting up & pushing on again, with an incessant deafening roar of musketry, & hail of balls in one's face, & constant explosion of shell around.

[General James] Reilly's men pushed on & the colors of one regt, the 8th Tenn. were planted on the breastworks themselves, but the column had so melted under the fire that it was no longer strong enough to do any good, & the color bearer was either captured or killed. Our men lay down within two rods of that work, & still kept up a fire which forced the rebs to keep hidden, & remained there until the examination of the place showed that pressing the assault further would be a waste of life, when on consultation with Gen. Schofield I withdrew them, a little way only however, for we kept so close, & the other divisions of our corps made such a threatening movement to their flanks, that they abandoned the works in the night, & we occupied them yesterday.

It was terribly sad to go over the ground yesterday, & see our brave fellows lying dead all over the ground where they made the charge, & to realize that they tried to rush up there under fire, when I could hardly get through when I could give my whole attention to my feet. I was with the support during the charge, & as these brigades were kept under cover at the foot of the hills, was in no imminent danger except from chance shots or shell. The attack was made by Reilly's brigade.

My loss is not as heavy as we at first supposed, but is about three hundred & sixty, of whom a hundred were killed outright. Gen. Schofield sent a complimentary message to the troops yesterday, saying that they must not regard themselves failed, for though they did not carry the works in the first assault they forced the enemy to evacuate so shortly after that it was a substantial success, & all knew they had gone as far & done as bravely as men could go & do.

We have heretofore escaped the duty of assailing fortified positions in front except at Resaca, where in the general assault we alone were successful in carrying the breastworks, & our success there is the only one of the kind either party can boast through the whole campaign. It is no wonder that the troops begin to regard it as hopeless work.

In this case it was not entirely certain that strongly made works would be found there, or we should not have been ordered to attack, but faltering 'doless' conduct of others during the two days before had given the enemy time to fortify, & as Gen. Sherman said, a paltry quibble about rank could cost the army perhaps two thousand lives!

The feeling of the rebels on the subject is well shown by one of the picket conversations which is reported. In one of the 'chaffing' talks the pickets sometimes have in the intervals of skirmishing, a 20th corps man hailed a rebel, 'Well, Reb, how many more men have you got left by this time?' 'Oh' answers reb, 'about enough for two more killings.' It is said the opposition to Hood's policy of hurling them against our works has become so strong that he has had to give it up. At any rate they have made no more assaults during the flank movements of last week.

Before Atlanta 11th Aug 1864
Since I wrote last I have not changed my position, except to work in closer to the rebel lines, our own being substantially where they were. A constant & galling fire of pickets and sharp shooters is kept up, & a brisk artillery fire so that shot & shell fall pretty freely in all parts of our camp. I can count half a dozen trees cut off by cannon balls as I sit at my hd. qrs. & stray bullets fly around promiscuously.

My horse brown Peter was shot through & through a couple of hours ago by a rifle ball, as he stood tied to a sapling near our tents. The rebels cannot see us owing to a slight ridge in front, but the curve of the ball's flight brings it down over the slope while it has abundant force yet to kill man or beast. But as this has been the rule rather than the exception ever since we approached Dallas, we have become accustomed to it, & think little of it, except to be thankful that so few accidents happen.

Just before I moved my hd. qrs., as we advanced three days ago, a poor fellow came from the trenches to the ammunition train close to my tents, & was sitting on the tongue of a wagon, when a solid 12 pound shot came over & striking near him ricocheted & took off his leg. He never recovered from the collapse caused by the shock & died in a short time.

Just within my lines & not ten paces from the breastworks stands a loghouse owned by an old man named Wilson. A little before the army advanced to its present position several relations of his with their families came to him from houses regarded in more imminent danger, & they united their forces to build, or dig rather, a place of safety. They excavated a sort of cellar just in rear of the house on the hill side, digging it deep enough to make a room some fifteen ft. square & six ft. high. This they covered over with a roof of timbers, & over that they piled the earth several feet thick, covering the whole with pine boughs to keep the fresh earth from washing.

In this bomb-proof four families are now living, & I never felt more pity than when, day before yesterday, I looked down into the pit & saw there, in the gloom made visible by a candle burning while it was hard day above, women sitting on the floor of loose boards, resting against each other, haggard & worn, trying to sleep away the days of terror, while innocent looking children of four or five years old clustered around the air hole, looking up with pale faces and great staring eyes as they heard the singing of bullets which were flying thick above their sheltering place. One of the women had been bed-ridden for several years before she was carried down there. One of the men was a cripple, the others old & gray. The men ventured up & took a little fresh air behind the breastworks, but for the women, unless they come out at night there is no change. Yet they cling to home, because they have nowhere else to go, & hope we may pass on in a few days & leave them in comparative peace again.

Before Atlanta 13th Aug. 1864

Yours of the 4th inst met me as I came in last evening after a most wearisome day's work. My division was relieved in the morning at day break & marched out of the trenches for a reconnaissance beyond the sight of the army. The original intention was to try to reach the rail-road running from Atlanta to Montgomery but information we received early in the day made it evident that this was impracticable in the time assigned to the duty & we devoted ourselves to the work of moving along the front of the enemy's lines to discover how far & in what directions they extended, the nature of the country, character of the roads, streams, ridges, &e. &e. This is done under fire of course & is a slow & laborious process.

As soon as we passed beyond our picket line we met the enemy's cavalry. These kept up a continuous skirmish, falling back only as they were driven, blocking roads, making as much show of force as possible & in every way annoying us, hindering our advance & endeavoring to discover the object of our movement.

Beside the hindrances of these active demonstrations of opposition, we have to go carefully enough to avoid falling into traps, & leaving ways open by which the enemy could interpose a superior force between us & our own army &e. &e. These are the things which make a 'reconnaissance in force' upon the flanks of a great army a very delicate & hazardous operation, especially when, as in our case, the country is entirely unknown, & we learn it only as we fight for its possession.

Our whole day's work took us over some three miles & back, but it gave us very valuable knowledge, & was therefore labor well spent though it was very hard labor. I got back to my quarters about an hour after dark, got my dinner, read your letter, & went to bed very early. Today we are quiet in camp.

In mid-August, Hood decided to try to cut Sherman's supply line back to Chattanooga and thereby force his retreat. Hood later claimed that while his cavalry made significant strides toward cutting the line, there simply were not enough men to complete the job.[19] Sherman, frustrated by earlier efforts to cut the Macon Railroad, now implemented a comprehensive flanking maneuver aimed at that objective. By the 27th, "all of Sherman's army except the XX Corps was between Atlanta and Sandtown, with Cox's Division the inner part of the 'wheel.'"[20]

While Sherman had not intended this movement to be a subterfuge, it became one when Hood concluded that his effort to cut Sherman's supply line had succeeded. Moreover, an incident on August 27 in which Cox was involved was, by some accounts, critical to convincing Hood that Sherman had in fact retreated.[21] It seems that, on the 27th, a female spy told Hood's subordinate General W. T. Hardee that she had been within Schofield's lines on August 18, where she asked for food. Cox wrote in his *Military Reminiscences* that he told Hardee that allegedly she had met personally with Cox, who refused her and said he had been "living on short rations for seven days, and now that your people have torn up our railroad and stolen our beef cattle, we must live a damn sight shorter." One of Cox's men wrote later, "Those who knew Gen. Cox best never heard an oath pass his lips, and also that no hungry man or woman ever left his presence as long as he had a loaf to divide with them."

In his memoirs Cox wrote a description of the incident, noting that he heard about it from Confederate General Hardee after the war while Cox was Military Governor of western North Carolina. Cox wrote, blushingly, "a laugh was raised at my expense as Hardee in telling the story repeated some profane camp expletives as having added emphasis to the refusal, according to the old woman's account of it. Schofield merrily rallied me on a change of habits of speech when not with my usual associates, and refused to credit my protestation. . . . Hardee helped the fun by pretending to think of other proof that the woman was right; but he went on to give the matter real historical interest by telling how he had taken the woman to Hood that he might learn what she said she had seen and heard." After telling the story, Hardee said, "Hood exclaimed, 'There, Hardee! It proves that it is just as I told you. Wheeler has broken Sherman's communications; he is short of provisions and is retreating north by the Sandtown road. The troops that have moved from the north of the city have gone that way.'"[22]

Cox's letters before these events include a warning that, because he would be on the move, he might not write for a while. In one, he described his movements as Sherman practiced his "zig-zag" strategy.

Before Atlanta 17th Aug. 1864
The rebs are following our example in making raids upon the railroad as [Joseph] Wheeler is now at our rear committing mischief of that sort, it is by no means certain when this will reach you, though the interruption is not likely to be of long duration.

I have been expecting for some days that our continuation of our lines by our right around Atlanta & East Point would result in cutting off our communications for a short time with the North, & you must not be surprised if you should find us in that predicament any time.

East Point, Ga. 21st Aug. 1864
You enquire how it is necessary to change the relative position of the parts of the army so often. I don't know that I can give any intelligible explanation which would not be too long for a letter, but the gist of the reason is that as two armies parallel to each other, both being in entrenchments cannot easily move the whole line at once, the way by which one flank can be most readily extended without the opposite party discovering the movement is by taking troops off from one flank and carrying them over to the other.

Thus suppose the lines of our army to be represented by the marks numbered 1 to 7, representing corps, & the dotted line within to represent the enemy's line. No 1 is taken off the left & put in on the right of No. 7, then No. 2 is taken off & put in again beyond No. 1, & so on, the line being thus extended around until we get behind the enemy's position by gradual stages, when he must abandon his position or be cut off from his supplies & line of retreat. The effort is to make the movement as successful as possible & so leaving pickets out, No. 1 moves quietly off in the night & endeavors to get into the new position partially turning the enemy's flank before he is aware of it or can change his own line in like manner. This is substantially what you hear so much about in this campaign under the name of flanking.

Open field fights between large armies are almost impossible in most parts of this country because the forests are so extensive & so dense that it is impracticable to handle a great force with the unity & precision necessary, only a small part of the line being visible from any one point. Hence has grown up the practice of entrenching behind earthworks, & endeavoring mutually to force one's adversary to make the attack, whilst the aggressive party proper, endeavored to force his adversary to quit his position by the measures described above.

We have been demonstrating for three days past, my command moving out about two miles to see if we could coax the rebs out of their works, & returning at night.

Yesterday one of my aides, & one of the very best staff officers I have ever had, was captured whilst carrying orders. He must have got lost as to his direction on going through a wood & came out plump into the midst of a rebel picket, so some prisoners say, whom we captured. It is a great loss to me, & I sincerely hope he may dodge them and get away.

Before Atlanta, Ga. 24 Aug. 1864

The week past has been one of the most quiet we have had during the campaign, for though my own command has been active in watching the flanks of the army & moved more or less every day, yet we have retired to our camp every night, & so have seemed to keep a home somewhere for a longer period than common.

As I wrote you once before, you must not be concerned if you find at any future period of this campaign that our mail arrangements are broken up. Situated as we are, nothing is more probable than that weeks may elapse at any time during the Fall without your hearing from me. Bear this constantly in mind so that you may not be disturbed if it happens.

7

The Taking of Atlanta

Even as Hood hoped the Union army was moving northwest, it was, in fact, storming to the south. On August 31, meeting minimal resistance, Cox's men cut the Macon Railroad line, effectively breaking Atlanta's last supply line. When Hood learned of this, he ordered his men to abandon the city on September 1. The Union had now taken the great prize, in part due to Cox's efforts.[1] On September 12, Schofield recommended Cox's promotion to major general, noting that "he is the senior brigadier general of volunteers in active service . . . I have never seen a more able and efficient division commander."

With the Atlanta campaign over, Sherman wanted to rest his men for a new campaign against Hood, whose army had moved south. He also was musing about an idea which he had been considering for some time: marching to the sea.[2] As Sherman considered his approach, Schofield went on leave for five weeks, leaving Cox in command of his army. It was during this period when Sherman, who normally derided the military skills of nonprofessional soldiers, told Cox that he wanted him to take part in his march to the sea as commander of the XXIII Corps.

Hood did not wait for Sherman; instead, he marched to Sherman's west in late September, again hoping to break his supply line. He was aided by the addition of the Confederacy's most able cavalryman, Nathan Bedford Forrest, to his command.[3] However, Hood was desperate for supplies and he retreated through Alabama to Florence in early November.[4] Sherman, as he wrote in his memoirs, was tired of the "wild goose chase," so he then turned his eyes to the sea.

Grant gave Sherman permission to march to the sea on November 2, but he was still concerned about Hood's army. Sherman, having sent Thomas to Nashville in order to prepare repelling a Confederate campaign in that direction, reassured Grant that "Thomas will have ample time and sufficient troops to hold Hood until re-enforcements reach him from Missouri and recruits."[5]

Among the "sufficient troops" supporting Thomas would be the XXIII Corps, as well as the IV Corps, led by Major General David

Stanley. Schofield had convinced Sherman that Cox and the XXIII would be more important in fending off Hood than in marching to the sea. Cox was disappointed that he would not have the corps command or be with Sherman. However, he appreciated being treated as an equal in this key discussion, stating in his memoirs, "I still look back with pleasure to this incident as proof of the hearty comradeship between Sherman and his subordinates, which continued to be shown toward me by both him and Schofield to the end."

Sherman now split his force in two. One wing would march east through the fields of Georgia, laying waste to the South while facing no real opposition. The other, under Schofield and George Thomas, would engage in the last major campaign of the war in the West, culminating in the climactic battles of Franklin and Nashville.[6]

Cox's last letters during this campaign described his happiness at having played a crucial role in taking Atlanta, his anticipation at potentially having a corps command on the march to the sea, and his preparations for the Franklin-Nashville campaign. In a bit of wishful thinking, he told Helen that Schofield might not return to command, leaving him in that position.

Decatur, Ga. 8th Sept 1864

The day after I wrote my last (Aug. 24) our army moved, dropping for the time all communications with the north & striking out for the rear of Atlanta. I could not venture to tell you plainly what we proposed doing, because Wheeler with his rebel cavalry was upon our railroad line, & our letters ran no small risk if falling into his hands. Hence it was necessary to be very reticent as to our plans, even to keeping our own families ignorant of our projected movement.

We got back this morning to this place, where we first struck the Augusta R.R., when we approached Atlanta after crossing the Chattahoochee. That was the 19th July. Since then we have passed around Atlanta by the North, down on the West side to where we were on the 25th Aug. then struck off across country for the Macon R.R. six miles below Jonesboro & about thirty miles below Atlanta, completely destroying the R.R., as we went.

The rebels fell back precipitately, destroying immense quantities of stores as they abandoned Atlanta, & after being beaten in several partial engagements, they finally succeeded in concentrating their forces in a strong defensible position near Fosterville.

Having compelled them to evacuate Atlanta, Sherman had no desire to invest them in their new position, & our own supplies running short, we came back as at first intended, our Corps coming up the East side of the R.R. to this place completing the entire circuit of Atlanta. The center of the Army is at that place, we being again on the left wing, & about six miles away from the rest of the forces.

This closing movement it will be conceded by all, has been a very brilliant one, & has closed the campaign with a coup d'eclat which will place Sherman very high in the list of successful commanders of great armies.

We are now expecting several weeks rest, & preparation for a new campaign. It is not probable that the principal body of the rebel forces will venture this way again, & except an occasional cavalry skirmish, we look for quiet times.

Gen. Schofield expects to go to Knoxville & thence to Ken. in a few days, & will probably be gone till we are ready for active operations again, leaving me in command of the Corps. He & Gen. Sherman will now press the promotion, & we may hear something from it before a great while.

This is a little old town of some five or six hundred inhabitants, but is cleaner & neater than most small southern towns. We chose it as our position, knowing that we could have it to ourselves whilst Atlanta will be crowded with the bulk of the army.

Decatur 11th Sept. 1864

Our habits are not varied materially by our being in a town for my tents are pitched on a vacant grassy lot, and we live as if in the field, the only change being the absences taking place on leave.

Col. Sterling has resigned on account of his mother's health, & is going home in a day or two. Lt. [Levi] Scofield, my topographer, started today on leave. Dory hopes to get a leave also in a day or two, & I shall be almost alone.

I myself am tied down by the Corps being left in my command, making it vain for me to hope to get away at present. Indeed, the administration expects so much from the army here, that I understand they think at Wash. that we should go ahead upon a new campaign at once. Have you ever tried to realize what it is to live by the year in a canvass tent? In some respects I always enjoy it & never tire of it; but in others it becomes very irksome.

Since the first of May we have been constantly under fire, till this week. Our quarters have always been in reach of shell, & scarce a day has elapsed that we were not exposed to musket shots. Yet even this, habit makes comparatively easy, such creatures of circumstance we are.

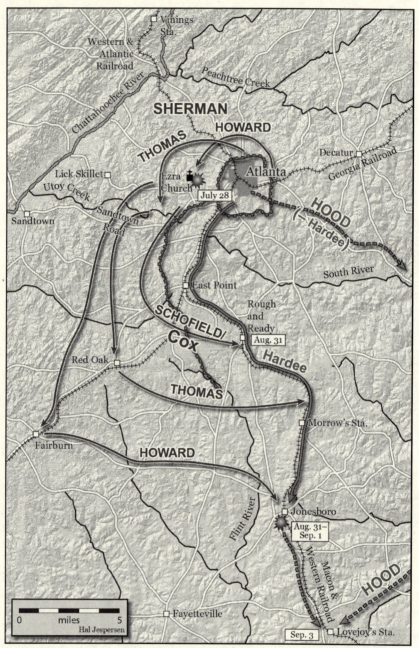

Map 4. The Taking of Atlanta, August 31–September 1, 1864. Map by Hal Jespersen.

Kingston, Ga. 11th Oct. 1864

While the rear of my column is passing I snatch a moment in the telegraph office to write a line, this being the first time I have been in mail communication with home for a fortnight.

Hood is making desperate efforts to destroy our R.R. but is getting badly foiled. He can't starve us, for we have full three months food for the whole army safe & snug. He dare not fight us unless he catches a detachment out of reach of support & that he cannot often do. [General John] Logan may feel confident that though we are having rough marching & hard work, we are doing well & in high feather.

I am still commanding the Corps, the breaks of communication probably preventing Gen. S. from joining us. We were not in the fight at Allatoona, that being a garrison left there when we went down the country. I telegraphed you from there day before yesterday, fearing from the similarity of names you might think Gen. [John] Corse's hurt was mine.

Villanow, Ga. 17th Oct. 1864

I wrote you from Kingston on the 11th when we were on march, the second day after the rebels cut our R.R. again at Resaca. Today is the first day we have communication open with Chattanooga again.

We have been on the march every day for two weeks chasing Hood, who has been making desperate efforts, but without any other advantage than the destruction of some R.R. which we shall soon re-open again.

If he goes North, we believe he will never get back again, & his only chance seems to be, to turn South, on the other side of Pigeon mountain ridge & make for Alabama, where we shall doubtless follow him.

Gen. Schofield has not yet joined us & I continue in command of the Corps. I am not yet fully informed of Gen. Sherman's intention in regard to us, but doubt whether Gen. Schofield will remain with us even if he comes down.

Gaylesville, Ga. 22 Oct. 1864

Gen. S. overtook us yesterday, relieving me of the command of the Corps, & I am back again at div. hd. qrs. Our marching has also come to a temporary halt. We reached this place day before yesterday, & are awaiting now to draw fresh supplies & see whether Hood will make any serious efforts at going into Tenn.

The damage he has done the R.R. is completely restored today, & beyond the expense & trouble of chasing him, he has done nothing to pay for the destruction he has brought upon one of the finest sections of Ga. & one which had hitherto escaped the devastation of war.

We have done more marching during the past month than in any other month of the campaign & my command has been the most active. I was at Gen. Sherman's hd. qrs. yesterday when Gen. Schofield arrived, & Gen. Sherman was very complimentary in regard to the manner our Corps has been handled, while I have been in command. He said to Gen. S. 'Your command has been handled in your absence to my complete satisfaction, indeed it has been beautifully handled.' He then went on to say that if Gen. Schofield chose to remain in command of his Dept. North of the Tenn. leaving the active field command to me, he might do so. Gen. S. prefers however to retain the field command himself, so I retain the Div.

The almost constant separation from our lines of communication has made it impracticable to write or to receive letters or papers often. We have never been so completely shut out from the world as at present, & the prospect now is that our Fall & Winter campaign will be no better, so that you will have to make up your mind for a dearth of correspondence during the coming season.

Cedar Bluffs Ala. 27 Oct. 1864

The weather is hardly propitious to my fete day. We are having the first rain we have had since the 7th and fear our fair Fall weather is permanently broken up.

We have been & still are expecting a good deal of active campaigning this Fall & Winter. I should like to tell you all we propose & expect to do, but the risk of capture of mails makes it improper to do so, & I can only promise to write as often as our circumstances permit.

There was some talk of our Corps being sent to hold the country north of the Tenn, & to protect the rear of the army, but I did not favor it although it would have put us in more regular & easy communication with home.

I have thoroughly settled the question in my own mind that I want no garrison duty or position in the rear. Till the war is ended I want to be with the biggest & most active moving column in the West.

We are now encamped in a beautiful situation on the North bank of the Coosa river in Al. but only three or four miles from the Ga. line & about twenty five miles west of Rome.

Yesterday I made a reconnaissance with my div. to Centre, a place seven miles from here, down the Coosa on the South side. We found nothing but some cavalry of the enemy there. The question now is where have they gone?

Southward toward Talladega, or North westward toward Tenn. The solution of this question will probably determine our movements.

Dalton, Ga. 3d Nov. 1864

Our perambulations continue, & appear to be growing 'more so'. I am here putting the rear of the Corps upon the cars, Gen Schofield having gone on with the advance. For fear of accidents I cannot give you many particulars of our movements either past or future, but hope before long to have so safe a line of communication that I may give you a full history or at least a clear sketch of the campaign of the month past.

We have had two days of cold rain & wind, with no signs of abatement yet. I fear it is but the beginning of the rainy season, though we have the right to expect the Indian summer yet. Lucy [Opdycke's wife] has of course heard that Opdycke was not in the skirmish at Snake Creek Gap, which was an insignificant affair at most. His corps & ours are to operate together, so that if you know his present position, you may guess our movement.

═ 8 ═
Final Campaigns

VICTORY IN THE WEST
AND IN NORTH CAROLINA

> I exerted myself [at the Battle of Franklin], as did most of the brigade & regimental officers to rally the broken regiments, & as Opdycke's men came up, the whole went back with a rush driving the rebs over the parapet again. Gen. Stanley commanding 4th Corps came up as we were rallying them & assisted, but was almost immediately wounded, & the battle was fought out under my orders.
>
> —Dolson to Helen, December 2, 1864

As Sherman prepared to depart Atlanta, George Thomas was in Nashville preparing for a potential advance by Hood. Cox wrote in his book, *The Battle of Franklin*, that "the task before Thomas was to conduct a cautious and purposely dilatory campaign till his reinforcements should be well in hand, and then, resuming the aggressive, to drive Hood southward and follow him wherever he should go."

Thomas ordered Schofield's and Stanley's two corps to play the primary role in stemming Hood's advance. Schofield was to base his men at Pulaski, a village on the railroad line between Decatur and Nashville. They were to be augmented ultimately by three divisions of the XVIth Corps under General A. J. Smith (then in Missouri). The risk was, Cox wrote in his book about the Battle of Franklin, "the time within which Thomas should be concentrating his forces." But he did not concentrate them and Smith's division was delayed for several weeks.

Unsure of Hood's objective in moving north, Thomas spread his forces widely around the region.[1] Hood had about fifty-five to sixty thousand effectives, including cavalry, for the new campaign. The XXIII and IV Corps numbered less than thirty thousand, though they were soon augmented by a few thousand reinforcements, many of them untried and untested men, and some fifteen hundred cavalry under General James Wilson. Nevertheless, Schofield soon recognized that he was in a difficult situation, not sure in which direction Hood would advance to the north. On the other hand, and fortunately for the Union army, Hood waited for supplies and did not advance promptly.[2]

When Hood finally moved north on November 21, he tried to outflank Schofield, aiming at Columbia via an advance led by Forrest.[3] By this point, Schofield had come to realize that Cox was his most reliable and capable subordinate. Thus, on November 24, he ordered Cox to lead his division, along with General George Wagner's IV Corps brigade, to stem the rebel advance, which they did late that day.[4] The next day, Schofield began to lay the groundwork for a strategic retreat toward Nashville. Giving Cox the critical role as the army's rear guard, Schofield's forces crossed the Duck River north of Columbia on the 27th.[5]

Cox wrote only three letters during this period, in part because of poor communications links and, in part because he and his men were constantly on the move. He noted in one letter his pride about fending off Forrest and Hood in Columbia.

Thompson's station, Tenn. 11 Nov. 1864
We arrived here last night from Ga. by way of Nashville, & should have gone on to Pulaski, but for the destruction of the railroad bridges by a freshet. We are thirty miles south of Nashville on the R.R. leading to Decatur Al. in a much richer & better cultivated country than any we saw in Ga. We left Dalton on the P.M. of the 6th & till last night were living on the cars. The trip was not so uncomfortable as we expected though the weather was stormy all the way. I took a box car for my hd. qrs. & we had our camp chairs during the day, & our blankets on the floor at night, & managed at the points where we were delayed to make some coffee, & so with boiled ham we provided before starting & a quarter of mutton we managed to get cooked on the caboose car, we got along very well.

The 4th Corps is at Pulaski, & we shall join them there as soon as the r.r. is repaired. New troops are coming in, & we expect to have an army here sufficient to make headway against Hood, while Sherman operates in Ga. Gen. Thomas retains command of the whole Western part of the military div., whilst it seems to be understood that Gen. S. is to command the two Corps in the field.

We passed through some of the most romantic scenery between here & Ga. in the night, but I was delighted with what I did see approaching Chattanooga from the South, & then from C. to Bridgeport next morning. I would like to attempt the description of some of it, but writing as I am by camp fire in the open air, you will hardly expect me to do more today than scribble briefly an account of myself & of our more immediate intentions.

Near Pulaski, Tenn. 17th Nov. 1864

We marched here in three days from Thompson's station where I last wrote you. The last three days have been miserably rainy & muddy. Today is not exactly fair, but neither is it rainy, & we are consequently hoping the storm is over. We are about fourteen miles from the Alabama line.

How long we shall remain quiet depends in great measure upon Mr. Hood. If he makes no effort to move Northward we shall probably use a short period in refitting our commands & preparing for a new campaign.

I voted at both the Oct. & Nov. elections. At the former we were on the march from Kingston to Rome, & at the noon halt on the banks of the Coosa, we opened the polls in an ambulance & I voted with the 99th Ohio regt. At the Presidential election we were on the cars from Chattanooga to Nashville, & we opened the polls at my own hd. qrs. box car, & voted for 'A. Linkum'. I have no doubt the votes have gone safely home & then counted according to law.

Columbia, Tenn. 27th Nov./64

The past ten days have been so full of movement & so uncomfortable from rain & cold that writing has seemed out of the question.

On the fourth morning after I wrote last the rain had changed to freezing cold, & we commenced a retrograde movement, the evidence being conclusive that Hood was making for some point in our rear toward Nashville. My command was therefore moved back to Lynnville, 19 miles, to check any movement that might be made on cross roads coming in there, & [George] Wagner's div 4th Corps followed us.

The remainder of the command followed us next day, and Hood appearing to be making for Columbia via Mt. Pleasant, I marched my div. that evening eleven miles to another intersection of roads covering the r.r. & started again two hours before day next morning, moving up to the two mile post from Columbia, where I cut across to the Mt. Pleasant pike, reaching it just in time to interpose between our retreating cavalry who were in precipitate retreat, & the rebel Gen. Forrest who was following them up sharply. We were not a moment too soon.

My skirmishers checked them, & I put my div. in position across the road, where we had a lively artillery & musketry skirmish, till the rest of the army came up about noon, when the whole took up a defensive line about the town. The rebs made no decisive assault though they have been keeping up a constant demonstration ever since.

We do not believe Hood will keep the bulk of his army here, but are looking for further flanking movements with a view to force us back toward Nashville. We however are looking for reinforcements which will enable us shortly to turn the tables upon him.

More disagreeable weather for campaigning we could hardly have. For two days we have had snow squalls, alternating between raining and freezing, & for two weeks the weather has been constantly stormy though not so cold as on those two days. We console ourselves however with the reflection that 'it's a long lane that has nae turning.'

Hood wrote in his memoirs that, on the 28th, he thought Schofield might feel so secure after having crossed the Duck River that he would not notice that Hood was engaged in a flanking movement to the east. His analysis was correct, for Wilson, a 26-year-old "boy wonder," who was supposed to watch Schofield's flank, had in fact lost contact with Forrest and did not report Hood's maneuver.[6] Also, at about 8 a.m. on the 29th, Hood's artillery began a vigorous cannonade against Cox and his men. The inevitable result was a confused Schofield, who now was even less sure how Hood had dispersed his forces or what his intentions were. It was exactly what Hood hoped for.

Schofield gambled by splitting his army, keeping Cox at Columbia and sending Stanley with two of his divisions north to Spring Hill, followed by another division of the XXIII Corps. He then issued a general order to all forces to retire to Franklin, with Stanley acting as the rear guard.[7] The ensuing Battle of Spring Hill on November 29 was one of the stranger encounters of the war. While the Confederates had a significant numerical advantage, they attacked only in spurts and they were stifled by a strong defense led by Stanley and Emerson Opdycke. Hood ceased the attacks after dark, thinking he would continue in the morning, presuming the Union army would still be in place.[8]

At about 7 p.m. on the 29th, Schofield arrived in Spring Hill and ordered a rapid withdrawal of all forces to Franklin, twelve miles to the north. Cox's division would be the first to arrive in the city, where he would set up a defensive line as the remainder of Schofield's forces were to retreat to Nashville over the pontoon bridge that Schofield presumed

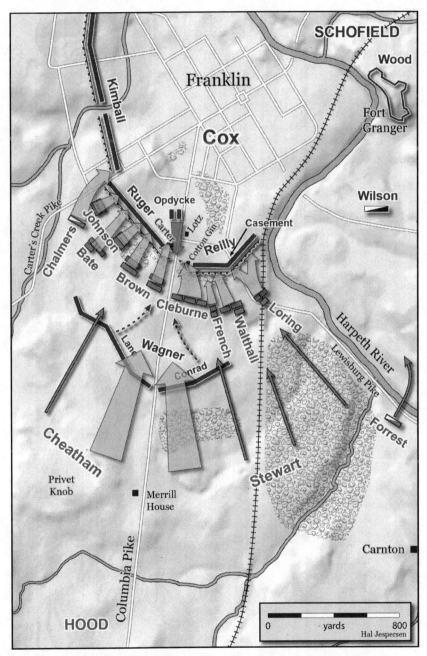

Map 5. Battle of Franklin, November 30, 1864. Map by Hal Jespersen.

would be waiting on the Harpeth River. During the night of the 29th and the morning of the 30th, the entire Union army engaged in forced, silent marches along the Columbia Pike, careful not to catch the attention of the Confederates in Spring Hill that they were passing just hundreds of meters away.[9]

In Franklin the morning of November 30, Schofield and Cox discussed their defense against Hood. Having a choice between West Pointer Stanley and Cox to command the defensive line, Schofield again chose the citizen general, in whom he had far greater confidence. Stanley would direct the operations of the rear-guard over the river as the wagon train passed through the town, followed by the troops. As a result, Cox commanded the XXIII Corps and most of the IV Corps during that fateful day.[10]

Hood learned that morning that all of the Union forces had left Spring Hill and were on their way to Franklin. After surveying the Union line from Winstead Hill outside Franklin at about 1 p.m., he announced, "We will make the fight" via a frontal attack against Cox's defensive line. His commanders were stunned, but they obeyed this misguided order. General Patrick Cleburne's famous comment "If we are to die, let us die like men" encapsulated this fatalistic approach.[11]

Cox did a superb job of quickly setting up adequate breastworks. However, in one of the necessary compromises he had to make, he left open the main road into town to allow the wagons and artillery to pass through toward the river north of town. He also created a second line of smaller works about two hundred yards behind the first line across the Pike just in case he needed it. That would prove crucial.[12] Also, he reiterated Schofield's order to General Wagner to remain in front of the line as a trip-wire, but then to withdraw if the Confederates attacked.[13]

However, conflict in Wagner's division caused major problems. Cox's friend Opdycke, worn out from the day's marching and fighting, and without sleep, refused a direct order from Wagner and took his men into the main line. There he was ordered by Cox to go into reserve. Then, when Hood attacked at about 4 p.m., Wagner ordered his men to stay put, where they were quickly overwhelmed. When he realized his mistake, Wagner tried to reverse his earlier impetuous order, but by then it was too late.[14]

As Wagner's men realized they were about to be overwhelmed, they began to retreat toward the fortified line, many in a panic. Rebel soldiers following behind passed through the open center and over part of

Jacob Cox at the Battle of Franklin. Kurz and Allison Painting, Library of Congress.

the front defensive line.[15] Within seconds, there began what Cox called the "superhuman exertions" by the Union forces to grasp victory from the jaws of seeming defeat. The 44th Missouri, a group of new recruits who by chance were on the main line and had never fired a shot previously, quickly filled the gap, aided by other new regiments. Cox sent orders to Opdycke to join the fray and Opdycke led his men into the maelstrom.

Cox himself became inspired, riding around the rear of the forces, encouraging his men to stem the tide, firing up his men. At that critical moment, for the first and only time in his military career, with disaster looming, Cox the warrior emerged from within Cox the stoic, unemotional commander. As one of Cox's men later wrote, "No finer picture could be painted of a commander in battle, rallying the breaking line . . . taking orders through the air from the waving sword of their general, they sprang forward."[16]

These combined efforts stemmed the tide, though the Confederates continued to attack late into the night. Cox wrote later that these assaults on the center "were obstinately repeated until night-fall . . . and easily repulsed," having been met by a "sheet of fire" from the Union forces.[17] Cox wrote that, after 10 p.m., the fighting seemed to die down "when the enemy definitely accepted defeat and sought only to reform his lines and collect the remnants of his broken divisions. . . . [Soon] we became satisfied that no further attack would be made."[18]

Based on Cox's report at 7 p.m. that victory was assured, Schofield ordered the continuation of the withdrawal to Nashville. Cox was very disappointed, perhaps recalling his and his men's regrets when the advantage at Antietam was lost. But Schofield was adamant. The Union forces retreated over the river about midnight, leaving the field to the Confederates.[19] On December 3, Schofield's forces moved on to the defenses around Nashville, where they stayed for two weeks before the next battle.

On December 1, Hood issued a proclamation congratulating "the army on the success achieved yesterday over our enemy by their heroic and determined courage,"[20] but it was a Pyrrhic victory at best. As Cox wrote in his book about the battle, "No intelligent officer on either side was ignorant of the fact that the heart of the Confederate army was broken."[21] Most Confederate soldiers who fought there agreed. Private Sam Watkins wrote later that "it was a grand holocaust of death," adding "[i]t is the blackest page in the history of the Lost Cause."[22] Nevertheless, Hood plunged on, taking a position about two miles from Nashville on December 2.[23]

Cox wrote only three letters during this period because of the intensity of the fighting at Franklin. His letter on December 2 in particular is important because it described, in some detail, the Battle of Franklin. Cox's matter-of-fact tone belies the fact that he recognized that this battle, along with Antietam, were the titanic events of his military career. Also, perhaps seeing how he was not being mentioned in accounts of Antietam, he made sure Helen understood that he alone was in command on the defensive line. He also gave credit to his friend Opdycke for saving the day, a statement which would lead to considerable and ongoing debate among the participants and in Civil War historiography.

Nashville Tenn, 2 Dec. 1864

Since I wrote you last, I have had a busy & exciting time of it. Hood has pressed determinedly upon us, detaining us whenever it was possible in the hope of forcing us to a decisive engagement before we received our reinforcements, & while his force was decidedly superior.

At Columbia we held him at bay & repulsed his advances upon our lines, but he swung round our left, crossing Duck river about five miles above us. This necessitated a change of position of our army, & my division was left to hold in check one Corps of the rebels which remained in Columbia & prevent them from putting a bridge over the river during the day of our movement. This gave me warm work, as I had a lively skirmish all day & a sharp combat a little before night.

The rebels were repulsed in my front, & between dark & midnight I drew off according to orders & rejoined the remainder of the army, marching within rifle shot of the camps of the enemy who had crossed above. We reached Franklin next morning Nov. 30, just before day break & went into position to cover the rest of the army's movement, thus passing from rear-guard to advance guard by a long night's march of twenty miles.

The trains came up & were getting slowly over the Harpeth river by a miserable ford when the news came that the enemy were following closely upon the rear, in force. Both the divisions of our corps were acting under my orders in covering the movement, being in position South of the town & around it on that side. Two div of the 4th Corps were ordered to report to me as they came up, which they did, thus putting four divs. out of the five under my command, the remaining div. crossing the river & taking up a position on the North side.

Gen. Schofield succeeded in getting two temporary foot bridges for troops done, when about three o'clock P.M. Hood advanced to the attack of my lines with his whole army, when he had assured that he had us in his grasp, & that a decisive victory should now be theirs, ruining our army.

I had my own div. on the left, the 2d of our Corps in the centre, & [General Nathan] Kimball's div of the 4th Corps on the right. Wagner's div. of the 4th had two brigades in advance (not yet having come in) & one Opdycke's was held in my reserve.

The enemy soon drove in the two advance brigades who were ordered to fall back before getting warmly engaged & were in fault only in fighting too long, as it made their retreat to our breastworks so hurried as to cause some confusion.

The enemy came on in magnificent style, in three lines of battle, the central point of attack being the turnpike which ran out between the divisions of the 23rd Corps. The country was open & nearly level, & we had the grandest fight I have seen since Antietam [this sentence was underlined in blue pencil in the original transcript].

The retreat of the two brigades of Wagner's was not understood by some of our men from new regts, which were on the left of the 2d Div, 23d Corps & as our men from the front rushed back over the breastwork, these broke too.

The enemy were close after them & came over the work immediately. It looked very squally for awhile. I ordered up Opdycke's brigade on the charge, but I believe he had anticipated the order & was coming before it reached him.

I exerted myself, as did most of the brigade & regimental officers to rally the broken regiments, & as Opdycke's men came up, the whole went back with a rush driving the rebs over the parapet again. Gen. Stanley commanding 4th Corps came up as we were rallying them & assisted, but was almost immediately wounded, & the battle was fought out under my orders, Gen. Schofield being in a fort north of the river where he could see the whole field, but did not find it necessary to interfere in my plans.

Opdycke's charge saved the day for though all the rest of the line stood firm, if the enemy had succeeded in penetrating there we could not have held the place.

Again & again they came on but were foiled every time. I have never seen fighting continue so late. It was nearly eleven o'clock before they gave up their attacks or feints.

About midnight we were withdrawn as originally intended, since the enemy could easily pass around our position.

We are concentrated here with a view to prepare our reinforcements for field work, & take the field with superior force. Hood may be fool enough to attack us here meanwhile. We hope he will as he will have a smaller army left for future operations. He lost more than 5000 in the battle of Franklin, of whom a thousand are our prisoners.

My aid Lt. Coughlin was killed instantly while we were rallying the men at the center. Lt. [Levi] Scofield of my staff had his horse killed, but was not hurt himself. I fully expected to be hit, but as before Providence willed it otherwise & I was unscathed, though not even at South Mountain was I under hotter fire. Our loss is about 1000.

Nashville 5th Dec 1864

Hood's army is before the town, but I cannot think he will be fool enough to assault us, & a blockade merely will waste time he may need before the Winter is over.

My hd. qrs. are in the East part of the town just in rear of Fort Morton, looking out on the Nolensville & Franklin turnpikes. I have two rooms in a large house with Corinthian pillars of full height with the house, in the Southern style of pretentious Greek architecture. We have part of our tents outside & get along very comfortably.

I spend most of my day on the forts in my part of the line, watching the rebs & occasionally enlivening their enjoyment of the day by practicing at them with thirty pound Parrot guns from Fort Negely.

My belief is that they are destroying the R.R. toward the South & will retire as soon as they have done enough of it to suit them.

The present complication of affairs makes all our future movements doubtful. Hood may retire any day, & then we shall up & off after him. I would very gladly get away for two or three weeks, but see no proper way of leaving my command at present, even if the leave would be granted for my asking, of which I am by no means sure.

Nashville 14th Dec. 1864

The cold has continued up to yesterday, when a change began which has changed our ice bound camp to mud. Today is damp & foggy, but mild, & we shall now expect some days of moderate weather, probably rain.

We have been in the dullest possible mood for a week, looking across at the enemy's lines in silence, even the picket firing being almost wholly frozen up. The fact that we are in such close proximity to the enemy had made it necessary to keep very close to the lines, & I have therefore seen nothing whatever of the town. We shall be glad enough to get away as soon as field movements become practicable.

The situation Hood faced at Nashville was hopeless, though he refused to admit it. Nevertheless, primarily because of bad weather, Thomas did not attack Hood until December 15.[24] Thomas's first attack stunned Hood and forced him to contract his lines. Cox's division played only a small role that day, but, on December 16, his men were among those who took Shy's Hill, a key point which led to the breaking of the rebel line. Cox wrote later that at about 4:30 PM "the whole Confederate left was crushed in like an egg-shell." A crestfallen Hood wrote, "I beheld for the first and only time a Confederate army abandon the field in confusion."[25] The Confederate Army of Tennessee almost died that day and the war in the West was effectively over.

Hood retreated helter-skelter, his fearful, tattered army scattering to the south. But the effort to destroy Hood's force by the pursuing Union force proved more difficult than Washington had hoped. As the weather turned even worse, a chase in the mud and muck ensued for several days.[26] Unable to catch the rebels, Thomas logically decided to close the campaign and he ordered Cox and the XXIII Corps to Dalton for winter quarters.[27] For Cox, this was an opportunity to apply for a furlough, his first in two years, to go home to recuperate. His request was granted on the 30th and, on January 2, he wrote to Helen, "last night my trunk was packed for home, & my leave of absence for thirty days was snug in my pocket."[28]

However, Thomas was ordered to continue the campaign and, as Cox wrote later, he "engaged in a hearty bit of private grumbling" as his furlough was cancelled. In the end, Grant determined that the threat was over and that Hood could not be caught. He also noted that many of the remainder of Thomas's forces would be transferred "where they can be used."[29] On January 18, Cox finally was allowed to go home for a one-week furlough.

Cox's letters during the chase after Hood and before his furlough reflect his pride in his accomplishments and his bitterness that Washington did not give proper support to the troops in the field.

Spring Hill, Tenn. 21st Dec 1864

The first fine days have been full of hard work. The battle of Nashville you have seen accounts of in the papers more full than I should have time to give. It was great in results, though the fighting was not severe. The rebels were evidently dispirited & easily panic stricken, & we captured nearly six thousand prisoners & over fifty pieces of cannon with less loss to ourselves than we have sometimes experienced in a mere affair of outposts.

My command was engaged on the final charge which broke the enemy's line, in conjunction with Gen. [A.J.] Smith's Corps, & the cavalry. My first brigade carried a fortified hill by assault capturing eight pieces of cannon.

We look upon this engagement as finishing Hood's career for the present & having pressed him to Columbia already, we anticipate little difficulty in pushing him South of the Tenn.

The two or three days & nights after the battle were among the most uncomfortable I have ever experienced. The first night we could not get up a wagon, & the servants could not find us to bring us anything to eat, so we lay down before a camp fire, in the mud, hungry & damp. About midnight the rain began again & poured. This made any posture but an upright one impossible & we stood shivering & weary &—let it rain—which it did with right good will till morning.

Our boys then found us, & brought some coffee with hard tack. It has rained or snowed, sometimes both, ever since, & is still at it. My overcoat keeps me dry, but weighs about fifty lbs. with water in it.

The night after the one mentioned passed in a similar way, except that we borrowed a tarpaulin from the artillery, & by the help of a few fence rails made a shelter tent of it, which with a camp fire in front kept us pretty comfortable. When our wagons fail to come up, we officers are infinitely worse off than the privates, since we have neither food nor shelter.

Columbia, Tenn. 2nd Jan 1865

Last night my trunk was packed for home, & my leave of absence for thirty days was snug in my pocket.

During the night came orders to march, the War Dept. insisting upon our continuing the Winter campaign, though we are conscious that we shall probably make little headway.

Under the circumstances, however, my sense of duty forces me to forego the pleasures of a visit home & instead of starting Northward with a light heart this morning, I swallowed my disappointment & head the column Southward. We shall strike the Tenn. river & move up it, probably to Florence. I fear our mail arrangements will be much broken for a time.

Clifton Tenn. 7th Jan 1865

We arrived here yesterday in a rain storm changing to sleet & snow, & after a very hard four days march from Columbia. Two days we were in the barrens, or 'barus' as the natives called them, being the high barren ridges which divide the water courses in this part of the state.

We went nearly twenty miles through unbroken forest, finding but a single family living near the roadside in the whole distance. We then came down into the narrow valley of a creek, in which the road crosses the stream several times in every mile, making it necessary for the troops to ford it in water knee deep & from ten to twenty yards wide. From this we passed over a high ridge, & down into another similar valley, with similar creek, & similar fordings. We followed this latter Rockhouse creek down to Buffalo river, forded that stream which was some eighty yards wide, & three feet deep, & then by a rough mountain road reached Waynesboro at the end of the tired day. The fourth day, (yesterday) we marched here, & are bank of the Tenn. river.

The place is called Carollville on most maps, though its name is Clifton. It was once a flourishing village containing half a dozen stores & several hundred inhabitants, but it has suffered the fate of many other such places, & a few stone chimneys are all that stand to show that it was ever inhabited.

We shall probably be delayed here several days waiting for transportation to take us up the river. I am as yet quite ignorant of the plans of the campaign, & I find Gen Schofield has as little information on the subject as I.

The extreme wetness of the season & the consequent bad conditions of the roads, makes me very skeptical as to any great results being attained by continuing active operations, such being understood to be the peremptory

[sic] orders from Washington, we have nothing for it but to go ahead as far as possible.

Our first move will take us very near the old battle ground of Shiloh or Pittsburg landing, & it is possible, though not probable that we may get another battle there, or in the vicinity.

Clifton Tenn. 13th Jan. 1865

The total interruption of our communications with the outer world is more vexatious than anything of the sort I have before had to endure.

We left Columbia on the 2nd & since that time have not had a word from any source. A stray newspaper of the 4th is the latest news of any sort we have seen. This when I have some interest in knowing what is done at Washington is peculiarly trying.

We were ordered off with the understanding that we were to go right into Alabama in chase of Hood, but here we have been more than a week, waiting for transports to take us up the Tenn. & we are likely to wait a week longer, so that it is now certain that so far as movements are concerned I might have had my leave of absence & been back before anything could be done in the way of campaigning. We have been in tents, there being no houses here to shelter anyone.

The probability is that after we get transports to take us up the river, we shall be unable to get beyond Eastport, & that is represented as being a viler, muddier, & more uncomfortable camping place than this. You need to see this to appreciate the delights of our anticipations.

The weather for the past three months has been quite uniform in its changes. We have first, about three days drenching rain, one day sleet & snow, one day frozen cold, one day mild & fair, one day mild & murky, the rain gathering, then the three days rain again, & so on ad infinitum.

I am getting ragged & barefoot. My boots are worn out, my coat is worn out, my waistcoat are worn out, my hat is worn out, & I am only whole & respectable when I am in my shirt & drawers. If I ever get near civilization again, I shall be obliged to hide in bed somewhere till I can get some clothes made.

I don't wonder Washington people want to have the campaign go on, & if they would apply a little of the 'go ahead' to the Army on the James, would appreciate it still better. Here we know to an absolute certainty that the army is stuck in the mud, but the administration would not believe Gen. Thomas when he told them so, & force him to pretend to move with the fear of being superseded hanging over him, whilst he knows that any effective movement is impossible.

We can ruin our horses & mules, & put half our men in hospital without getting twenty five miles from the Tenn unless the weather changes, & this is all we can do. Hood can laugh at us, unless the Mobile & Ohio r.r. can be repaired as we go, & he made to furnish us supplies.

If this could be done, or if the season would permit us to chase the rebels right into the gulf, I would be perfectly content to stay, & in fact couldn't be coaxed to go home, but knowing what I know, I feel perfectly sure that I might as well be making a biennial visit to my family as not.

Cox enjoyed his furlough in Warren and then was ordered to the East Coast for a new venture in North Carolina under Schofield.[30] Thomas was ordered to make arrangements for the XXIII Corps to go to Annapolis and, on January 14, he authorized the movement. Cox learned of the new orders on the 15th, the same day he heard that his long-awaited "re-promotion" to major general of Volunteers had finally been confirmed.

Cox originally thought that he and Schofield would be sent to Petersburg to reinforce Grant, but, on January 25, Halleck ordered Schofield to capture Wilmington, North Carolina, one of the few remaining ports under Confederate control. Thereafter, his forces would prepare the way for Sherman's movement into North Carolina toward Goldsboro, where the two armies would be reunited. Schofield would be in command of the new department of North Carolina with two provisional corps, one of which Cox was ultimately to command, in addition to the XXIII.[31]

Cox passed through Washington on his way south and he spent some time preparing for a renewal of his political career, as both Garfield and Chase urged him to run for Governor of Ohio that October. He also was in the gallery of the House of Representatives when that body passed the 13th Amendment, a titanic event for everyone, especially for a graduate of Oberlin College, one of the North's institutions most virulently against slavery.[32] It was at this point that Cox likely began planning for how he would deal with the issues of abolition and Reconstruction during a campaign for Governor of Ohio. He had already posited in letters to colleagues that internal colonization of Blacks might be part of the "solution" and that concept would be a core element of his future policy proposals.

Cox's voyage south with eighteen hundred of his men was by sea and, as on the land, Cox came through it in great health, unlike most of his troops. Many of the troops were green and, as it turned out, their lack of experience both on the sea and on land would cause problems later. Once the men landed, the new army's movement toward Wilmington began on February 9. On the 11th, Cox ordered them to march from Fort Fisher north on Federal Point to meet General Alfred H. Terry's corps, which had landed there earlier. Terry, also a talented political general, had led the forces which had taken Fort Fischer earlier that year.

Cox's letters from this period depict his wonderment at his sea voyage—he would later become an avid sailor—and his pleasure at having been in the House gallery when the 13th Amendment was passed.

Washington 2nd Feb. 1865

I have never been more full of aches & completely tired than since I have been in this restless city. Every moment has been a busy one, & its magnificent distances are terribly hard upon feet made tender by long habit of riding instead of walking.

We reached Phil. Sat. evening after leaving you, & sending Miss Ford forward to Baltimore. I went out and I found not only Ma [Cox's mother] & Lottie [Cox's sister Charlotte] with Redelia [Cox's sister], but also Sarah Brainard who had come on from N.Y. with Dory. You may easily believe we had a happy family reunion.

I left there Sun. eveg. & came to Wash. reaching here on Mon. about nine in the morning. I found our troops were arriving, but the frozen condition of the Potomac has hindered us from shipping them as yet, though we are expecting now that we shall get off within twenty four hours.

I called on Gov. Dennison at the P.O. Dept & found him as cordial as ever. In the evening I called on the family, & of course enjoyed myself.

The next day I was in the Capitol during the debate on the Constitutional Amendment abolishing slavery, which finally passed amid the most tremendous excitement.

In the morning yesterday I called on [Secretary of War Edwin] Stanton, who was exceedingly cordial, congratulating me on my promotion & saying I owed nobody thanks for it, as I had fairly & fully won all I had got. It was pleasant to get so much of a recognition even. I am assured the confirmation will be made today. Dory's promotion to Major was also promised me.

Hd. 3d Div. 23d Corps, Steamship Atlantic 3d Feb. 1865

I have my command on ship board, & am expecting to sail at daybreak, unless the ice should prevent. The whole Potomac is full of it, & we have

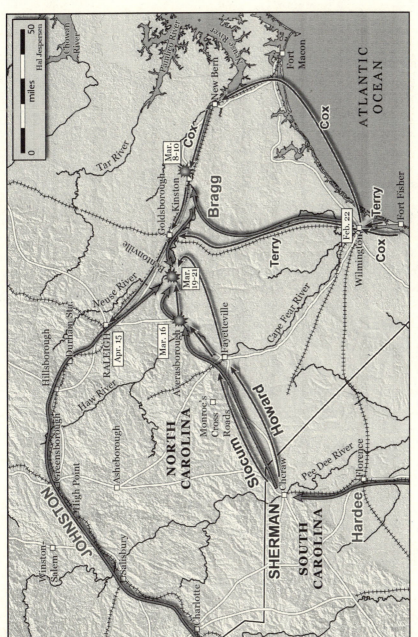

Map 6. The North Carolina Campaign, 1865. Map by Hal Jespersen.

to make our way some sixty miles through the frozen mass before we shall reach open water.

Our ship is the Atlantic, one of the famous Collin's line of Liverpool steamers. Gen. Schofield & myself with our hd. qrs. &e. & about eighteen hundred soldiers are on board.

Many of our Western men are seeing the ocean for the first time, and expect enjoyment in full of the delights of sea-sickness. Our voyage will not be quite so long as we expected when I was at home, though the general object will be the same.

My hurry today has not permitted me to learn whether my confirmation was made as expected, but the assurances as given me are such as to remove all uneasiness as to the matter in the end.

Steamship Atlantic off Cape Fear N.C., 8th Feb 1865

Most of our troops are ashore, but the roughness of the sea has prevented our landing our baggage, & so I write tonight from the cabin of the good ship Atlantic, though a heavy ground swell makes her roll so at her anchor that writing is not altogether easy.

This is our fifth day since leaving Alexandria. We got on board on the 3d. The morning of the 4th was foggy, & the pilot would not venture from the wharf till the fog lifted, which was nearly noon. The ice in the Potomac was a great obstruction & we made only fifteen or twenty miles that day, & reached the Kettle Bottom shoals just before dark. These shoals were too dangerous to pass at night, so we anchored till morning.

On the 5th we ran out of the Potomac down the Chesapeake bay to Fortress Monroe, the rest of the fleet lying near Cape Henry while we ran into Hampton Roads.

I landed in a small boat & went into the fort, which is said to be in area one of the largest in the world. I had a good view of it by moonlight, the moon being very bright. I believe some thirty acres are enclosed by the fort, & the grounds are neatly laid off: the officers quarters being substantially built dwellings shaded by live oak trees, a species of evergreen which I saw here for the first time.

The ditch of the fort is some sixty feet wide, & filled by the tide from the sea, so as to add greatly to the strength of the place. We had some ammunition to load here, & this gave me considerable time to look around. The wall of the fort is of heavy masonry some twenty-five or thirty feet high with embrasures for casemated guns in the walls, & other guns upon the top 'en barbette'. I have many doubts whether it would prove a very strong work against modern projectiles.

As we rounded to enter Hampton Roads we got the first taste of a swell, which gave the ship much motion, & many began to question how they should be affected outside the cape if this made them uneasy. We weighed anchor again about 4 o'clock A.M., & stood out to sea, giving Cape Henry a wide berth of some fifteen miles, & then turning southward along the coast.

Sometimes the land would be entirely out of sight, & then again would be portions of the coast, looking like low clouds hanging between the heavens and the waters. The sea was not rough, but there was still motion enough to make quite a number of our officers squeamish, though very few of the men between decks showed any symptoms of sea-sickness.

The day passed on the whole very pleasantly. I was on deck all the while making as usual friends of the Capt. & his mates, & 'ship' to them by way of pouring my within sight of salt water [sic].

We passed Cape Hatteras just before night having distanced the rest of the fleet, leaving them out of sight in the rear. We turned in that night, thinking we were not to see any very thorough ocean experience. But we were not to be let off so.

Next morning 7th I woke about daybreak, feeling the ship rolling heavily, & hearing the driving of the rain upon the deck above me. I lay quietly for awhile & then rolled out of my bunk, slid open my state room window & looked out. A heavy driving fog accompanied the rain. the wind was blowing 'very fresh' as sailors say, not quite a gale, that is, but what they call 'very dirty weather'. No land was in sight, the swell was heavy & the ship plunged and rolled as thoroughly as any old salt could have desired, had he wished to give us a taste of real ocean experience.

The four or five feet between my state room window & the bulwarks were filled with soldiers in all stages of seasickness. I felt my own stomach rebelling at the sight aided by the motion, & closed the windows, & began to dress. I found it difficult to keep one leg off the deck long enough to put it into my pants, & now I was pitched forward against my bunk & now seated rather summarily as suddenly on the seat under the window. This confusion of up & down, right & left proved rather too much for me for a few minutes & I confess to some decided symptoms of nausea.

I lay down again & grew quiet in stomach & concluded however not to venture to the breakfast table, & lay still in my bunk till about ten o'clock, when I turned out & went on deck. There I was completely myself.

The air was bracing, the rain had ceased though the wind was high, & the swell rolled magnificently. I thoroughly & completely enjoyed it, & hardly left my station in the wheel house till the gong sounded at two o'clock for dinner.

Then I went below & ate hearty meal & back on deck again, feeling as rigorous as a young lion.

The weather continued foggy all day, & we lay off and on the coast, having gone as far as we needed, & only awaiting a clearing up to run in shore. Just before night the fog lifted enough to let us see the coast, & we came in to our anchorage about a mile off the beach in seven fathoms water.

There is no bay here which we can enter, & we lie in the open roadstead, ready to run out to sea if the wind should haul off shore. We now expect to get our baggage out in the morning & go ashore to stay.

I have been gaining in strength & vigor every day since I have been within smelling distance of salt water.

Federal Point, N.C. 11th Feb. 1865

We landed yesterday morning on this long strip of sand beach between the Cape Fear river & the ocean. Gen. [Albert] Terry occupied the point, & we moved in behind him. Our transfer from the steamship to the shore had to be made first to a propeller drawing less water than the Atlantic, so that she could pass the bar at high tide.

We got away from the ship about midnight of the 9th & came in over the bar next morning. Our troops were put ashore about nine o'clock by a small steamboat which took them off the propeller, which could not get up to the little wharf, so that we had two transfers before we got landed. I then went off in the steamboat to the ship on which Gen. Schofield had his hd. qrs. & from there to Admiral [David Dixon] Porter's flag ship, where we got a lunch of fresh oysters & crackers.

We had a little breakfast on the steamboat in the morning so that we fared better than we expected, for when I left the Atlantic I had not the slightest idea how I was to get any meals during the day.

Toward evening we got our tents pitched in the sand about three miles up the point from the landing, & succeeded in getting some supper cooked by our own servants. Today we made an advance of about a mile & a half—pushing back the rebels within their line of entrenchments, & establishing a new line of our own.

We expected to be transferred tonight to the other side of the river, but the order was countermanded. As we have none of our wagons or saddle horses ashore yet we are not in a very comfortable condition, & movements are very difficult for us in consequence.

In the narrow strip of land we are at present confined to, there is no growth of anything but pines & scrub live oaks. The sand is in most places bare, & is as white as snow. When it is thrown into breastworks it is of the most dazzling whiteness &, at this cold season one can hardly believe it is not snow.

Gen. Terry I find a very pleasant quiet tempered man. He was kind enough to lend me four horses today, so that I was able to mount myself & ride in the movement we made.

Gen. Schofield is put in command of the Dept. of N.C. & will have two full corps here, when the rest of our troops arrive.

As we advanced today, the naval fleet moved up the river, & one of the monitors going in advance engaged the rebel Fort Anderson on the other side of the river, & we had a very pretty view of the encounter. The monitor fired slowly with her heavy guns, but with beautiful precision, the shells striking into the parapet & blowing the earth high into the air at almost every shot.

The ground within Fort Fisher shows the effect of the naval bombardment at the time of the assault. The ground is almost literally covered with the fragments of shells, mingled with many unexploded ones, the great fifteen inch spherical shells lying like so many great bowling balls all over the hard sand beach, while here and there are also unexploded conical shell & solid shot of six or eight inches in diameter. I have never seen anything which gave so vivid an idea of the effects of a Navy bombardment with these great guns. The assault could not have been successful but for this.

> On February 21, 1865, Cox arrived at Brunswick Ferry, opposite Wilmington. The Confederates could then see their situation was hopeless, so they abandoned the city. Before that happened, Cox had received an order from Schofield to delay his advance. However, relying on their close relationship, Cox responded to Schofield that it would be better to continue the attack because he thought the rebels were vulnerable. Showing his confidence in Cox, Schofield rescinded his original order. Cox proved to be correct and, on February 22, when the federal troops occupied Wilmington, they received no active opposition.[33] The taking of Wilmington, coupled with Sherman's occupation of Columbia, South Carolina a day before, were major blows to the dying Confederacy. The fact that Joseph Johnston had been put in command of the Confederate army in North Carolina was of minimal concern to Cox or the Union leadership. They knew momentum was on their side.[34]
>
> Cox wrote a lengthy letter to Helen describing how he and the others took the city of Wilmington.

Wilmington N.C. 23d Feb. 1865

At last in Wilmington, after a little campaign involving more discomforts than we usually have encountered in the same time, & resulting chiefly from the fact that we have not had our wagons with us, they not having arrived & there being a great anxiety to get possession of this point at an early day to facilitate Sherman's movements.

On the night of the 12th we made a movement up the sea-beach with a view to getting above the enemy's lines & so turning their flank. The wind was blowing a gale from the north & as we moved silently up the shore, the surf came swelling in like thunder, the moon-beams glittering over the breakers as they tumbled in, & our long black line on the white sand looking like a great snake as we moved along. The wind was piercing, finding every button hole, & penetrating our clothing in a way I never before experienced.

We marched about four miles, when the order was countermanded in consequence of the gale preventing the steamer from towing around on the outside the boats which were to convey us over myrtle beach sound, a long narrow strip of water which separated us from the enemy.

We marched back to camp before midnight, to find part of our tents blown down, & the gale coursing over the narrow strip of sand on which we were encamped. Next day was milder, & we endeavored to get our camp in some shape again.

On the 14th the same movement was attempted again, this time the pontoons being drawn along the banks upon trucks. The night was not as cold & stormy as the 12th, but much darker, & the surf was rolling in heavier. We worked along with the pontoon train till two o'clock in the morning when it became evident that we should be hindered by it, till it would be too late to complete the movement that night, & it was again & finally abandoned. We did not get back to camp until nearly morning & slept nearly all day of the 15th.

Early on the 16th we were ordered aboard steamers to go down to Smithville, on the opposite side of the Cape Fear river, near the Southern inlet, & the whole day was used in this maneuver, our baggage not getting down till after dark. So when our tents were up we had barely time to get supper & go to bed at a reasonable hour.

Immediately after breakfast on the 17th we marched northward from Smithville, driving back the enemy's skirmishers & cavalry till we reached a point within a mile of Fort Anderson, a strong fort some six miles above Fort Fisher, & on the opposite side of the river. Here we halted & extended our lines to the river on our right, to communicate with Gen. S. on his hd. qrs. ship & with the fleet.

At 7 next morning we pushed in close to the fort, driving the enemy pickets inside the works, which extended from the fort itself to a large marshy pond called Orton pond, 3/4 of a mile from the river. We made a careful reconnaissance of the position, keeping up a sharp skirmishing fight with the enemy who opened on us hotly with both musketry & artillery, the fleet meanwhile bombarding the fort, though as we afterward learned, without doing any serious injury.

Being satisfied that it would cost too much to assault the works directly, Gen. S. ordered me to leave two brigades, & take two others on a long detour around the Orton pond to turn the position. The circuit was about 13 miles, the pond or lake being some eight miles in length.

A div. of Gen. Terry's command met me about five miles out and joined my forces just at dark. We encamped for the night at the head of the pond, after a very sharp skirmish with the rebel cavalry, at the crossing of a creek with tangled swampy banks. At that place the creek was an impassable swamp & thicket some sixty or eight yards wide, the undergrowth being high enough to prevent our seeing over or through it, & the bank being quite steep down to the single narrow causeway which ran through it.

The rebels had some rifle pits completely covering the further end of the causeway, & as our advance guard threw a few skirmishers through the defile they were met by a volley of rifle shots as soon as they showed themselves. There followed a lively fight in which we tried to deploy skirmishers enough in the swamp to match the force in front, & finally succeeded in doing so after losing 8 men. The rebs ran off, & on their report that we had turned the head of the pond, Fort Anderson was evacuated during the night, & our march around to its rear was effected on the morning of the 19th without further opposition.

In making this movement & onward through the next day, we took no tents or baggage with us, carrying some coffee & crackers on a pack animal, & a blanket apiece on our horses, & sleeping on the ground by the camp fires.

The div. of Terry's command was then sent back to him, & my other brigades having joined me I pushed on after the rebels to Town Creek, a deep tide water stream about 8 miles from Wilmington. Here the rebels had torn up the bridge & occupied a fortified position on the other side, very difficult of approach. I skirmished with them some that evening, & got possession of a flat boat further down the stream, with which next morning the 20th I ferried over part of my command, got them through the rice swamps where we could not take a horse, & made a circuit of some three miles to the enemy's rear where we attacked them just before evening, routing them, capturing their artillery, three hundred & seventy five prisoners including nearly all their officers from the brigade commander down, & three flags.

On the 21st we pushed right on to the river bank opposite Wilmington being delayed by the necessity of rebuilding burnt bridges & etc., so that we reached the ferry about three o'clock. We skirmished across the river exchanging some cannon shots, & they set fire to their stores of cotton, turpentine, &e. & evacuated.

Thus my little command opened the road for Gen. Terry to march in, he having been unable to force either of the lines below the city, till our movements caused them to be evacuated.

My troops are temporarily encamped about this city, & I think we shall be here a few days. My hd. qrs. are in a magnificent house, but it is totally unfurnished, so that its magnificence is barn like, the marble mantles & splendid pier glasses making the bare floors with our camp chairs for furniture look all the more desolate.

I am finishing this in haste as Gen. Schofield has sent for me & I must go down to his headquarters.

With the first part of his mission completed, Schofield now turned to opening the line of communication from Beaufort and New Bern, North Carolina into the interior to Goldsboro. He ordered Cox to take command of the District of Beaufort and the three divisions which were assembling there. His task was to protect the reconstruction of the railroad to Goldsboro so that it could supply Sherman when he arrived there. The same day, Schofield asked the War Department to permanently assign Cox as commander of the XXIII Corps.[35]

Cox began his move into the interior from New Bern on March 2. Unfortunately, many of the troops that he had been given were untried, and even his veterans had not seen any fighting for several weeks.[36] On March 6, in one of the last gasps of the Confederacy, Braxton Bragg tried to stop Cox at the Battle of Wyse Forks, near Kinston, North Carolina. On March 7, Bragg routed one of Cox's green regiments, but Cox quickly brought up the rest of the division, which checked the Confederate advance. After several further unsuccessful attacks, Bragg retreated on March 10 and Cox continued his railroad repairs to Goldsboro.[37] This would prove to be his last fighting of the war. On March 14, Cox marched into Kinston. He occupied Goldsboro on March 22, the same day that Sherman announced the retreat of Johnston and the uniting of the armies at Goldsboro, which was completed on March 24th.[38]

On March 23, the three armies Sherman had led to Atlanta were re-united and engaged in a celebratory parade. In his memoirs, Cox described the festivities in a way that underlined the camaraderie of the men who had fought so long and hard together in the West and who now, reunited in the East, could sense that the end of the war was not far off. He wrote,

On Thursday, the 23rd, Sherman joined us in person, and we paraded the Twenty-third corps to honor the march-past of Slocum's Army of Georgia, the Fourteenth and Twentieth AC, as they came in from Bentonville. Sherman took his place with us by the roadside, and the formal reunion with the comrades who had fought with us in the Atlanta campaign was an event to stir deep emotions in our hearts.

The men who had traversed the Carolinas were ragged and dirty, their faces were begrimed by the soot of their camp-fires of pine-knots in the forests, but their arms were in order, and they stepped out with the sturdy swing that marked all our Western troops.

By contrast, Cox noted, his men greeted Sherman's in new uniforms, which they had just received from the quartermaster, and the veterans presumed Cox and his men were all "rookies." Cox commented, "tatterdemalions who had made the march to the sea were disposed to chaff us as if we were new recruits or pampered garrison troops. 'Well, sonnies!' a regimental wag cried out, 'do they issue butter to you regularly now?' 'Oh, yes! to be sure!' was the instant retort; 'but *we* trade it off for soap!' The ironical emphasis on the 'we' was well understood and greeted with roars of laughter, and learning that our men were really those who had been with them in Georgia and had fought at Franklin and Nashville before making the tour of the North to come by sea and rejoin them in North Carolina, they made the welkin ring again with cheers."[39]

Cox's last letter in the typescript was written before these events on March 17. In it, as in the preceding three letters below, he discussed his fighting, his concern for his men, and his happiness that his men had shown their appreciation for his leadership by giving him a new horse as a parting gift. He clearly sensed that the war was going to end soon, but would not risk saying so.

Wilmington, N.C. 25th Feb. 1865
I am about to run up the coast tonight to take command temporarily of

our forces operating from Newbern. I shall take my aides, & Maj. Dow my Inspec. Gen. with me, the rest of the staff I shall leave here.

The country here is a queer mixture of sandy fine lands thickly interspersed with swamps & small lakes. It is all as flat as a pancake, & I presume will not be found different till we get about a hundred miles up the river.

I find my movement on the West side of the river has given us more éclat than we had reckoned upon, & has at once put our Western troops on the footing we like to see them on with other troops.

Gen. Schofield informs me that he has made application to the War Dept. for my permanent assignment to the command of the 23d Corps & Dory to the 24th with a view to consolidate all the troops in the two Corps.

Newbern N.C. 2d March 1865

I left Wilmington to come here on the 28th, but was delayed two days at Ft. Fisher by a gale of wind which made the Capt. of our vessel afraid to put to sea. Gen. [Innis] Palmer who has been commanding here, had come down to see Gen. S. & was of our party returning, together with his wife & mother-in-law, his surgeon with his wife & sister-in-law, & several members of Gen. Palmer's staff. Also Gen. [Samuel] Carter of E. Tenn. who has come on to join our command.

As we lay at Ft. Fisher in the midst of the fleet, the presence of the ladies, soon attracted the many officers, & in spite of the weather we had a very gay time.

We took breakfast & lunch on board one of the ships, called on the Admiral on his flag-ship, visited the Monitor Montauk, & several of the gun boats, & the whole party went over Ft. Fisher. On the 28th we started though the weather had not yet cleared trusting that the heavy rain of the previous night had beaten down the sea. We had a rough stormy trip across to Beaufort, but not a long one, as we were at sea only about nine hours.

We then took a freight train & came on to Newbern, reaching here about eight o'clock. We found a tavern here in an old fashioned sort of house, but our living has been quite good, & for those so long away from the seaboard, quite to our taste, fresh shad & oysters forming the staple articles of diet.

The troops here are odds & ends, & will not be as efficient as our own Corps, but I hope they will accomplish all we expect of them, & we shall soon be reunited with our own command, & not long after with Sherman's army. It will be a happy day for us when we get once more into good regular shape for field work, but I fear it will be many a day before we get transportation &e in the condition we had at Nashville.

I shall go up the country tomorrow with my troops which are collecting here now, & our movement will of course be toward Kinston & Goldsboro, building the railroad behind us as we go.

Near Kinston N.C. 12th March 1865

The first ten days have been days of life in a swamp, ending up with two days of battle, in which I met the remains of Hood's old army of the Tenn, together with Hoke's division, & defeated them.

My troops here were raw & inexperienced in the field as were also two out of three of my Div. commanders, so that I had an unusual weight of responsibility on my shoulders. We were wholly without wagons & so were delayed till the railroad could be rebuilt behind us as we advanced. The enemy sensible of the danger of allowing us to push much farther, & learning that the other two divisions of the 23d Corps were en route to join me, concentrated S.D. Lee's & Stewart's Corps of Hood's army & [Robert] Hoke's Div which had been in front of Wilmington & came at me.

The first day they hit a small brigade which was a little in advance, & which was not handled by its commander as it should be, & routed it, capturing probably five hundred men. I came on the ground just as the Div. commander had learned of his misfortune.

The first work was to make disposition of the rest of the div. to hold the rebs in check while I brought up other troops. The rest of the command was then quickly brought into position, the enemy checked & no ground lost except that which had been held by the advanced brigade. My lines were made as strong as the nature of the position would admit, & the next day was spent in strengthening them & feeling the enemy.

On Fri the 10th their reinforcements having come up fully, they made a desperate effort to crush me, swinging well out on my left flank. I have never had to handle troops so rapidly. I brought part of my right wing over to the left, taking first about half from my centre, all at double quick, & hurled them in on the enemy as he swept around my left. He was evidently surprised at meeting me there, & in about one hour, I had him completely routed at that point & in disorderly retreat.

Our men then sent up a rousing cheer, which I think the enemy mistook for a signal of their success on my left, & in they came on my centre with a yell. I then double quicked men & artillery back to the centre from the left, where I had kept only one rank of men, & at it we went again. We continually repulsed them, but they were anxious to win & though badly cut up, did not finally retreat till about four o'clock when they fell back to their works.

I didn't know but I should catch it on my right next, & so did not dare push far in pursuit beyond my own line of breastworks. During the night they withdrew entirely beyond the Neuse river, abandoning Kinston, which was the prize for which we were contending, & we are only waiting for the R.R. to progress far enough to bring us supplies before we advance again.

My loss in Fri's engagement was about fifty killed & two hundred fifty wounded. The rebels could not have lost less than a thousand.

The field is as flat as a board, & became a decidedly warm place under the fire, but my usual personal good luck attended me & I was unhurt. One of my orderlies has his arm carried off by a shell, another was shot through the knee, another through the ear, & several had their horses killed within five paces of me.

Gen. [George] Greene, who was volunteering as a staff officer had his horse shot under him as we sat side by side. My personal staff were kept on the gallop carrying orders & bringing up troops & were less exposed. The other two div. of the Corps were some twenty miles away, & hearing the rapid cannonade marched rapidly forward.

During the night couriers reached them informing them of the battle, but of the probability also that it might be renewed the next day. They marched again at two in the morning, & the officers said they never saw the old 3d div. march as it did when the word was passed along the line that I might be in peril before they could get up. They plunged through swamps & streams, & closed up in a rapid energetic effort to reach me in time.

Their aid however was not needed, though it was affecting to get the assurances that the officers & men burned with zeal to get up to the help of their old commander. At one place the men were slowly filing over a narrow foot bridge across a stream waist deep. Col. Hartsuff Corps Inspector, rode up & said, 'Gen. Cox has been fighting the enemy two days & may be in danger of defeat unless the 3d div. make haste.' The men with one cheer dashed into the stream & through it, waiting for no bridge, though it was a cold frosty night.

Kinston N.C. 17th March 1865

I had intended writing you yesterday, as we reached this place the day before, but having got damp in a sudden shower which came up just as we were going into camp here, I was too nearly sick yesterday to do anything but lounge on my cot & keep as quiet as possible. I was sore all over & had some fever all day, but at night after drinking some hot tea, I got to bed & covered up so warm as to be soon in a sweat, & this morning I am all right again.

The day after the battle in front of this place, the enlisted men of the

16th Kentucky regiment surprised me by sending me a very fine roan mare, a splendid animal of good Ken. blood, easily worth six hundred dollars, as horses are selling. Coming as it did just as the old command came up & joined us after the fight, it was a very pleasant reminder that the soldiers of the 3d Div. have a real attachment for me. I enclose the note which accompanied the gift.

Sherman will be within communicating distance very soon. We hear from him by couriers & scouts every few days, & the junction of the armies cannot be many days distant. Bragg thought he had me at great disadvantage on the 10th & began to 'crow before he was out of the woods,' as I understand he had telegraphed to Richmond that he had routed us on the 8th when he had only struck one brigade which was carelessly handled, & on the 10th he got handsomely whipped.

Of course the rebs pictured that their evacuation of this place was due to the fears of Sherman but he was altogether too far off to hurt them then, & we should have had a different story if they had succeeded in driving us back on Newbern.

Sherman was planning an advance with his re-united army in early April, but it would never take place. On April 11, Sherman received word that Lee had surrendered to Grant at Appomattox, and he sent word to his subordinates, including Cox, to let the troops know the good news. The following description of the reaction of Cox and his men to Lee's surrender, written by one of Cox's classmates at Oberlin then serving under him, is a fitting finale to this chapter in Cox's life:

> On a bright day in April, 1865, Major-General J. D. Cox, commanding the Twenty-third Army AC, with his staff and escort, was riding leisurely at the head of the marching column. . . . Though hourly expecting news of important movements, we had no expectation of decisive victory . . . an orderly rode slowly toward us, bearing a message. General Cox opened it in the usual businesslike manner, and read it over as he would have done an ordinary official communication.
>
> Happening then to cast my eyes toward the general, I noticed his face suddenly brighten, and in great animation he turned and directed the escort and staff to be drawn up in line, that he might read to them a message from General Sherman. It was done in a hurry, and with head uncovered he read a brief dispatch stating

that General Lee, with his entire army, had surrendered to Grant at Appomattox. It was the message long looked for, long fought for, and though it came to us on the roadside so unexpectedly, its full significance was at once appreciated. It meant home, and wife, and children, and happy meetings, throughout the land. Before the message was read, General Cox ordered all hats off and throats cleared for three rousing cheers.

As Cox wrote in his diary for the day, "The army nearly went crazy with joy. ... [W]e hope the last battle of the war has been fought."[40]

Afterword

Confederate Commander Joe Johnston, after trying to find a way to keep fighting, ultimately saw the futility of his position. Defying orders from Jefferson Davis, then on the run from pursuing Union troops, Johnston agreed in mid-April to discuss peace terms with Sherman. After several controversial days, including Washington's rejection of the first agreement, Sherman and Johnston signed their final agreement on August 26, 1865. The inevitable joy of knowing that the war was now over for Cox was tempered by the news of the assassination of President Lincoln. Cox had great faith in Lincoln and he wrote prophetically in his diary, "Mr. Johnson's disgrace of himself at the inauguration gives no little room for satisfaction in thinking of him as the President."[1]

With the surrender in place, Cox was assigned to be military governor of western North Carolina. He spent the next few weeks paroling Confederate troops and instilling order in the region. Separately, he and his campaign manager, Aaron Perry, finalized arrangements for him to contend for the nomination as Republican candidate for Governor of Ohio. On June 21, Cox won the nomination and, on June 30, he was re-assigned to Columbus as commander of the District of Ohio. His official responsibility there was to muster out Union troops, but he would spend most of the next few months campaigning for Governor. He won the election in October by over thirty thousand votes. He resigned from the Volunteer Army in early January of 1866, a few days before he was inaugurated as Governor.

It perhaps is not surprising that Cox chose to be pictured in his dress two-star general's uniform for his official portrait as Governor (see below). In many ways, his unexpected military career was the most successful period of a life in which this self-made Renaissance man excelled in many areas. The support and love he had from his beloved "Lilla" during his trying and triumphant times on and off the battlefield were integral elements of that success.

―――

The Coxes had been married for almost fifty-two years when Cox died in 1900 at the age of seventy-two. Two years earlier, they had celebrated their

Jacob Cox's Official Portrait as Governor of Ohio. Image provided by the Capitol Square Review and Advisory Board, Ohio Statehouse; photographed by Garth's Auctioneers and Appraiser, Delaware, Ohio.

fiftieth anniversary at the sumptuous home of their eldest son, Jacob Cox III, a Cleveland industrialist. Their six children who lived to adulthood became either successful businessmen or the wives of influential men. The eldest daughter, Helen Finney, married John Black, a mathematics professor at Wooster College, on August 6, 1878 and lived there afterward. The eldest son and namesake, Jacob Dolson Cox III, became, through a $2,000 loan from his father, the owner of a successful business, the Cleveland Twist Drill Company. Son Kenyon trained as an artist in Paris, and later became one of the best known and finest mural painters in the United States. Some of his paintings are on display today at the National Museum of American Art in Washington. Charles Norton Cox, the youngest son, became an entrepreneur in Colorado, specializing in orchard growing and cattle raising. The

The Coxes on their porch in Cincinnati, circa 1889, along with their daughter Hope Charlotte and three of their grandchildren. Courtesy of Oberlin College Archives.

The Coxes' gravesite in Spring Grove cemetery, Cincinnati, Ohio. Photograph by Gene Schmiel.

youngest daughter, Charlotte Hope, born in 1871, married a son of General John Pope in 1897. Cox's stepson and first biographer, William Cochran, became a respected lawyer in Cincinnati and the author of legal textbooks. For all those years, Helen Cox presided over the family as an aloof, aristocratic, but loving mother and wife. She died in 1911.[2]

Dolson, Helen, and many members of the family are buried in Spring Grove Cemetery in Cincinnati. In the center of the family plot is an obelisk on which is inscribed, "Jacob Dolson Cox, 1828: Soldier, Statesman, Scholar, Patriot. *Integer Vitae.*" Beneath that are the words, "Helen Finney Cochran, Wife of Jacob Dolson Cox, 1828–1911."

Notes

Preface

1. This incident is discussed in chapter 2, note 33. The original letter, with the description of the embarrassing family situation, is in the Cox Papers in the Oberlin College Archives, hereinafter referred to as Cox Papers.

Introduction

1. Cox to James Monroe, 23 October 1873, Cox Papers.
2. William Cox Cochran, *Political Experiences of Major General Jacob Dolson Cox*, vol. I, unpublished manuscript Cincinnati, 1940, Oberlin College Archives, Oberlin, Ohio, I, 1–4. The sources on Cox's early life are extremely scarce, but the most important source is this work, the biography of Cox by his stepson, which the latter wrote as a companion piece to Cox's *Military Reminiscences*.
3. Jacob Cox, "Why the Men of '61 Fought for the Union," *Atlantic Monthly* LXIX (March 1892): 25–26.
4. Allan C. Guelzo, "Charles Grandison Finney," in *The Human Tradition in the Civil War and Reconstruction*, ed. Steven Woodworth (Wilmington, DE: Scholarly Resources, 2000), 156.
5. James B. Stewart, *Holy Warriors: The Abolitionists and American Slavery* (New York: Hill and Wang, 1997), 59–60; Robert S. Fletcher, *A History of Oberlin College* (Oberlin: Oberlin College, 1943), 236–70.
6. William Cochran, Unpublished and untitled autobiography, William Cochran Papers, Oberlin College Archives.; https://www.gospeltruth.net/Finneyletters/finlets/finlet%201840-1849/finlet1846-05_19.htm
7. Cochran, "Helen Finney Cox," *Oberlin Alumni Magazine* (October 1911): 9.
8. See Eugene D. Schmiel, *Citizen-General: Jacob Dolson Cox and the Civil War Era* (Athens: Ohio University Press, 2014), 8–11. This source supplies his family background.
9. Charles E. Hambrick-Stowe, *Charles G. Finney and the Spirit of American Evangelism* (Grand Rapids, Michigan: Wm. B. Eerdmans, 1996), 271.
10. Cochran, *Political Experiences*, vol. I, 1314; Charles Hambrick-Stowe, *Charles*

Finney and the Spirit of American Evangelism. (Grand Rapids: Wm. B. Eerdmans, 1996), 271. Cox himself made no specific reference to this incident and its aftermath; however, in several letters in the 1850s to friends with whom he had studied theology, he made references to his honesty having been questioned. The letters are in the Cox Papers found in the Oberlin Archives.

11. See Schmiel's Chapter 1 of *Citizen General* for background about Cox's political evolution and his racial views. See Stephen Maizlish, *The Triumph of Sectionalism: The Transformation of Ohio Politics, 1844–1856* (Kent, Ohio: Kent State University Press, 1983). Maizlish provides background on the formation of the Ohio Republican Party. See Nat Brandt, *The Town that Started the Civil War* (Syracuse, NY: Syracuse University Press, 1990). Brandt discusses the Wellington Rescue and its aftermath.

12. While Cox always adamantly professed his distaste for patronage, it should be noted that he used his influence and position to get the militia appointment for himself. He never explained what seems to have been an illogical and inconsistent step, although perhaps he thought that, since it was to benefit himself and not others in return for favors, it was acceptable.

13. Jacob Cox, *Military Reminiscences of the Civil War,* vol. 1 (New York: Scribner's Sons, 1900), 67.

14. Cox, *Military Reminiscences,* vol. 1, 102.

15. Cochran, *Political Experiences,* 538. These sentiments, recounted to the author by Mary Rudd Cochran, Helen's granddaughter, were contained in a footnote to the edition of her father's book in the Oberlin Archives and were based on her recollections of a conversation with Helen Cox some years after the war.

16. Helen Cox to Lucretia Garfield, 6 April 1862, and July 19, 1863, Lucretia Garfield Papers, Library of Congress.

17. Helen Cox to Lucretia Garfield, 19 July 1863, Lucretia Garfield Papers, Library of Congress.

18. Jacob Cox to Helen Cox, 19 and 28 April 1861, Kenyon Cox Papers, Avery Library, Columbia University. These letters, written from Columbus, were not in the typescript.

19. Schmiel, *Citizen-General,* 44.

20. Helen to William Cochran, 13 January and 18 June 1862, Helen Cox Papers, Oberlin Archives.

21. H. Wayne Morgan, *Kenyon Cox, 1856–1919: A Life in American Art* (Kent, OH: Kent State University Press, 1994), 3. Schmiel, *Citizen-General,* 10–11.

22. See Schmiel's *Citizen General* for a description of Cox's military record.

23. Jacob Cox, *Military Reminiscences,* vol. 1, 165–91.

24. Cox to Dennison, July 9, 1865, Cox Papers.

1. The Making of a Soldier

1. Jacob Cox, *Military Reminiscences*, vol. 1, 1–2.
2. For a summary of these bills, see: *Ohio Senate Journal*, 54th General Assembly, Second Session, April 15–18, 1861, 200–302, and George B. Porter, *Ohio Politics During the Civil War Period*, (New York: Columbia University Press, 1911), 75–7 for a summary of these bills.
3. Cox, *Military Reminiscences*, 1, 9–10.
4. R. U. Johnson and C. C. Buell, eds., *Battles and Leaders of the Civil War*, vol. I (New York: Charles Scribner's Sons, 1887–1888), 89–90; George B. McClellan, *The Mexican War Diary of George B. McClellan* (Princeton University Press, 1917), 51 Stephen Sears, ed., *The Civil War Papers of George B. McClellan* (New York: DaCapo Press, 1988), 67. As seen in Sears, George B. McClellan telegrammed Cox on July 22, 1861.
5. See Eric J. Wittenberg, Edmund A. Sargus, and Penny L. Barrick, *Seceding from Secession: The Civil War, Politics, and the Creation of West Virginia* Savas Beatie, 2020). These authors offer an in-depth analysis of the political and legal aspects of the statehood creation effort.
6. Johnson and Buell, eds., *Battles and Leaders*, vol. 1, 96. For a discussion of the history of the militia, activities at Camp Dennison, and the first months of the war, see Matthew Oyos, "Ohio Militia in the Civil War," *Ohio History* 98 (Summer-Autumn 1989): 147–174.
7. Cox, *Military Reminiscences*, vol. 1, 3. These events are also described in the official history of the 11th Regiment: J. H. Horton and Solomon Teverbaugh, *A History of the Eleventh Regiment, Ohio Volunteer Infantry* (Dayton, Ohio: W. J. Shuey, 1866), 276–77.
8. Gustavus Bascom was the 20-year-old son of William Bascom, Ohio Republican Party leader and newspaper editor. Gustavus would stay on Cox's staff for two years before taking a staff position in the regular army.
9. General William Rosecrans was a West Point graduate who would eventually rise to become commander of the Army of the Cumberland.
10. Jacob and Helen Cox's daughter, Helen Finney Cox (b. July 8, 1850). Other children born before the war are: step-son William Cochran (b. March 29, 1848); Jacob D. Cox, Jr. (b. May 15, 1852); Kenyon Cox (b. October 27, 1856); Charles Norton Cox (b. July 28, 1858); and William Brewster Cox (b. January 26, 1861, died in infancy on September 14, 1861]. Another son, Dennison, was born in 1867, but died in 1868.
11. As would be seen, Cox learned eventually that DeVilliers was all dash, but little substance.

12. Here, Cox lets the reader know that both he and Helen understand French and that they agree that "men propose, but God decides."
13. The War of the Rebellion: A Compilation of the Official Records [hereinafter referred to as OR] of the Union and Confederate Armies (Washington, D.C.: Government Printing Office, 1880–1897), 51, pt. 1 338–39. For a discussion of these plans, see also Stephen A. Sears, *George B. McClellan, the Young Napoleon* (New York: Ticknor and Fields, 1988), 74–76.

2. Baptism of Fire

1. See Festus Summers, *The Baltimore and Ohio in the Civil War* (New York: G. P. Putnam's Sons, 1939); Thomas Weber, *The Northern Railroads in the Civil War, 1861–1865* (Bloomington: Indiana University Press, 1952); and John E. Clark, *Railroads in the Civil War* (Baton Rouge: Louisiana State University Press, 2004).
2. Cox, *Military Reminiscences*, vol. 1, 144–45.
3. Johnson and Buell, eds., vol. I, 127–28; *OR*, 2, 51–52, 64–65; Oyos, "Ohio Militia in the Civil War," *Ohio History* 98: 167.
4. *OR*, 2, 239–44.
5. *Ibid.*, 197.
6. Sears, ed., *The Civil War Papers*, 55–56. McClellan to Cox on July 14, 1861.
7. *Ibid.*, 67. McClellan to Cox on July 22, 1861.
8. Cox, *Military Reminiscences*, vol. 1, 250; Gavin Mortimer, *Double Death: The True Story of Pryce Lewis, the Civil War's Most Daring Spy* (New York: Walker Publishing, 2010), 46–50, 8084. This George Patton was the grandfather of the famous WWII General George Patton.
9. Cox, 25 July 1861, Roy Bird Cook Papers, West Virginia University Collection; *OR*, 51, pt. 1, 425–26.
10. Cox, *Military Reminiscences*, vol. 1, 73–79. See Clayton R. Newell, *Lee vs. McClellan: The First Campaign* (Washington: Regnery Publishing, 2010), 178–79.
11. *OR*, 2, 1011–12; *OR*, 51, pt. 1, 440; Newell, *Lee Vs. McClellan*, 267.
12. Pierpont led the political effort to create the state of West Virginia. For a discussion of these issues, see Wittenberg, Sargus, and Barrick, *Seceding from Secession*.
13. Tompkins was an 1836 graduate of West Point. After retreating from Cox's advance, Tompkins spent most of the war in Richmond in staff positions.
14. Cox, *Military Reminiscences*, vol. 1, 49–50, 76–78; Charles Whittlesey, *War Memoranda: Cheat River to the Tennessee 1861–1862* (Cleveland: William W. Williams, 1884), 78. For accounts of this incident, see William D. Sloan and Lisa M. Purcell, *American Journalism: History, Principles, Practices* (Jeffer-

son, NC: Macfarland, 2002), 231; Mark W. Summers, *The Press Gang: Newspapers and Politics, 1865–1878* (Chapel Hill: University of North Carolina Press, 1994), 21–22.
15. *New York Times*, September 18, 1861, 2.
16. Cox, *Military Reminiscences*, vol. 1, 93–96; Johnson and Buell, eds., vol. 1, 145.
17. See T. Harry Williams, *Hayes of the 23rd, the Civil War Volunteer Officer* (New York: Alfred A. Knopf, 1965), 120–21. Williams was an esteemed historian, and he analyzed accurately Cox's military leadership during this period.
18. *OR*, 5, 148–49.
19. Cox to Helen, 17 October 1861, Cox Papers. Cox's aide Gustavus Bascom called the movement back to Gauley an "ignominious retreat" and boasted to his father that if Rosecrans hadn't ordered it, Cox would have wiped out Wise and Floyd. This information comes from a letter from Bascom to W. T. Bascom, 15 October 1861, William Bascom-Hiram Little Papers, Western Reserve Historical Society, Cleveland, Ohio.
20. As quoted in James McPherson, *Battle Cry of Freedom: The Civil War Era* (New York: Oxford University Press, 1988), 302–3.
21. Cox, *Military Reminiscences*, vol. 1, 131–32.
22. Benham's biography is in Mark M. Boatner, III, *The Civil War Dictionary* (New York: Vintage Books, 1991), 58–59; *OR*, 51, pt. 1, 251; *OR*, 5, 657.
23. Johnson and Buell, eds., vol. 1, 148.
24. *OR*, 5, 691.
25. Cox to Garfield, 9 September 1861, James A. Garfield Papers, Library of Congress.
26. Hayes's letter to Lucy, 29 September 1861, and a notation in his personal diary, 2 February 1862. Both of these are found in Charles Richard Williams, ed., *Diary and Letters of Rutherford Birchard Hayes*, vol. 2 (Columbus: Ohio Archeological and Historical Society, 1922–26), 104, 198.
27. Cox to Garfield, 8 November 1861 and 2 February 1862, James A. Garfield Papers, Library of Congress.
28. Cox, *Military Reminiscences*, vol. 1, 168.
29. For background on the "other Civil War," the guerrilla conflict, see, among others: Daniel Sutherland, *American Civil War Guerrillas, Changing the Rules of Warfare.* (Santa Barbara, CA: Praeger, 2013) and Kenneth Noe and Shannon Wilson, eds., *The Civil War in Appalachia* (Knoxville: University of Tennessee Press, 1997).
30. See *OR*, 5, 54 for McClellan's report in 1863 about all of his operations, in which he included the full text of Lincoln's announcement creating the Mountain Department on March 11.
31. Cox, *Military Reminiscences*, vol. 1, 202–22. During this period, future president William McKinley joined Cox's force as a commissary sergeant. Hayes

was McKinley's commanding colonel in the 23rd Regiment. These facts are in William H. Armstrong, *Major McKinley: William McKinley and the Civil War* (Kent, OH: Kent State University Press, 2000). For the Shenandoah campaign, see Peter Cozzens, *Shenandoah 1862: Stonewall Jackson's Valley Campaign* (Chapel Hill: University of North Carolina Press, 2008).

32. George Crook was a West Point graduate who served under Cox until after the Battle of Antietam. He was one of the most renowned "Indian Fighters" of the nineteenth century, but one whom the Indians trusted to treat them fairly.

33. *OR*, Series 2, 2, 829–57; Cox to Helen Cox, 26 June 1862, Cox Papers. The transcript version of the letter from June 26 differs only slightly from the original, which is in the Cox Papers at Oberlin. However, it provides an example of at least one kind of material Helen and Jacob Cox did not include in the transcript. It seems that in September 1861, the husband of Cox's sister Redelia, a Canadian named William Gilchrist, a merchant in Philadelphia, was arrested for allegedly selling contraband to the Confederacy. Gilchrist claimed that he had been deceived by others and denied the charges. Redelia wrote to Secretary of State William Seward underlining that her brother (Cox) was fighting for the Union in West Virginia and that she could not believe her husband would break the law. Ultimately, the British authorities intervened and, with Seward's agreement "upon grounds of national comity and wise policy, Gilchrist was released the following April. Cox made no specific mention of this incident in his papers or memoirs, but in the original, unedited version of this letter, he wrote to Helen, "I am very sorry to hear that Redelia's hardships do not seem to be much relieved by the release of William. You may send the receipt from the attorneys to her"—implying that Cox had paid their legal bills.

34. McPherson, *Battle Cry of Freedom*, 502–3; Sears, *Young Napoleon*, 227–28; Mark Grimsley, *The Hard Hand of War: Union Military Policy toward Southern Civilians, 1861–1865* (Cambridge: Harvard University Press, 1995), 23, 94–95.

35. *OR*, 12, pt. 3, 435, 451.

36. Interestingly, the Coxes' youngest daughter, Charlotte Hope, would marry one of John Pope's sons and Cox would become more sympathetic about General Pope once the latter became a member of the family.

37. *OR*, 12, pt. 3, 560–67.

38. *OR*, 12, pt. 3, 941–46; 19, pt. 1, 1069. Cox, *Military Reminiscences*, vol. 1, 392–93; *OR*, 19, pt. 1, 142–43.

39. Ewing was one of the sons of the powerful Ohio politician Thomas Ewing, Sr. and also the foster brother of General William T. Sherman. Ewing had been expelled from West Point during his senior year for unexplained reasons. However, he was an alcoholic, which seemingly was the root cause.

3. On the National Stage

1. *OR*, 19, pt. 3, 805.
2. Joseph Harsh, *Taken at the Flood: Robert E. Lee and Confederate Strategy in the Maryland Campaign of 1862* (Kent, OH: Kent State University Press, 1999), 21; *OR*, 19, pt. 2, 601–2.
3. See D. Scott Hartwig, *To Antietam Creek: The Maryland Campaign of September 1862* (Baltimore: Johns Hopkins University Press, 2012) for one of the best overviews of this time in the war.
4. Hayes to S. Birchard Hayes, 7 September 1862. This document can be found in Williams, ed., *Diary and Letters of Rutherford Birchard Hayes*, vol. 2, 347. Hayes here disregarded the fact that the Army of the Potomac had been engaged in many significant battles over the previous months, whereas he and his men had essentially been doing garrison duty.
5. *OR*, 19, pt. 2, 255, pt. 1, 758; Stephen W. Sears, *Landscape Turned Red: The Battle of Antietam* (New York: Ticknor and Fields, 1983), 106–10. McClellan's exaggeration of the numbers of his enemy are discussed in Edwin Fishel, "Pinkerton and McClellan: Who Deceived Whom?," in *Civil War History* 34, no. 2 (September 1988): 118, 137, 142.
6. Johnson and Buell, eds., *Battles and Leaders*, vol. 2, 583–85; Cox, *Military Reminiscences*, vol. 1, 271–77.
7. Ibid., 303–4. In this section of his memoirs, Cox identifies Porter as the *eminence grise* behind this decision. See Cox to Emerson Opdycke, 24 January 1876, Oberlin College Archives. In this letter, Cox wrote, "it is the luck of men who are second in command to get ignored for a good deal of the work they do and it several times happened to me in the war . . . thus at Antietam I actually commanded the 9th corps and Burnside was nominally in command of the 'wing' consisting of the 9th and Hooker's corps." Additionally, for a discussion of these issues, see Hartwig, *To Antietam Creek,* and Ethan Rafuse, *McClellan's War: The Failure of Moderation in the Struggle for the Union* (Bloomington: Indiana University Press, 2005). Hartwig sides with Cox, while Rafuse sides with McClellan.
8. Sears, *Landscape Turned Red*, 291–92; *OR*, vol, 51, pt. 1, 844 In *McClellan's War*, 326, historian Rafuse, who generally supports McClellan, admits that not sending Porter forward "clearly cost him a golden opportunity to destroy Lee's army and possibly end the war" (326). See Eugene D. Schmiel's *Lincoln, Antietam and a Northern Lost Cause* (Seattle, WA: Amazon Publishing, 2019) for an alternative history which posits that the Union could have won an overwhelming victory if Cox had advanced at 2 instead of 3 p.m.
9. *OR*, 19, pt. 1, 65–66.

4. Paper General

1. *OR*, 19, pt. 2, 380; Cox, *Military Reminiscences*, vol. 1, 391–92.
2. Tod was Governor of Ohio, Pierpont of the "Restored" Government of Virginia and, in effect, of the incipient state of West Virginia.
3. Cox to Perry, 9 February 1863, Cox Papers. See Schmiel, *Citizen-General*, 179–90. While Cox did not specifically address the issue, it seems likely that he thought that keeping freedmen in the South after the war was preferable to allowing them to migrate North.
4. Cox to Chase, 1 January 1863, Cox Papers.
5. Cox, *Military Reminiscences*, vol. 1, 42735; Cox to Chase, 25 March 1863, Salmon Chase Papers, Historical Society of Pennsylvania Thomas Ewing to Hugh Ewing, 12 March 1863, Thomas Ewing Family Papers, Ohio Historical Society; Schmiel, *Citizen-General*, 96–97, 106.
6. Cox, *Military Reminiscences*, vol. 1, 455.
7. Helen Cox to Lucretia Garfield, 19 July 1863, Lucretia Garfield Papers, Library of Congress. Helen wrote, "I was with my husband, which you know was enough in itself to insure complete happiness."
8. *OR*, 23, pt. 2, 237; Cox, *Military Reminiscences*, vol. 1, 454.
9. *OR*, Series 2, 5, 633–46, 23, 316. Stanton was notorious for switching sides when he saw it as politically wise.
10. Cox, *Military Reminiscences*, vol. 1, 458–72.
11. Ibid., 495509; Allan Keller, *Morgan's Raid* (New York: Bobbs-Merrill Company, 1961).
12. See *OR*, Series 3, 3, 1023–25 for the correspondence among Cox, Tod, and Stanton regarding this effort.
13. Helen Cox to Lucretia Garfield, 19 July 1863, Lucretia Garfield Papers.
14. *OR*, 31, pt. 3, 314, 457.

5. East Tennessee and the Struggle for Position

1. Cox, *Military Reminiscences*, vol. 2, 99–103. For an overview of the campaign in and around Knoxville, see Earl Hess, *The Knoxville Campaign: Burnside and Longstreet in East Tennessee* (Knoxville: University of Tennessee Press, 2012).
2. Glenn V. Longacre and John E. Haas, eds., *To Battle for God and the Right: The Civil War Letterbooks of Emerson Opdycke* (Urbana: University of Illinois Press, 2003), 149.
3. Cox, 10 February 1864, Cox Papers. This letter detailed Special Order no. 41 from the headquarters of the Department of Ohio. The best biography of

Schofield is Donald Connelly, *John M. Schofield and the Politics of Generalship* (Chapel Hill: University of North Carolina Press, 2006).
4. *OR*, 32, pt. 3, 245.
5. This phrase means getting into a more difficult situation than you expected.
6. Cox, *Military Reminiscences*, vol. 2: 203–6.
7. This section underlines that Cox did not want to get involved in guerrilla warfare and that the "chivalry of fair field warfare" was where he wanted to be. See Noe and Wilson, *The Civil War in Appalachia*, for a discussion of guerrilla warfare in Tennessee during this period.

6. *The Atlanta Campaign*

1. Cox, *Sherman's Battle for Atlanta* (New York: Scribner's, 1882), 23–24; *OR*, 32, pt. 3, 245.
2. B. H. Liddell Hart, *Strategy*, 2nd rev. ed. (New York: Penguin Group, 1967), 131–34.
3. Cox, Sherman's Battle for Atlanta, 50.
4. *Ibid.*, 24.
5. Cox, 14 and 16 May 1864, Cox Papers; Cox, *Military Reminiscences*, vol. 2, 222–23; Johnson and Buell, eds., *Battles and Leaders*, vol. 4, 269.
6. *OR*, 38, pt. 4, 243; *OR*, 38, pt. 2, 511, 581, 610–11.
7. Johnson and Buell, eds., *Battles and Leaders*, vol. 4, 267–69; Albert Castel, *Decision in the West: The Atlanta Campaign of 1864* (Lawrence: University Press of Kansas, 1992), 197–200; Cox, *Military Reminiscences*, vol. 2, 230–31; Cox, *Sherman's Battle for Atlanta*, 55–56; *OR*, 38, pt. 4, 242.
8. William T. Sherman, *Personal Memoirs*, vol. 2 (New York: Charles L. Webster, 1891), 511–12; Cox, *Military Reminiscences*, 237; *OR*, 38, pt. 4, 273. See Edward Hageman, *The American Civil War and the Origins of Modern Warfare* (Bloomington: Indiana University Press, 1992), 175–210 for a discussion of the evolution of tactics toward the defensive and trench warfare.
9. *OR*, 38, pt. 4, 582; Cox, *Military Reminiscences*, vol. 2, 259; Johnson and Buell, eds., *Battles and Leaders*, vol. 4, 271–72.
10. Cox, *Military Reminiscences*, vol. 2, 260; Cox, *Sherman's Battle*, 117–18; Sherman, *Memoirs*, vol. 2, 530–31; John M. Schofield, *Forty-Six Years in the Army* (New York: Century Company, 1897), 143; Castel, *Decision in the West*, footnote 71, 598. See Earl Hess, *Kennesaw Mountain* (Chapel Hill University of North Carolina Press, 2013).
11. *OR*, 38, pt. 4, 607, 617, 621; Cox, 27 and 28 June 1864, Cox Papers; Connelly, *John M. Schofield*, 183; Schofield, *Forty-Six Years in the Army*, 144; Johnson and Buell, eds., *Battles and Leaders*, vol. 4, 273.

12. Sherman, *Memoirs*, vol. 2, 543–44; Cox, *Military Reminiscences*, vol. 2, 270; *OR*, 38, pt. 5, 193.
13. Johnson and Buell, eds., *Battles and Leaders*, vol. 4, 339–41; Cox, *Military Reminiscences*, vol. 2, 280; *OR*, 38, pt. 5, 219, 900.
14. *OR*, 38, pt. 5, 247; Sherman, *Memoirs*, vol. 2, 561; Johnson and Buell, eds., *Battles and Leaders*, vol. 4, 341.
15. *OR*, 38, pt. 5, 909.
16. Cox, *Sherman's Battle*, 183–87; Cox, *Military Reminiscences*, vol. 2, 280; Johnson and Buell, eds., *Battles and Leaders*, vol. 4, 341; *OR*, 38, pt. 5, 289.
17. *OR*, 38, pt. 5, 364–66.
18. *OR*, 38, pt. 5, 368–72, 378–85, 391–94, 438; Cox, *Sherman's Battle for Atlanta*, 189–94.
19. *OR*, 38, pt. 5, 940–43, 946; Johnson and Buell, eds., *Battles and Leaders*, vol. 4, 342; Cox, *Sherman's Battle*, 196–98.
20. Sherman, *Memoirs*, vol. 2, 576–77; Cox, *Military Reminiscences*, vol. 2, 299; *OR*, 38, pt. 5, 642, 649.
21. *OR*, 38, pt. 5, 990–93; Cox, 26 August, 1864; Cox Papers; Cox, *Sherman's Battle*, 198; Castel, *Decision in the West*, 486–87.
22. Cox, *Military Reminiscences*, vol. 2, 526–27; Frederick Fout, *The Dark Days of the Civil War, 1861–1865* (Indiana: F.A.Wagenfuhr, 1903), 403–4. The woman certainly did not meet with Cox, who of course would not have cursed. Cox's comments underline that, while he was an intensely-serious person, he could take a joke.

7. The Taking of Atlanta

1. *OR*, 38, pt. 5, 732–35, 1023; Johnson and Buell, eds., *Battles and Leaders*, vol. 4, 343.
2. Cox, *Sherman's Battle*, 218–19; *OR*, 39, pt. 2, 411–13, 432.
3. Johnson and Buell, eds., *Battles and Leaders*, vol. 4, 344; John Bell Hood, *Advance and Retreat: Personal Experiences in the United States and Confederate Armies* (New Orleans: G. T. Beauregard, 1880), 206; *OR*, 38, pt. 5, 1023–24
4. Cox, *Sherman's Battle*, 225–39; Johnson and Buell, eds., *Battles and Leaders*, vol. 4, 254; Castel, *Decision in the West*, 552–53; Hood, *Advance and Retreat*, 263–64.
5. *OR*, 39, pt. 3, 357–58, 377–78, 594–95.
6. Cox, *Military Reminiscences*, vol. 2, 320–22; *OR*, 39, pt. 3, 511, 534, 535, 537.

8. Final Campaigns

1. *OR*, 39, pt. 3, 756; Cox, *Sherman's March to the Sea* (New York: Scribner's 1882), 6–7; Cox, *Military Reminiscences*, vol. 2, 328.
2. *OR*, 45, pt. 1, 1245, 1254.
3. *OR*, 45, pt. 1, 958, 989, 998; Schofield, *Forty-Six Years*, 167–68; Cox, *Military Reminiscences*, vol. 2, 340.
4. *OR*, 45, pt. 1, 1019–21; Hood, *Advance and Retreat*, 282; Schofield, *Forty-Six Years*, 168; *OR*, 45, pt. 1, 1017.
5. *OR*, 45, pt. 1, 358, 1015–17, 1039, 1086–91; Cox, *Military Reminiscences*, vol. 2, 344; Schofield, *Forty-Six Years*, 175; Hood, *Advance and Retreat*, 282.
6. Cox, *The Battle of Franklin, Tennessee, November 30, 1864: A Monograph* (New York: Scribner's, 1897), 97, 26; Cox, *Sherman's March*, 69; *OR*, 45, pt. 1, 1109–16, 1144. Wilson's biographer paints a picture of a befuddled commander. See Edward Longacre, *Grant's Cavalryman* (Mechanicsburg, PA: Stackpole Books, 1972), 168–74; Hood, *Advance and Retreat*, 283–84.
7. *OR*, 45, pt. 1, 1138–42.
8. Cox, *Sherman's March*, 73–74; Cox, *Battle of Franklin*, 31; Longacre and Hass, eds., *To Battle for God*, 249. Hood, *Advance and Retreat*, 284–85; *OR*, 45, pt. 1, 653.
9. Cox, *Battle of Franklin*, 34; *OR*, 45, pt. 1, 342, 1138; Schofield, *Forty-Six Years*, 174.
10. Cox, *Battle of Franklin*, 38–39; *OR*, 45, pt. 1, 1172; Schofield, *Forty-Six Years*, 175.
11. There are several books which describe the Confederate decision-making process for the Battle of Franklin. See Brian Craig Miller, *John Bell Hood and the Fight for Civil War Memory* (Knoxville: University of Tennessee Press, 2010); William L. White, *Let Us Die Like Men: The Battle of Franklin, November 30, 1864* (El Dorado Hills, California: Savas Beatie, 2019); as well as Hood's memoirs and his report in the *OR*, 45, pt. 1, 657–58.
12. Cox, *Sherman's March*, 84–85, 88; *OR*, 45, pt. 1, 349–56; Cox, *Battle of Franklin*, 53, 60.
13. *OR*, 45, pt. 1, 342–44, 352; Cox, *Sherman's March*, 87; Connelly, *John M. Schofield*, 133; Wiley Sword, *Embrace an Angry Wind: The Confederacy's Last Hurrah: Spring Hill, Franklin and Nashville* (New York: Harper Collins, 1992), 198.
14. Cox, *Battle of Franklin*, 64–82; *OR*, 45, pt. 1, 239–41, 269–70, 352, 653–54, 1174. Cox's *Battle of Franklin* describes the background and related orders regarding the imbroglio between Wagner and Opdycke.
15. *OR*, 45, pt. 1, 353; Cox, *Sherman's March*, 89. Two recent books by Eric Jacobsson, *For Cause and Country* (Franklin: O'More Publishing, 2008) and *Baptism of Fire* (Franklin: O'More Publishing, 2011) are excellent summaries of the battle and its context.

16. See Jacobson, *Baptism of Fire*, 151–81 for an in-depth analysis of the movement of all relevant Union forces to meet the challenge to the center of the line.
17. Cox, *Sherman's March*, 91–95; *OR*, 45, pt. 1, 343–55; Cox, *Battle of Franklin*, 218. In the latter, Cox notes that several of his men had repeater rifles which made their ability to keep up a constant "sheet of fire" that much easier.
18. Cox, *Battle of Franklin*, 167.
19. *OR*, 45, pt. 1, 1171–74; Cox, *Battle of Franklin*, 169, 192; Schofield, *Forty-Six Years*, 187–88.
20. *OR*, 45, pt. 2, 628; *Ibid.*, 45, pt. 1, 654.
21. Cox, *The Battle of Franklin*, 11; *OR*, 45, pt. 1, 35, 343–47, 356, and 650 contain the Union reports of casualties on both sides.
22. Samuel Rush Watkins, *Company Aytch, or A Side Show of the Big Show, and Other Sketches* (Nashville: Cumberland Presbyterian Publishing House, 1882), 201, 203.
23. Hood, *Advance and Retreat*, 299; *OR*, 45, pt. 1, 654; *Ibid.*, pt. 2, 640.
24. *Ibid.*, 1520, 84.
25. Cox, *Sherman's March*, 122–23; Hood, *Advance and Retreat*, 303; Watkins, *Company Aytch*, 216; *OR*, 45, pt. 1, 405–7, 699. Cox's report on the battle of Nashville is on pages 405 to 407 and Hood's report is on page 699.
26. Cox, *Military Reminiscences*, vol. 2, 367–68, 371–72.
27. Cox, *Sherman's March*, 126; *OR*, 45, pt. 1, 402–3, 409.
28. *OR*, 45, pt. 1, 361; Cox to Helen Cox, 2 January 1865, Cox Papers.
29. *OR*, 45, pt. 2, 419–20, 441, 781.
30. *Ibid.*, 377–78; Schofield, *Forty-Six Years*, 254–55; Cox, *Military Reminiscences*, vol. 2, 379. Later, Schofield's request would be seen by Thomas's partisans as yet another attack on their commander because Schofield was "abandoning" him and leaving him to the dull routine of the West, while he got to go to main battle arena with Sherman.
31. *OR*, 47, pt. 2, 131, 154–56; Cox, 30 January and 2 February 1865, Cox Papers; Cox, *Military Reminiscences*, vol. 2, 391–96.
32. Cox, *Military Reminiscences*, vol. 2, 395; McPherson, *Battle Cry of Freedom*, 838–40.
33. *OR*, 47, pt. 1, 910–11, 927–31; Cox, *Sherman's March*, 147–54.
34. Cox, *Military Reminiscences*, vol. 2, 420; *OR*, 47, pt. 2, 1247–48, 1256–57, 1271. At the time Sherman's forces numbered about sixty thousand and Schofield's about thirty thousand; Johnston had about thirty thousand eventually.
35. *OR*, 47, pt. 2, 579–80, 559. In the same request to Grant, Schofield asked that Terry be named corps commander of the other troops in Schofield's department and that they be designated the X Corps. It meant that both of Schofield's corps commanders were political generals.

36. Cox, *Military Reminiscences*, vol. 2, 427; Cox, *Sherman's March*, 155.
37. Cox, *Military Reminiscences*, vol. 2, 444; Wade Sokolosky, *To Prepare for Sherman's Coming: The Battle of Wise's Forks, March 1865* (Savas Beatie, 2015).
38. Cox, *Military Reminiscences*, vol. 2, 445; *OR*, 47, pt. 1, 44, 1055.
39. Cox, *Military Reminiscences*, vol. 2, 447–48.
40. *OR*, 47, pt. 3, 129, 140; Augustus J. Ricks, "Carrying the News of Lee's Surrender to the Army of the Ohio: A Paper Read Before the Ohio Commandery of the Military Order of the Loyal Legion of the United States," *Sketches of War History* II (Cincinnati, OH: Robert Clarke & Co., 1890 235. Ricks was one of Cox's friends from Oberlin. In his memoirs, Cox wrote that he "acted as fugleman" (i.e., like a bugler) in announcing the news (460).

Afterword

1. Cox *Diary*, Cox Papers.
2. My book, *Citizen-General*, is the definitive biography. It discusses in great detail not only the war years, but Cox's pre-war and post-war life.

Selected Bibliography

Listed here are only the writings and source materials that have been of the greatest importance in the making of this book. The notes include the full range of sources used and there were many others consulted which are not referenced here. A full listing of all the relevant elements of the extensive literature on the Civil War would require a multi-volume study of its own.

Primary Sources

Interviews and Personal Communications

Cochran, Mary Rudd. Personal interview with author. March 25, 1969, Monroe, Ohio.
———. Personal letters to author. December 14, 1968, to April 6, 1969. In the author's possession

Manuscripts

Chase, Salmon. Papers. Historical Society of Pennsylvania.
Cochran, William Cox. Papers. Oberlin College Archives.
Cook, Roy Bird. Papers. West Virginia University Collection.
Cox, Helen. Papers. Oberlin Archives.
Cox, Jacob Dolson. Papers. Library of Congress.
———. Papers. Oberlin College Archives.
———. Papers. Western Reserve Historical Society, Cleveland, Ohio.
Cox, Kenyon. Papers. Avery Library, Columbia University, New York.
Thomas Ewing Family Papers. Ohio Historical Society.
Garfield, James A. Papers. Library of Congress.
Garfield, Lucretia. Papers, Library of Congress.
Schofield, John M. Papers. Library of Congress.
William Bascom-Hiram Little Family Papers. Western Reserve Historical Society, Cleveland, Ohio.

Documents

United States Congress. *Report of the Joint Committee on the Conduct of the War.* Washington, D.C.: Government Printing Office, 1863–1865.

United States War Department. *The War of the Rebellion: A Compilation of the Official Records of the Union and Confederate Armies.* Washington, D.C.: Government Printing Office, 1880–97.

Letters, Diaries, and Memoirs

Cochran, William Cox. *Political Experiences of Major General Jacob Dolson Cox.* 2 vols., unpublished manuscript. Cincinnati, OH: Oberlin College Archives, 1940.

———. Unpublished [untitled and undated] autobiography. Oberlin, OH: Oberlin College Archives.

Hood, J. B. *Advance and Retreat.* New Orleans: Beauregard, 1880.

Horton, J. H., and Solomon Teverbaugh. *A History of the 11th Regiment, Ohio Volunteer Infantry.* Dayton, OH: W. J. Shuey, 1866.

Johnston, Joseph. Narrative of Military Operations Directed During the Late War Between the States. New York: D. Appleton and Co., 1874.

McClellan, George B. *McClellan's Own Story.* New York: Charles L. Webster & Co., 1887.

Reid, Whitelaw. *Ohio in the War.* Columbus, OH: Eclectic Publishing Co., 1867, 1893.

Sherman, William T. *Personal Memoirs.* 2 vols. New York: Charles L. Webster & Co., 1891.

Watkins, Samuel R. *Company Aytch, or A Side Show of the Big Show, and other Sketches.* Nashville: Cumberland Presbyterian Publishing House, 1882.

Secondary Sources

Ambrose, Stephen. *Duty, Honor, Country: A History of West Point.* Baltimore, MD: Johns Hopkins University Press, 1966, 1996.

Boatner, Mark M., III. *The Civil War Dictionary.* New York: David McKay Publications, 1988.

Brown, Harry J., and Fred B. William, eds. *The Diary of James A. Garfield.* 2 vols. East Lansing: Michigan State University Press, 1967.

Castel, Albert. *Decision in the West: The Atlanta Campaign of 1864.* Lawrence: University Press of Kansas, 1992.

Clemens, Thomas, ed. *The Maryland Campaign of 1862.* 3 vols. Written by Ezra Carman. New York: Savas Beatie, 2010, 2012, 2017.

Selected Bibliography

Connelly, Donald B. *John M. Schofield and the Politics of Generalship*. Chapel Hill: University of North Carolina Press, 2006.
Cox, Jacob D. "Why the Men of '61 Fought for the Union." *Atlantic Monthly* LXIX (March 1892): 25–6.
———. *Atlanta*. New York: Charles Scribner's Sons, 1882.
———. *The Battle of Franklin, Tennessee, November 30, 1864: a Monograph*. New York: Charles Scribner's Sons, 1897.
———. *Military Reminiscences of the Civil War*. 2 vols. New York: Charles Scribner's Sons, 1900.
———. *Nation*, 161 articles, 1874–1900.
———. *The Second Battle of Bull Run: As Connected with the Fitz-John Porter Case*. Cincinnati, OH: Peter G. Thompson Co., 1882.
———. *Sherman's March to the Sea; Hood's Tennessee Campaign and the Carolina Campaigns of 1865*. New York: Charles Scribner's Sons, 1882.
Fischel, Edwin C. *The Secret War for the Union: The Untold Story of Military Intelligence in the Civil War*. New York: Houghton Mifflin, 1996.
———. "Pinkerton and McClellan: Who Deceived Whom?" *Civil War History* 34, no. 2 (June 1988): 115–142.
Fletcher, Robert S. *A History of Oberlin College*. Oberlin, OH: Oberlin College, 1943.
Glatthaar, Joseph. *The March to the Sea and Beyond*. New York University Press, 1985.
Goss, Thomas J. *The War Within the Union High Command: Politics and Generalship during the Civil War*. Lawrence: University Press of Kansas, 2003.
Grimsley, Mark. *The Hard Hand of War: Union Military Policy toward Southern Civilians, 1861–1865*. Cambridge University Press, 1995.
Guelzo, Allen C. "Charles Grandison Finney." In *The Human Tradition in the Civil War and Reconstruction*, edited by Steven Woodworth, Wilmington, DE: Scholarly Resources, 2000.
———. *Fateful Lightning: A New History of the Civil War and Reconstruction*. New York: Oxford University Press, 2012.
Hageman, Edward. *The American Civil War and the Origins of Modern Warfare*, Bloomington: Indiana University Press, 1992.
Harsh, Joseph. *Confederate Tide Rising*. Kent, OH: Kent State University Press, 1998.
Hartwig, David S. *To Antietam Creek: The Maryland Campaign of 1862*. Baltimore, MD: Johns Hopkins University Press, 2012.
———. *Taken at the Flood: Robert E. Lee and Confederate Strategy in the Maryland Campaign of 1862*. Kent, OH: Kent State University Press, 1999.
Hess, Earl J. *Kennesaw Mountain: Sherman, Johnston, and the Atlanta Campaign*. Chapel Hill: University of North Carolina Press, 2013.
———. *The Knoxville Campaign: Burnside and Longstreet in East Tennessee*. Knoxville: University of Tennessee Press, 2012.

Hoptak, John D. *The Battle of South Mountain*. Charleston, SC: The History Press, 2011.

Hsieh, Wayne Wei-siang. *West Pointers and the Civil War: The Old Army in War and Peace*. Chapel Hill: University of North Carolina Press, 2009.

Jacobsson, Eric, and Richard A. Rupp. *For Cause and For Country: A Study of the Affair at Spring Hill and the Battle of Franklin*. Franklin, TN: O'More Publishing, 2008.

———. *Baptism of Fire: The 44th Missouri, 175th Ohio, and 183rd Ohio at the Battle of Franklin*. Franklin, TN: O'More Publishing, 2011.

Johnson, R. U., and C. C. Buell, eds. *Battles and Leaders of the Civil War*. 4 vols. New York: Charles Scribner's Sons, 1887–88.

Jordan, Brian. *Unholy Sabbath: The Battle of South Mountain in History and Memory, September 14, 1862*. New York: Savas Beatie, 2012.

Lesser, W. Hunter. *Rebels at the Gate: Lee and McClellan on the Front Line of a Nation Divided*. Naperville, IL: Sourcebooks, 2005.

Liddell Hart, B. H. *Strategy*. 2nd rev. ed. New York: Penguin Group, 1967.

Longacre, Glenn V., and John E. Hass, eds. *To Battle for God and the Right: The Civil War Letterbooks of Emerson Opdycke*. Urbana: University of Illinois Press, 2003.

Maizlish, Stephen. *The Triumph of Sectionalism: The Transformation of Ohio Politics, 1844–1856*. Kent, OH: Kent State University Press, 1983.

Marvel, William. *Burnside*. Chapel Hill: University of North Carolina Press, 1981.

McClellan, George B. *The Mexican War Diary of George B. McClellan*. Princeton University Press, 1917.

McPherson, James M. *Battle Cry of Freedom: The Civil War Era*. New York: Oxford University Press, 1988.

———. ed. *The Atlas of the Civil War*. Philadelphia, PA: Running Press Book Publishers, 2005.

Miller, Brian C. *John Bell Hood and the Fight for Civil War Memory*. Knoxville: University of Tennessee Press, 2010.

Newell, Clayton R. *Lee vs. McClellan: The First Campaign*. Washington: Regnery Publishing, Inc., 2010.

Noe, Kenneth, and Shannon Wilson, eds. *The Civil War in Appalachia: Collected Essays*. Knoxville: University of Tennessee Press, 1997.

Rafuse, Ethan. *McClellan's War: The Failure of Modernization in the Struggle for the Union*. Bloomington: Indiana University Press, 2005.

Ricks, Augustus J. "Carrying the News of Lee's Surrender to the Army of the Ohio: A Paper Read Before the Ohio Commandery of the Military Order of the Loyal Legion of the United States." *Sketches of War History* II (Cincinnati, OH: Robert Clarke & Co., 1890).

Roseboom, Eugene H. *The Civil War Era, 1850–1873*. Columbus: Ohio Archeological and Historical Society, 1944.

Schmiel, Eugene D. "The Career of Jacob Dolson Cox, 1828–1900: Soldier, Scholar, Statesman." PhD diss., Ohio State University, 1969.

———. *Citizen-General: Jacob Dolson Cox and the Civil War Era*. Athens: Ohio University Press, 2014.

Sears, Stephen W. *George B. McClellan, the Young Napoleon*. New York: Ticknor and Fields, 1988.

———. *Landscape Turned Red: The Battle of Antietam*. New York: Ticknor and Fields, 1983.

———, ed. *The Civil War Papers of George B. McClellan*. New York: The DaCapo Press, 1989.

Smith, Jean E., *Grant*. New York: Simon and Schuster, 2001.

Sokolosky, Wade. *To Prepare for Sherman's Coming: The Battle of Wise's Forks, March 1865*. Savas Beatie, 2015.

Stewart, James B. *Holy Warriors: The Abolitionists and American Slavery*. New York: Hill and Wang, 1997.

Summers, Mark W. *The Press Gang: Newspapers and Politics, 1865–1878*. Chapel Hill: University of North Carolina Press, 1994.

Sutherland, Daniel E. *American Civil War Guerrillas, Changing the Rules of Warfare*. Santa Barbara, CA: Praeger, 2013.

Sword, Wiley. *Embrace an Angry Wind: The Confederacy's Last Hurrah: Spring Hill, Franklin and Nashville*. New York: Harper Collins Publishers, 1992.

Tap, Bruce. *Over Lincoln's Shoulder; The Committee on the Conduct of the War*. Lawrence: University of Kansas Press, 1998.

Weigley, Russell F. *The American Way of War: A History of United States Military Strategy and Policy*. New York: Macmillan Publishing Co., Inc., 1977.

White, William L. *Let Us Die Like Men: The Battle of Franklin, November 30, 1864*. El Dorado Hills, California: Savas Beatie, 2019.

Williams, Charles R., ed. *Diary and Letters of Rutherford Birchard Hayes*. 5 vols. Columbus: Ohio Archeological and Historical Society, 1922–26.

Williams, Kenneth P., *Lincoln Finds a General*. 4 vols. New York: The MacMillan Co., 1957.

Williams, T. Harry. *Hayes of the 23rd, the Civil War Volunteer Officer*. New York: Alfred A. Knopf, 1965.

Index

Page numbers in **boldface** refer to illustrations.

abolitionism: at Oberlin (*see* preface); Cox's views, 34, 211; Thirteenth Amendment debate in House, 211–12

Antietam, battle of: preliminary events, 75–85; command controversy at, 85–87; Burnside's bridge, 88–92, **88**; missed opportunities, 75, 89–93

antislavery: Cox as radical, 5–7; teachings of Thedia Cox, 1–2

Army of the Cumberland, in Atlanta campaign, 137–40, 153–54

Army of the Ohio: in Atlanta campaign, 137–45; and Schofield, xii, 153; Cox's command *ad interim*, 161, 191–94

Army of the Potomac, xxii, 39, 76–77, 86–87, 91, 95–96, 114; and Maryland campaign, 75–89

Army reform, 102–4; political Generals, xxiii, xxv, 179; Cox's views of, 102–4

"Atlanta," Cox's writing of, xxiv

Atlanta campaign: Cox's role (*see* chapter 6); Sherman's leadership and tactics, 147, 153–54, 179, 187; power of the defensive, 158. *See also* Hood, John Bell; Johnston, Joseph

Baltimore and Ohio Railroad (B&O), 13; Federal focus on retaking it, 13

Bascom, W. T., xxii, 3,5,6,9, 49, 90, 139

Battle of Franklin, Tennessee, November 30, 1864, a Monograph, xiii, xxiv

Benham, W. H.: failure in West Virginia campaign, 38–39, 41–42; and reputation of West Point, 44

Bragg, Braxton, 62, 141; and battle of Kinston, 220, 225

breastworks: power of the defensive, 91, 160, 163, 176, 179, 183–85, 217, 224; Johnston's use of Fabian tactics, 154, 158, 165; at Franklin, 202, 205

Burnside, Ambrose: Cox's views of, 92; Maryland campaign, 76–93; and Fitz-John Porter, 87, 90; commander, District of the Ohio, 104–11; commander in Tennessee, 110

Camp Dennison: formation of, 2–4; Cox's policies at, 3–8

Carnifex Ferry, battle of in West Virginia campaign, 28–29

Carter house, Cox's headquarters at Battle of Franklin, 83, **83**

Casement, John (Jack), in West Virginia campaign, 28, 30

Charleston, WV: Cox taking the city in 1861, xxii, 10–20; Cox retaking the city in 1862, 96–100

Chase, Salmon P., xiii, xxi, 73, 102, 105, 117; as patron of Cox, 8–9, 79, 95, 97, 211

Cochran, William, xiii, xviii, xxi; as Cox's biographer, 231, 248

colonization, internal, Cox's views of, 103, 211

Columbia, battle of, Cox's role, 198–90

Copperheads, 110. *See also* Vallandigham, Clement

counter-insurgency policy, Cox's approach in West Virginia, 20, 22

Cox, Helen Finney: as Oberlin student, xviii, xix; attitudes of, xviii, xx, xxi; as sounding board for Dolson, xx, xxiii, xxiv, 104–6; views of the war and Dolson's participation, 8–12, 61–64, 126–30; love for Dolson, xx; and mourning about death of son, William Brewster, xxi, 29–33

Cox, Jacob Dolson, **228**; long-term impact of Cox's writings, xiii; upbringing, xvii, xviii; and Charles Finney, xviii, xix; studies at Oberlin, xix; relationship with Helen Finney Cox, xviii, xx, xxi; personality, xvii, xviii, xxii, xxiii; views on race, xxiii; relations with Garfield, xx; and founding of Republican party, xix; leader in Ohio Senate, xxi; named Brigadier General of Ohio militia, xx; military chief of staff for Gov. Dennison, 1; named Brigadier General of U.S. Volunteers, xx; relations with McClellan, 1–2, 5–6,17, 22, 24, 26, 79, 85; commander of Camp Dennison, 1–12; relations with Rosecrans, 5, 10, 14, 19, 22, 24, 28–34, 42; autonomous command/first campaign in western Virginia, 10–12; naïveté early in the war, 14; defeat at Scary Creek and implications, 17, 18, 22; taking of Charleston and Gauley Bridge, 20–22; dealing with journalists, 25–26; Battle of Carnifex Ferry, 28; death of son William Brewster, 29, 32–34; final defeat of Floyd, 39; thoughts about nature of war in West Virginia, 13, 20, 26; campaign with Fremont, 45–63; atop Flat Top Mountain, 50–54; and John Pope, 62–70, 80; movement to Maryland campaign, 75–80; meetings with McClellan during/after Second Manassas, 75–76, 78–80; relations with Burnside, 76, 81, 85–87; comparing Kanawha troops with Army of Potomac, 77, 83, 91–92, 96; takes Frederick, 82; Battle of South Mountain, xxii, 76, **84**, 85–86; and Fitz-John Porter, 87, 89; Battle of Antietam, 87–93, **88**; retaking of West Virginia, 95–101; interregnum in Ohio and West Virginia (*see* chapter 4); thoughts about army reorganization, slavery, West Point, 102–3; dismay at loss of promotion in 1863, 95, 104, 106–8; commander, Department of the Ohio, 104; and Morgan's raid, 69, 110–11; and Confederate attempt to raid Sandusky prison, 111, 119–20; movement to Tennessee as commander of XXIII corps,

120–23; chief of staff to Schofield, relations with Schofield, 137–40, 145; commander, 3rd division, Army of the Ohio, 149; launching of Atlanta campaign, 153–54; relations with Sherman, 147–48; Battles of Resaca and Cassville, 154, 158–59; Battle of Kennesaw Mountain, 158, 164–69; successful flank attack at Kennesaw, 159, 169; stealth crossing of the Chattahoochee, 171–75; dismay at Hovey's promotion, 158–59, 171, 176–77; dismay at Palmer's actions, 180, 182; a "cursing Cox," 186; taking of the Macon RR, fall of Atlanta, 190–92, **192** (*see also* chapter 7); commander of Army of the Ohio ad interim, 189, 191–93; Sherman's desire to take him on March to the sea, 189, 194; decision to stay with Schofield, 190, 194; Thomas's strategy for Franklin-Nashville campaign, 197–98; deterring of Forrest at Columbia, 199–200; Schofield's confusion, 200; and march to Franklin in after Battle of Spring Hill, 200; given responsibility to command two divisions from 4th AC, 202; nature of entrenchments, 202; and Opdycke and Wagner, 202–6; success at Franklin, **201**, 204–6; Battle of Nashville and destruction of Confederate army, 207–8; return home on furlough, 209, 211; Washington trip, new politics, political future planning, 211; and North Carolina campaign, 212–25, **213**; victory at Wyse Forks, 223–25; as Reconstruction administrator, 227; preliminary thoughts on race and Reconstruction, 227; victory as governor, xxiii, 227; decision not to run for reelection, xxiv; decision to challenge administration policies, xxxiv; resignation, xxiv; and division with Grant, xxiv; retirement to Oberlin; death, burial, family tombstone, 230; legacy and overview, xxiv, **229**, 230

Cox, Jacob Dolson I, (father), career, xvii
Cox, Jacob Dolson III (son), 229
Cox, Kenyon (son), xiv, xxi, 229
Cox, Thedia R. (mother), xvii, 212
Cox, Theodore (brother), 90; as Cox's aide, 101, 121, 128, 131, 135, 136, 139, 144, 146–47, 176, 191, 212, 222
"Cursing Cox," Confederate spy and, 186

defensive, power of the, 154, 179; Joseph Johnston's strategy, 154, 158–59, 179; Confederate soldiers' recognition of it, 179–80; and Battle of Franklin, 201–4
Dennison, William, Ohio Governor, xxii; appoints Cox military chief of staff, xxii, 1; as postmaster general; 212

Election of 1865, Cox's decision to run for governor, 227; final results, 227
Eleventh (11th) Ohio regiment: at Camp Dennison, 2; on Kanawha campaign, 14; at Second Bull Run, 72, 78
Ewing, Hugh, 70, 238n39; at Antietam, 103; role reversing Cox's promotion, 103–4

Finney, Charles Grandison, xiv; clash with Cox, xix; personality of, xiv, xviii
flanking maneuvers, 20, 38, 91, 153–54, 163, 165, 182, 187; the "indirect method," and Sherman, 154, 186; Johnston tactics Atlanta campaign, 154
Floyd, John, 28; campaigns against Cox, 28; retreat to Big Sewell Mountain, 34; disputes with Wise, 28, 34; attack against Rosecrans and final retreat, 37–41
Forrest, Nathan B., 189; Cox's success against at Columbia, 198–99; flanking cavalry attack at Franklin, 200
Foster, John G., Cox's commander in Tennessee, 120–22, 128, 130, 132, 135–39, 141
Fourth (4th) Corps and Atlanta Campaign, 144–45, 161, 181; and Franklin-Nashville campaign, 197–99, 205–6
Franklin, Battle of, 197–206, **201**; Cox's description of, 204–6; painting of, 203; Cox's books about, 249
Fremont, John C., 45–47; 1862 campaign planning in West Virginia; Campaign, failure, 48–62

Garfield, James A.: in Ohio Senate, xxiii, xxii, 1; preparations for going to war, xiii, xx, xxii; military career, 43, 48, 111, 116; as "lobbyist" for Cox's promotions, 44, 96, 111, 118, 130, 138; urges Cox to run for governor in 1865, 211
Garfield, Lucy, friendship with Helen Cox, xx, 111

Grant, Ulysses, supports Cox to be secretary of war, xxiv; chooses Cox as secretary of interior, xxiv; split with Cox, xxiv

Halleck, Henry, negative views of political generals, 107; military chief of staff, 67, 96–97; Cox's views of, 71, 101
"Hard Hand of War," changing Northern attitudes in 1862, 62
Hardee, W. J., and a "cursing Cox," 186
Harpeth River, and Battle of Franklin, 202, 205; retreat over after Battle of Franklin, 205
Hayes, Rutherford: views about Cox, 44; and Maryland campaign, 70, 77
Hood, John Bell: frontal attack at Battle of Franklin, 202–6; and battle of Cassville, 158; replaces Johnston, 179; "General Field Order" on safety and security, 179; and a "cursing Cox," 186; post-Atlanta strategy, 186, 189, 193, 197; strategy for Franklin-Nashville campaign, 198; tactics against Schofield, 198–200; failure at Spring Hill, 200, 202; weaknesses as an army commander, 158, 179, 184; and Battle of Nashville, 207–8
Hovey, Alvin, incompetence of, 158; controversy over his promotion, 172, 176–77

Jackson, William (Stonewall), and Fremont, 49; and Shenandoah campaign of 1862, 60; at Second Manassas, 78–79
Johnson, Andrew, considers Cox for secretary of war, xxiv, 229

Index

Johnston, Joseph, 141; and Atlanta campaign, 153–54, 158–59, 164, 166, 171–72, 175; tactics/Fabian policy, 154; replaced by Hood, 179; return to battlefield in North Carolina, 217, 220; negotiations with Sherman to end war, 227

Jomini, Antoine-Henri: Cox's reading of, 68; influence on Civil War military strategy and tactics, 63, 68

journalism: and attacks on Cox during West Virginia campaign, 25–28, 32; and "puffs" about Benham, 41–42

Kanawha Division: creation in West Virginia, xxii; Maryland campaign, 70, 72, 76–9; Cox's command of, xxii; and South Mountain, 85–86; and Antietam, 87–92; ordered back to West Virginia, 92, 95

Kanawha Valley and West Virginia campaign, xxii, 10, **11**, 14–20; Lee's failures in 1861, 38; Lee's attempt to regain control of, 70, 95; Cox regains control, 95–96, 99–101

Kennesaw Mountain, battle of, Sherman's strategy, 158, 164, 166; Cox's relief at not participating in, 153; Cox's successful flanking movement, 159, 166–67

Kessler's Cross Lanes, incident at, Tyler's mistakes, 25, 28–29

Kinston/Wyse Forks, battle of, Cox's role, 220, 223–24

Lee, Robert E.: in West Virginia, 14, 28, 38, 70, 95; early failures, 34, 38; objectives in Maryland campaign, 76, 83; decision to withdraw after Battle of South Mountain, 85; Battle of Antietam, 87–89; surrender 225–26

Lincoln, Abraham: policies 1, 62, 75–6, 82, 110; assassination/after-effects, 227

"Lost Order," the (Lee's Special Orders no. 191), 85; contents not divulged by McClellan to subordinates, 85

Macon and Western Railroad: key supply line for Atlanta, 179–80, 186; Cox's role in cutting the line, 189–90

Manassas, Battle of Second: Pope's mistakes in losing the battle, xxii, 70, 76; McClellan's dragging of his feet to support Pope, 76, 79–80

"March to the Sea": Sherman's vision for, 189, 190; Sherman briefs Cox and Schofield, 190; Sherman wants Cox to lead XXIII corps, 190

Maryland Campaign, the. *See* Antietam, battle of

McClellan, George B.: view of Cox, xxii, xxv, 1, 2, 17, 22, 24, 26, 79, 85; takes command in Ohio, xxii, 1; the "Young Napoleon," 14; and West Virginia campaign, 2, 6–9, 10, 13–15, 17, 19; and Lincoln, 62; and Burnside, 87; and Pope, 62, 71, 75–76, 79–80; and Fitz-John Porter, 82, 239n7; and Maryland campaign, 80–91; and "Lost order," 85; decision to divide Burnside's "wing" and its implications, 85; decision not to reinforce Burnside, 90–91

military administration: Cox's counterinsurgency policy, xxii, 20, 22; Cox's distaste for, 4, 109–10, 120 military education: Cox's views of West Point, 103; and self-made men, 103

Morgan, John H., failed raid in Ohio, 110, 114

Mountain Department, and John C. Fremont, 45; Cox's command in 1862, 48–69

Nashville, Battle of, result of Battle of Franklin, 190, 207–8; Cox's role in, 208; final defeat of Confederates in West, 208

New York Times, and reporting on the Civil War, 28

IXth corps: Cox's "home corps" in Maryland campaign, 80–97; Cox's command, 87–92. See also Burnside, Ambrose

North Carolina campaign: Sherman's/Schofield's objectives, 211, **213**; Cox and Wilmington, 217–20; Cox and Battle of Kinston, 220–24; taking of Goldsboro, union of Union troops, 225

Oberlin College: foundations of, xviii, xix; and Charles Finney, xix

"Oberlin Letter," xxiii

Oberlin Rescuers, the, and Fugitive Slave law, xix; impetus to Cox's career, xix

Ohio Senate, the, Cox is elected to, xix, xx; role in war preparations, 1–2

Opdycke, Emerson, friendship with Cox, 48, 111, 117, 128–29, 154; and Battle of Spring Hill, 200; and Battle of Franklin, 202–6

Palmer, John: refusal to follow orders from Schofield, 180; delays which stopped Union advance, 180; Cox's anger at, 182

Perry, Aaron: friendship with Cox, 98, 112; as Cox's "sounding board," 102, 117; gubernatorial campaign manager, 227

political generals, conflict with professional generals, xxiii

Pope, John, Commander, Army of Virginia, 62, 71, 75–6, 79–80; political views, 62–63; orders Cox to Washington for campaign, 69–70; poor leadership at Second Manassas, 75–76, 79–80; recommendation to court-martial Fitz-John Porter, 82

Porter, Fitz-John: friendship with McClellan, 82; "conspiracy" against Burnside, 87; decision not to reinforce Burnside at Battle of Antietam, 75, 90

Princeton, Battle of, 48–54

race, Cox's views of, 102–3; and colonization, 103. See also "Oberlin Letter"

railroads, importance at the War's outset, 13, 58

Reconstruction: Cox's views, xxiii, xxiv, 211; Cox and military reconstruction in North Carolina, 227

Republican Party: Cox's role in forming party in Ohio, xix, xx, xxi; party concern about/opposition to Cox, xxiii, xxiv

Rich Mountain, battle of, and West Virginia campaign, 17. See also McClellan, George B.; Rosecrans, William

Rosecrans, William: and Cox training Ohio troops, 5,9; relationship with Cox, 9–10, 22, 24, 33–4, 39,

42; Battle of Rich Mountain, 17; and Battle of Carnifex Ferry, 2; decision to retreat in October, 1861, 34–6; rout of Floyd, 38; arrest of Benham, 39

Rough and Ready (city): key point of attack on Macon RR, 189–90, **192**

Scary Creek, Battle of: Cox's first battle experience, 17–18, 26; McClellan's criticism of Cox at, 18

Schofield, John M., Background of, xxii, xxiii; becomes commander of Army of the Ohio, 137; relationship with/praise of Cox, 137, 139–40, 157–58, 176; Cox's assessment of, 137, 145; absence after Atlanta campaign, 190–91, 193; management of Franklin-Nashville campaign, 198–204; placed Cox as "commander on the line" at Battle of Franklin, 202; North Carolina campaign, xxiii, 216–22; military governor of North Carolina, xxiii

Second Manassas/Bull Run, Battle of: and John Pope, 70, 75–76; McClellan's views, 83; role of Fitz-John Porter, 83; implications for Maryland campaign, 80–81

Sherman, W. T.: and Atlanta campaign, 137; views on strategy, 148, 153–54; Cox's view of, 147; and Battle of Kennesaw Mountain, 158–59, 167–68; asks Cox to go on "March to the Sea," 189–90, 194; orders to Thomas aabout Franklin-Nashville campaign, 190, 197; negotiates surrender of Johnston, 225–27

slavery: Cox's views of, 34, 63, 139, 211–12; Cox's education against, xvii-xx; and Ohio Senate before the war, 1–2. *See also* colonization; Oberlin College

South Mountain, Battle of: Cox's role, xxii, 76, 82–86, **88**; McClellan's praise of Cox, 85

Special Orders no. 191, 82. *See also* "Lost Order"

spies, 186

Spring Hill, Battle of, Hood's failure, 202

Stanton, Edwin: meetings with Cox, 70, 73, 79, 97, 212; Cox as possible replacement, xxiv

Stuart, Jeb, finds Cox's orders leading to reinvasion of West Virginia, 70

Thirteenth Amendment, Cox present at vote, 211. *See also* slavery

Thomas, George, Army of the Cumberland, 153, 168; strategy for Franklin-Nashville campaign, 189–90, 197–98; Battle of Nashville victory, 207–8

Twenty-third (23rd) army corps: and Burnside, 122; and Foster, 121; Schofield assumes command, 145–46; Cox as chief of staff, 140–41; Cox as commander of 3rd division, 148; and Atlanta campaign, 147, 153; Cox as acting commander, 189–90, 225; and "Army of the Ohio," 153–54, 189–90

Twenty-third (23rd) Ohio regiment: led by Rutherford B. Hayes, 44, 70; arrive in Washington for Maryland campaign, 72–73

Tyler, E. B.: colonel under Cox in West Virginia campaign, 25; overwhelmed at Kessler's Cross

Tyler, E. B. (*cont.*)
Lanes, 28–29, 31; beats Garfield in election to become regimental commander, 4–5

Union army: Scott's organization at beginning of the war, 4; and West Point, xxii, xxiii
Union Party. *See* Republican Party

Vallandigham, Clement: Cox announces he would be arrested if returned, 110, 112–15; candidacy for governor in 1863, 110, 117
Virginia and Tennessee Railroad: route for Confederate reinforcements, 49, 58; Cox's failure to take the railroad, 49–54
Volunteer army: creation of at beginning of the Civil War, xv; Cox's positive views, xx, 103

Wagner, George: role in diverting Hood at Columbia, Spring Hill, 198; relations with Opdycke, 202; misguided decisions at Franklin, 202, 205
war, Cox's preparations for, 1–5

Warren, Ohio: Cox's first home as a married man, xix; and Western Reserve politics, xix
West Point: Cox's views of, 41, 44; and volunteer soldiers, xxv, 39, 103–4
West Virginia: Cox's role in stabilizing and preserving the new state, xxii; creation of, 2, 10; terrain and topography of, 13, 63; Cox returns to retake WV in 1862, xxii, 95–100
Western Reserve, attitudes of, xviii, xix
Wilson, James, and Franklin-Nashville campaign, 198; failures of, 200
Wise, Henry, Confederate commander in West Virginia, 14, 15, 17; Cox forces retreat from Charleston and Gauley Bridge, 21–22; refusal to cooperate with Floyd and benefit for Cox, 28; defeat at Carnifex Ferry, 28; removed from command, 34

"Young Napoleon," McClellan's sobriquet after West Virginia campaign, 14

zig-zag movements, role of Army of the Ohio on Atlanta campaign, 179, 187